SHAKESPEARE

SET FREE

Also from the Teaching Shakespeare Institute

Shakespeare Set Free: Teaching *Hamlet* and *Henry IV, Part 1*
Shakespeare Set Free: Teaching *Twelfth Night* and *Othello*

Published by WASHINGTON SQUARE PRESS

SHAKESPEARE

SET FREE

TEACHING

A MIDSUMMER NIGHT'S DREAM

•

ROMEO AND JULIET

•

MACBETH

PEGGY O'BRIEN, GENERAL EDITOR
JEANNE ADDISON ROBERTS, SCHOLARSHIP EDITOR
MICHAEL TOLAYDO, PERFORMANCE EDITOR
NANCY GOODWIN, CURRICULUM EDITOR

•

Teaching Shakespeare Institute
Folger Shakespeare Library
Washington, D.C.

WASHINGTON SQUARE PRESS

New York   London   Toronto   Sydney

**For Louisa Newlin,
the mother of it all**

 Washington Square Press
1230 Avenue of the Americas
New York, NY 10020

Copyright © 1993 by The Folger Shakespeare Library

ISBN-13: 978-0-7432-8850-7
ISBN-10:   0-7432-8850-5

This Washington Square Press New Folger Library
Trade Paperback Edition August 2006

10 9 8 7 6 5 4 3 2

WASHINGTON SQUARE PRESS and colophon are
registered trademarks of Simon & Schuster, Inc.

Manufactured in the United States of America

For information regarding special discounts for bulk purchases,
please contact Simon & Schuster Special Sales at
1-800-456-6798 or business@simonandschuster.com.

CONTENTS

ᔆ | Part Three
IN THE CLASSROOM
NANCY GOODWIN, EDITOR

ACKNOWLEDGMENTS

The Teaching Shakespeare Institute was born to the high standards and with the warm encouragement of Carolynn Reid-Wallace; its work continues to be made possible by the National Endowment for the Humanities, for which I am daily and actively thankful.

The latter third of this book belongs entirely to the collective genius of the faculty and participants of "Teaching Shakespeare's Language" who were in residence at the Folger Shakespeare Library during the hot summers of 1988 and 1989:

Andrea Alsup, *Woodstock, Vt.*
Tom Berger, *Canton, N.Y.*
Susan Biondo-Hench, *Carlisle, Pa.*
Stephen Booth, *Berkeley, Calif.*
Kathleen Breen, *Louisville, Ky.*
Susan Cahill, *Whippany, N.J.*
Carlos Castillo, *Denver, Colo.*
Martha Christian, *Kingston, Mass.*
Barbara Crabb, *Helen, Ariz.*
Donna Denizé, *Arlington, Va.*
Ellen Diem, *Inola, Okla.*
Judy Dill, *Columbia, S.C.*
Susan Donnell, *St. Louis, Mo.*
Judith Elstein, *Somers Point, N.J.*
Lynn Frick, *Madison, Wis.*
Nancy Goodwin, *Clinton, Okla.*
Martha Harris, *Golden Valley, Minn.*
Diane Herr, *Lansdale, Pa.*
Tony Hill, *Stratford-upon-Avon, U.K.*
Judith Klau, *Groton, Mass.*
Michael LoMonico, *Stony Brook, N.Y.*

Jerry Maguire, *Columbia, Ind.*
Mary Beth Maitoza, *North Providence, R.I.*
Russ McDonald, *Greensboro, N.C.*
Diane Mertens, *Madison, Wis.*
Barbara Mowat, *Washington, D.C.*
John Murphy, *Claremont, Calif.*
Louisa Newlin, *Washington, D.C.*
Skip Nicholson, *Los Angeles, Calif.*
Suzanne Peters, *Tucson, Ariz.*
Mary Winslow Poole, *Washington, D.C.*
Christopher Renino, *New York, N.Y.*
Randal Robinson, *East Lansing, Mich.*
John Scott, *Hampton, Va.*
Susan Snyder, *Swarthmore, Pa.*
Annie Stafford, *New York, N.Y.*
Everett Stern, *Toledo, Ohio*
Robin Tatu, *Washington, D.C.*
Pat Thisted, *Colorado Springs, Colo.*
Michael Tolaydo, *Washington, D.C.*
George Wright, *Minneapolis, Minn.*

During those summers, institute members were aided immeasurably by the labors of Lauri Lewis, Heather Lester, and Mr. Freddie Lindsay, without whom no institute is ever possible. Subsequently, in classrooms across the country, several hundred students contributed greatly to the project; they are, of course, the best teachers of all.

From that summer to this day, this series has benefited from the enthusiastic direction of Jane Rosenman, our editor and guiding spirit at Washington Square Press.

Under the direction of Werner Gundersheimer (1984–2002), the Folger Shakespeare Library embraced the work of teachers and students, and the *Shakespeare Set Free* series was no exception. Dr. Gundersheimer and Director of Public Programs Janet Alexander Griffin gave their full and immediate support to these volumes from the first moment they were a gleam in my eye. Barbara A. Mowat and Paul Werstine, editing the New Folger Shakespeare editions at just the right time, have enabled us to work with splendid and exciting new texts.

As always, I am full of thanks to the staff of the Division of Public Programs, in particular Louisa Newlin, the truly extraordinary teacher who nudged the Library down the path of secondary-school students in the first place; to Jane Bissonette, Janice Delaney, Stephanie DeMouche, and Katy O'Grady, and most especially Molly Haws, who has kept this book close to her heart and under her thumb with great skill and humor. The Reading Room staff—particularly Betsy Walsh, Rosalind Larry, and Lu-Ellen DeHaven—provided assistance in all aspects of this work. The services of our dial-a-grammarian, *Shakespeare Quarterly* assistant editor Mary Tonkinson, have been invaluable.

I remain in debt to the "Folger Net," the burgeoning community of Teaching Shakespeare Institute alumni who thankfully won't let go, to head scholar Russ McDonald for his continued contributions to the life and work of the institute, and to master teacher Michael LoMonico, who edited part of this volume with the extraordinary generosity and insight I have come to take completely for granted.

This volume owes a great deal to the vision, inspiration, backbone, and industry of two spectacular women. Two years ago, I asked Nancy Goodwin to take on the impossible job of curriculum editor, and she continues to respond with a stream of miracles. She of the vast organizational mind lends to this project not only brilliance, honesty, persistence, and humor, but her long and exceedingly clear view of just about everything.

Well before this book, Jeanne Addison Roberts began shaping the Teaching Shakespeare Institute and the larger sphere of secondary education. The best kind of challenging and inclusive teacher, she has by her own example turned the attention and respect of first-rate university scholars to junior- and senior-high-school teachers and the value of their work, and awakened in many secondary-school teachers cravings for more learning and, of all things, graduate school. This volume and all of the institute's work reflect her intelligence, courage, insight, and support.

Finally, at the center of it all and in my heart's core are my own very finest teachers. Beth O'Brien, John O'Brien, and Michael Tolaydo know a thing or two about teaching and learning; I have been stealing from them for years. In the most profound sense, however, they keep me honest. They are the inspiration and spirit behind all of my work and much of this book.

P.O'B.
1993

In the thirteen years since *Shakespeare Set Free* first appeared, interest in the Folger's performance-based teaching techniques has grown dramatically. Under the leadership of Director Gail Kern Paster, the Folger continues to offer groundbreaking educational programs to teachers nationwide. With the generous support of the National Endowment for the Humanities, we have produced thirteen Teaching Shakespeare Institutes, continuing the tradition of the institutes that provided the content for these *Shakespeare Set Free* volumes. We regularly archive the work of more recent institutes on the Folger website at *www.folger.edu/teachingshakespeare,* along with other free lesson plans and study guides, in support of our commitment to further the very best teaching of Shakespeare.

We're pleased to offer the volumes in this revised edition, keyed to the New Folger Library Shakespeare Editions for convenience and incorporating other updates. We hope you'll use these books in conjunction with the ever-expanding database of materials available on our website. We thank the students from our 2005 Secondary School Shakespeare Festival who have given permission for their images to be used on the cover of this book, photographer Muriel Marquet, and our partners at Simon & Schuster for their hard work at revising this text. Finally, we continue to thank you for using our resources and trying out our techniques for teaching Shakespeare. We hope you will stop in to see us and our work the next time you find yourself in Washington, DC.

Jeremy Ehrlich, Head of Education
February 2006

INTRODUCTION
"Do We Get Credit for Reading This?"

❧

A LETTER FROM PEGGY O'BRIEN

I have worried a long time over this book. Not so much about editing it, because the writers and other editors involved in this project are the world's best, but about writing this introduction. I don't know why I am quite so worried because I never read introductions myself. They're always so *introductory,* and they get between me and the real stuff in books. On the other hand, this little bit of writing is important. I know this partly because, at this moment, I am sitting in a hot, cluttered room that seems to be crammed with thousands of teachers and students, all of whom I have worked with and all of whom are saying "Tell it! Say it right!" I sense hundreds more teachers and students—new faces to me—just beyond the door. The students are yawning and checking their watches. The teachers are correcting my grammar. These are truly a dangerous few pages.

I press on relentlessly, however, because I have a few things to say about the *Shakespeare Set Free* series and how it came to be, about teaching in general, and about teaching Shakespeare in specific. In one sense or another, all of this has to do with people. Unlike much of the education world, where texts and theories and methodologies often appear on the scene full-blown, disembodied, and described in personless prose, we are a bunch of real people with real voices—teachers, scholars, actors, and many students—at work figuring out about the sometimes tricky business of teaching Shakespeare.

This book, and the two volumes to follow, are born of a few Fiercely Held Beliefs and a critical mass of excellent people. Beliefs and people met at the Folger Shakespeare Library, a private research library tucked behind the U.S. Capitol in Washington, D.C. The Folger houses one of the world's largest—and perhaps the most significant—collections of materials pertaining to Shakespeare and the English and Continental Renaissance. And that's not all it houses. I am the Folger Library's Head of Education, a District of Columbia public-school English teacher at work in the world of Shakespeare. The Fiercely Held Beliefs are mine; they provide the foundation for the library's many education programs for teachers and students. They seem to have had some impact on the teaching of Shakespeare in American schools; they are basic and full of common sense.

For starters:

1. **The most significant work in the entire world goes on in schools. Period.** Not all learning happens in school, obviously, but what goes on daily in the mind of a student is the future creating itself. What goes on in your classroom—second grade, eighth grade, high-school sophomore, or undergraduate—is more important than anything that ever has or ever will take place in any boardroom or laboratory or launching pad. The true center of everything in school is what's happening in the mind of a

student. And the person who has the most direct influence on that is a teacher. *This is the world's most important work.*

2. **The people who know most and best about teaching are the folks who do it every day, with real kids in real classrooms.** The universe loses track of this fact because working teachers are short on time to document their findings, to undertake formal research, to write about their art. They are too busy working with up to 150 kids per day, reading journals, correcting papers, generally arranging for learning to happen on a daily basis. They are, however, the ones who *know*. And with all respect to the teachers of undergraduates and graduates and postgraduates among us, the people who really know the *how* of teaching are to be found in the classrooms of elementary, middle, junior, and senior high schools.

3. **Shakespeare is for all students: of all ability levels and reading levels, of every ethnic origin, in every kind of school.** In 1623, John Heminge and Henry Condell—two members of Shakespeare's acting company—compiled thirty-six plays and had them published in a volume called the First Folio. Their introduction to the book is entitled "To the great Variety of Readers." The introduction itself begins "From the most able, to him that can but spell. . . ." They meant it in 1623. I mean it right now. Teaching Shakespeare to all kinds of students is not only possible; it's essential.

4. **Shakespeare study can and should be active, intellectual, energizing, and a pleasure for teacher and student.** Students and Shakespeare have a great and natural affinity for each other; the classroom is the perfect and necessary place for its discovery. With a teacher as coach and collaborator, students learn Shakespeare by meeting him on his own ground—inside the play.

The man wrote *plays*. So is this about *acting?* No, it's about *doing.* Students get his language in their mouths, take on the work of actors and directors, get to know a play from the inside out. Don't worry about that stodgy academic notion that the body and the intellect can't be engaged simultaneously, that students moving about a classroom can't possibly be *really* learning anything. Make no mistake: learning Shakespeare through *doing* Shakespeare involves the very best kind of close reading, the most exacting sort of literary analysis.

Now take these Fiercely Held Beliefs and populate them with a load of extraordinary people. Tucked amid the Folger Library's dazzling—and quiet—collection of rare books and manuscripts is a brilliant—and noisy—whirlwind of rare people known as the Teaching Shakespeare Institute. Since 1984, thanks to these Beliefs, the vision of Professor Jeanne Addison Roberts of The American University, and the continuing support of the National Endowment for the Humanities, groups of scholars, actors, directors, and junior- and senior-high-school teachers have gathered together during summers for a month of rigorous Shakespeare exploration roughly divided into three geographies: scholarship, performance, and curriculum. Examinations of these areas are communal. Their relation to each other in the enhancement of our own teaching is a more individual journey as we talk, listen, act, react, argue, question, explicate, perform, write curriculum, and rewrite curriculum.

Surfacing again and again in discussions of work was the particular problem of language. Shakespeare's language, which for centuries has kept these plays fresh to all ages, remains the stumbling block that prevents many students from getting to them at all. "Teaching Shakespeare's Language" was a special institute that took place in the summers of 1988 and 1989 and the school year between. Its focus was the moment of truth when the student's eye meets the playwright's iambic. What's a teacher to do? What's a student to learn? How should it work? This was an institute about questions. I purposely set down for the participants few guidelines or interim deadlines or specific ways of working. Much of the process came from the collective genius of the group. The month was pressurized, unsettling, exhausting, enlightening, and satisfying.

The group agreed to work on seven plays that *should* be commonly taught in schools. They went along with my notion to leave out *Julius Caesar* altogether. (Believe me, the best thing to do with *Caesar* is to teach *Twelfth Night* or *A Midsummer Night's Dream* instead.) They worked on *Romeo and Juliet, Macbeth, A Midsummer Night's Dream, Hamlet, 1 Henry IV, Othello,* and *Twelfth Night.* Smaller groups of teachers collaborated on teaching plans for each play, taught them in classrooms around the country during the 1988–89 school year, and reshaped them further during the summer of 1989. Institute participants continued to teach and refine these strategies into 1990, when each play was entrusted to a single person to teach some more, then re-edit in a single voice. In this volume, the teaching strategies for *A Midsummer Night's Dream, Romeo and Juliet,* and *Macbeth* represent the combined and comprehensive knowledge of many fine working teachers and the practical journey of one.

Judith Elstein, Sue Biondo-Hench, and Chris Renino continued to teach full-time while taking up the challenge of this labor, working with curriculum editor Nancy Goodwin, herself teaching high school in Clinton, Oklahoma, as she masterminded the rest of the editing process. All of this serves to prove yet again that a good teacher can do *absolutely* anything.

Curriculum work is only one aspect of the Teaching Shakespeare Institute; the inclusion of scholarship and performance makes this *Shakespeare Set Free* series a set of true sourcebooks. David Bergeron, Russ McDonald, Meredith Skura, and Jeanne Roberts have contributed mightily to the work of teachers by presenting new ways of looking at old plays, offering us a revived and enlarged view of Shakespeare's words and of our own minds at the same time. Their articles here deal with topics that past institute members have found helpful, or mind-blowing, or both. Actor/director Michael Tolaydo has finally set down on paper the logistics of what has come to be known in many classrooms around the country as the "Tolaydo Method," the divinely simple way for students to discover and work with a piece of text *themselves,* with only the subtlest assistance from a teacher, and a teacher who doesn't even have to know anything about theater.

This book is by teachers, for teachers—for *all* teachers. The Fiercely Held Beliefs apply to students of any age or stage. While the methodologies here are the work of junior- and senior-high-school teachers, they are utterly possible in elementary school or in a college classroom. It only takes a good teacher to pick and choose, winnow or expand.

As books go, *Shakespeare Set Free: Teaching* Romeo and Juliet, Macbeth, *and* A Midsummer Night's Dream is too much a product of humans and the human experience to be perfect. It draws a bead on the delicate balance between a celebrated and complex writer and the slippery business of how people learn. How can perfection, or the definitive answer, be possible? It is, at this moment, the truth as we know it. And highly usable truth at that.

Use this book. Try something new. If you are used to grazing solely in the fields of practical classroom approaches, leap the fence into scholarship. Each of the articles in Part 1 can be a new pair of spectacles, helpful in seeing old plays with new eyes. Part 2—Michael Tolaydo's piece—is what many institute participants feel is a seminal ingredient, the basics of learning Shakespeare by doing Shakespeare. Part 3 is real live teaching: active strategies that are useful in their own right, and perhaps more important—with the addition of your own singular genius—as catalysts for even grander, more meaningful learning experiences for all kinds of students. When you reach those heights—in your A.P. class, your first-year survey, your learning-disabled class—let me know. I'm a good teacher, so I'm always looking for a better way to do it. And I hate to miss out on a great idea. So keep in touch. We're all in this together.

Peggy O'Brien
Folger Shakespeare Library
October 1992

PART ONE

Thinking About the
Plays

·

JEANNE ADDISON ROBERTS

EDITOR

Triple-Threat Shakespeare

 махе

JEANNE ADDISON ROBERTS
THE AMERICAN UNIVERSITY

Many students of Shakespeare know only a few plays, usually tragedies—most often *Romeo and Juliet, Julius Caesar, Macbeth,* and maybe *Hamlet.* This is, of course, a splendid beginning, and if we are able still to produce a generation that can identify "Parting is such sweet sorrow," "Friends, Romans, countrymen," "Is this a dagger which I see before me," and "To be or not to be," we've accomplished a great deal.[1] Nonetheless, if we restrict ourselves to tragedy, we communicate only a very limited appreciation of Shakespeare, and we miss the pleasure of discovering how one supremely creative mind experiments with forms, examines and reexamines themes, ideas, and characters, and constantly shapes and reshapes our vision of what the world is like.

Shakespeare wrote as many history plays as tragedies; and, judging from his total output, comedy may have been his favorite form. Some of his plays are hard to classify, but the new Folger edition of Shakespeare includes ten tragedies, ten histories, and eighteen comedies and romances (the First Folio categorized what we call "romances" as comedies). All of the comedies deal with young love, providing perspectives very different from that of *Romeo and Juliet,* and adding important dimensions to a topic barely touched on in any of the other great tragedies. It is, of course, a topic of intense interest to most students, although paradoxically the subject of young love is so close to most of them that they may have trouble dealing with it. The immediate emotional impact of the story of the doomed lovers in *Romeo and Juliet* may seem more accessible to them than the more detached rationality of the account of the multiple lovers in *A Midsummer Night's Dream,* but both attitudes need exploring; and the two plays are linked not only by subject matter but also by style and by their probable dates of composition (1595–96).

"Who ever lov'd that lov'd not at first sight?"[2] wrote Christopher Marlowe, Shakespeare's contemporary. The line is quoted by Shakespeare (*As You Like It* 3.5.82), and he employs the convention of love at first sight as an important element of *Romeo and Juliet* and, incidentally, in a few of the other comedies, notably *As You Like It* and *Twelfth Night.* But much more common in his studies of young love are illustrations of the maxim that "The course of true love never did run smooth" (*A Midsummer Night's Dream* 1.1.136). The lovers at the beginning of *A Midsummer Night's Dream* seem to have had a long history, now troubled in one case (Hermia and Lysander's) by parental disapproval, and in another (Helena and Demetrius') by the fickleness of the male. As for the third set of lovers, Theseus actually says he wooed Hippolyta with his sword

---

[1] Except where otherwise noted, all references to Shakespeare's works are to the New Folger edition (New York: Simon & Schuster, 1992–   ).

[2] *The Riverside Shakespeare,* ed. G. Blakemore Evans (Boston: Houghton Mifflin Company, 1974).

and won her love by doing her injury. Titania and Oberon are at war with each other, and each accuses the other of infidelity. And on the comical/tragical level, Pyramus and Thisbe are as doomed from the start as Romeo and Juliet. In this play it seems that Shakespeare may actually be making fun of love at first sight, since all who "love" in this way (Titania, Demetrius, and Lysander) do so under the spell of a magical potion, the effects of which are ludicrous and easily canceled. The very multiplication of lovers serves to deemphasize character—Demetrius and Lysander, for example, are almost indistinguishable—and to lend a farcical element to passion.

The instantaneous passion of Romeo and Juliet and the relentless movement toward their ill-fated end is tragic and deeply moving. But the multiplication of lovers and the changeableness of their infatuation in *A Midsummer Night's Dream* turns "love" into a game—albeit a serious one since it is the traditional prelude to the socially necessary process of propagating the race, a process often characterized by temporary insanity. The play-within-a-play, the rude mechanicals' *Pyramus and Thisbe,* can be read as a burlesque rerun of *Romeo and Juliet,* where love is not only blind, it is totally absurd. As Theseus says (5.1.3–7), the lunatic, the lover, and the poet are all obsessed with antique fables and fairy toys. Love is a life-and-death matter; it is also a joke, as the nonhuman Robin Goodfellow helps us to see.

In Shakespeare's English histories, most of them written before 1600, young "love" is either nonexistent or subordinated to practical politics. And by the time he writes the tragedy *Macbeth,* probably about 1606, ten years after *Romeo and Juliet* and *A Midsummer Night's Dream,* in the reign of James I, after all elements of the Elizabethan idyll had evaporated, Shakespeare's focus is no longer on young lovers. For Macbeth and his lady, love's effects are obsessive, sterile, and destructive. The spectrum of Shakespeare's representations of love is broad and diverse; and if one reads the three plays in this volume together, one gets a complex and stimulatingly contradictory view of one important topic of the poet's work.

There is no "message." It is tempting to try to isolate clear morals in these plays, but we need to resist the temptation to simplify them. I do not think that Shakespeare is trying to tell us that Romeo and Juliet were too young or that they shouldn't have defied their parents, or that the love of Demetrius and Lysander is simply sex drive in pursuit of an object, or that ambition devastates married love. He is rather showing us, in ways that drama is uniquely structured to do because it has no one narrative voice, the working out of genuine human conflicts for which there are no clear solutions. Different audiences will see the plays differently—you will notice that the essayists in this series do not always agree. Both these tragedies and this comedy resist simple, comfortable resolutions. The two tragedies show how conflicts wipe out the hoped-for future—the Montagues and the Capulets have no more children, and there is no certainty that Malcolm will not follow in the footsteps of Macbeth as he seems to do at the end of Roman Polanski's film version of the play. Even the comedy shows a future secured only rather uneasily—Demetrius is never freed from the magic spell that now links him to the previously rejected Helena; and, if one remembers Greek myth, one knows that Theseus will not long cherish Hippolyta.

In addition to their explorations of the effects of love, these three plays are linked by their brilliantly vivid and strikingly different uses of imagery of night. For better and for worse, night is traditionally associated with the eclipse of patriarchal cultural values. It is also frequently linked with females and with the ancient triple goddess, Hecate, who, as moon goddess, ruled the night. Night is a time when the rigidity of family feuds can be suspended, when lovers can be freed of societal dicta; but it is also a time when hierarchy, taboo, and humane principles can be violated. In *Romeo and Juliet* night is the benign and romantic time that shields the lovers and provides a cover for the consummation of their love. The nightingale is their bird, and in the privacy of their personal darkness Juliet is the sun (she begs Romeo not to swear by the "inconstant" moon [2.2.114]). Romeo, basking in her light, can forget family entanglements. Most of the disasters happen in daylight. But at the end the protective night shrivels into the darkness of the tomb, where human frailty and blindness lead to destruction and death.

In *A Midsummer Night's Dream* night again countenances the rebellion of young lovers, but it is the scene of both disorder and possibility. Changes are set in progress by the quarrel of Oberon and Titania, and by the magic that raises the specters of bestiality (Titania and the ass), sexual infidelity (Demetrius and Lysander, both Titania and Oberon), and the disruption of the "rational" order of society. The forest is a world bathed in moonlight—changeable, deceptive, and miraculous. It is also a place where problems are solved. Daylight seems dull and cold by comparison.

The prevailing imagery of *Macbeth* combines black night with blood. Night makes murders possible, and Macbeth's dark castle becomes Hell to the drunken Porter. When Banquo and Fleance arrive at the castle, the moon is down and heaven's candles are all out (2.1.2,7). Lady Macbeth sleepwalks in the dark, and Macbeth hears voices declaring that he has murdered sleep. The polar darkness, colored only by blood, leaves an audience yearning for dawn, with the hope that young Malcolm may indeed be the harbinger of a new orderly day.

Audiences of these three plays will notice significant differences in their poetic styles. The first two, written probably within a year, belong to what is called Shakespeare's lyrical period. There is persistent punning and playing with language. Both works take time out from the main plot for diversions like the ramblings of the nurse, the flights of fancy of Mercutio, and the delicious theatricals of Peter Quince and Bully Bottom. Students will quickly discover in both plays the pervasive use of couplets instead of the expected blank verse, and it is worthwhile to examine the varying effects of these couplets as they are differently used. Consider, for example, the effect of 2.3 in *Romeo and Juliet*, where the whole scene is written in couplets. And try to think of reasons why 1.1 of *A Midsummer Night's Dream* changes from blank verse to couplets when Helena joins the group on stage. There are other interesting changes in meter and rhyme patterns. Romeo and Juliet construct a sonnet between them at their first meeting, and the fairies speak in cadences different from those of the humans in *A Midsummer's Night's Dream*. *Macbeth*, by contrast, very rarely uses couplets, and the blank verse is less regular than it was in the earlier works. The action is stripped down, concentrated, relentless. The mood is intensified by the complex images focused on darkness, blood, murdered children, and clothes that cannot be made to fit their owners. There are no distractions. We cannot say surely why Shakespeare does these things, but we can try to analyze the effect on us as we read and watch.

Another extremely important topic for modern audiences to consider in reading these plays is their representation of women. Shakespeare was, of course, a member of a society even more patriarchal than our own, where women had no legal rights and were the property of their fathers or their husbands. Juliet's father can condemn his not-yet-thirteen-year-old daughter to "hang, beg, starve, die in the streets" (3.5.204) if she refuses the marriage he has arranged for her. Similarly, Hermia's father can credibly assert of his daughter

> As she is mine, I may dispose of her,
> Which shall be either to this gentleman
> Or to her death, according to our law. . . .
>   (1.1.43–45)

The women in Shakespeare's plays are presented primarily as young virgins, like Juliet and Hermia, valued for their marriageability, or as powerless mothers and wives, like Lady Capulet and Lady Macduff, valued for their fertility. Caesar's wife is blamed for sterility, which is automatically presumed to be her fault. Old women are either impotent like the nurse or frighteningly sinister like the witches.

And yet, in spite of the severe limitations on their scope, Shakespeare's women are nearly always memorable. In these three plays the examples are particularly striking. Juliet is the more active partner in the sudden romance. It is she on whom our main attention focuses, and it is she who has the best lines. She almost instantly introduces the subject of marriage; she arranges the rendezvous at Friar Lawrence's cell; she renounces her dependence on the nurse when the latter's practicality prevails over passion; and she risks the horrors of awakening in the tomb in order to be reunited with her husband.

Similarly, in *A Midsummer Night's Dream* the women are more individualized than the men. Hermia's strong-minded determination to have the lover of her choice precipitates the action. And Helena's wistful pursuit of her man complicates it. The quarrel of the two women is one of the funniest scenes in the play. (You might consider what makes audiences find it so funny. Would a quarrel between men be just as funny?) In both *Romeo and Juliet* and *A Midsummer Night's Dream* the patriarchal father is ultimately defeated—tragically in the one and comically in the other. At the start of *A Midsummer Night's Dream* the warlike Amazon Hippolyta has been subdued by Theseus, but it is she who sees most clearly at the end when Theseus dismisses the tale of the magical forest. Unlike him, she concludes

> But all the story of the night told over,
> And all their minds transfigured so together,
> More witnesseth than fancy's images
> And grows to something of great constancy. . . .
>
> (5.1.24–27)

Oberon and Titania seem well-matched opponents in the beginning of the play, fighting, in a sense, over the future as personified in the little changeling boy. Oberon clearly wins the boy in the end. But it is a muted victory. He means to make a fool of his wife by tricking her into loving an ass. And yet Bottom is such an appealing male presence (the ass was traditionally linked with extraordinary virility), and he and Titania seem to be having such a good time, that Oberon is somewhat undercut by his own device. Peter Brook's famous production of the play provided for sexual consummation between Titania and Bottom and for an extravagant celebration of the two as king and queen of festivity. The prospect of uninhibited female sexuality is permitted in Titania's erotic dalliance with the ass-headed Bottom. So strong is the festive atmosphere that the effect is only partly reversed at the end by her loss of the boy. Still, the major drive of the play is toward marriage, the socially sanctioned regulation of female eroticism.

The choice of females in *Macbeth* is between a murderous wife, a victimized mother, and the conniving witches. Indeed, I find *Macbeth* Shakespeare's most misogynistic play. Even Macduff, the savior of the country, must be distanced from female contamination by not being of woman born. Lady Macbeth, in some of the most shocking language in all Shakespeare, declares that she would sacrifice her own child rather than fail to pursue their murderous intentions:

> I have given suck, and know
> How tender 'tis to love the babe that milks me.
> I would, while it was smiling in my face,
> Have plucked my nipple from his boneless gums
> And dashed the brains out, had I so sworn as you
> Have done to this.   (1.7.62–67)

Her speech not only establishes her horrible repressed violence; it also raises the intriguing question of what has happened to her child. Lady Macbeth certainly eggs her husband on, and readers often blame her for the murder. But her future is totally dependent on Macbeth. Like Lady Capulet and even Lady Macduff, she is essentially powerless in spite of her formidable sense of purpose. Once her husband has moved into a realm where she cannot follow, her life disintegrates into madness and suicide. Without him she has no self.

Some modern productions have experimented with ways of modifying the limited and sometimes stereotypical representations of women in Shakespeare's plays. One company cast a woman as Banquo—not as a woman playing a man, but as a woman. The change, easily accepted by the audience, provided an interesting ironic parallel to the Macduffs: the savior of his country loses his prospects for progeny as his wife and son are murdered, but Fleance's mother, similarly murdered, leaves hope for the future. And, perhaps irrationally, the murder of a mother seemed more horrifying than the murder of a father. Students may find that experimenting with gender roles in their acting will illuminate both the past and the present.

In all three plays the end of the imagined woman's story is marriage. It is the end in both senses—the goal toward which the woman moves and the conclusion of her tale. Juliet's marriage is followed by almost immediate death. Hippolyta and Titania seem to dwindle into wives. And Hermia and Helena will presumably be tamed after achieving their respective marital goals. Even Lady Macbeth, formidable as she seems, is so linked to her husband for her identity that she has no independent life. Fully developed women's stories are notoriously rare in traditional literature, and Shakespeare's works are no exception. It is worth remembering that his plays focused on male experience for primarily male audiences. Modern readers need to recognize this as they read, watch, and study. We need to develop conscious resistance to the oft-repeated myth that a woman's story ends at the altar. There are many other paths than the marital one to be considered, and many possible journeys beyond marriage. Modern plays by women are only now beginning to chart what these journeys might be like.

If students read these plays together, they will find endless other avenues of approach. The following essays will suggest some. I hope that students will find their journeys challenging, stimulating, and enlightening—that they will learn more about Shakespeare and his age, more about the subtle manipulation of language and image, more about the dramatic construction of character, that they will formulate more questions, find it more difficult to isolate "messages," and explore more complex visions of the nature of their universe than they would from studying only one play.

The Flaw in the Flaw

❧

RUSS McDONALD

UNIVERSITY OF NORTH CAROLINA AT GREENSBORO

Modern thinking about Shakespearean tragedy derives from three main sources: the descriptive theory of Aristotle as set forth in the *Poetics*, Shakespeare's own practice, and the early-twentieth-century commentary of A. C. Bradley. But the distortions of time and translation, not to mention the difficulties of passing on complex ideas to millions of high-school and college students, have led us to simplify the question of tragic character, to seek ways of smoothing out its hairy and unruly surfaces. The most familiar and enduring of these simplifications is the doctrine of the tragic flaw, the notion that the tragic figure is cursed by an inescapable weakness of character leading inevitably—and perhaps properly—to death. Comfortable and useful though it seems, thinking about Shakespeare's heroes in terms of a tragic flaw amounts to a kind of intellectual bypass, a means of proceeding that permits us to move quickly but causes us to miss too much. It is time to challenge this orthodoxy and to replace it with a more balanced and appropriate conception of the Shakespearean protagonist and of tragedy in general.

The law of the flaw is a relatively recent phenomenon. To read Aristotle himself is to find the notion of tragic error associated specifically with an act, a mistake in judgment, not with a weakness of character, and while it is true that Bradley identifies a "fatal imperfection or error" and speaks of the hero's "trait" or "characteristic action," these nouns are part of a complex and balanced analysis in which Bradley pays equal attention to the competing energies in Shakespeare's creation of the tragic figure. The prevalence of the flaw theory owes much to its value as an instructional device: it permits us to apprehend a complex representation of a mysterious human experience and, by naming it, to master that mystery. It is a convenient way of explaining what happens to Hamlet and Oedipus and the other tragic heroes who are alien to us and, more importantly, to our students. It allows us to put the tragic hero in a box labeled "procrastination" or "ambition" or, in the somewhat fancier model, "hubris."

What is worse, its utility as a pedagogical aid has led us to overlook its serious and far-reaching interpretive implications. Deriving from the Victorian notion that "God's in his heaven, all's right with the world," the theory of the flaw suggests that those who experience bad fortune get what they deserve, that suffering must be the result of some kind of weakness, that the great tragic figures shouldn't have been surprised by and shouldn't resent their misery, that anybody who gets into big trouble is probably a pervert who ought to be punished. Phyllis Rose has complained that the doctrine of the tragic flaw "encourages self-satisfaction and the turning of one's back on other people's problems," and she wittily recounts her efforts to contest such conclusions in teaching *Oedipus the King:*

> Oedipus was my ace in the hole, because I think there's no way he can be seen as deserving his fate. An oracle has prophesied that he will sleep with his mother and kill

his father, so, horrified at the prospect of committing these crimes, he leaves the people he thinks are his parents. Of course, he runs smack into his real parents and commits the crimes he has been fleeing from. But how can he be seen as morally responsible? My students say he should never have left Corinth. He shouldn't have tried to escape the prophecy. His tragic flaw was arrogance. He flew off the handle. He shouldn't have killed that guy at the crossroads. Under the circumstances, he shouldn't have gone to bed with any woman without checking very carefully whether or not she was his mother.

("Hers," *New York Times*, Mar. 1, 1984)

If the flaw in the flaw is that it blames the tragic figure and exonerates the world—"I'm OK, Hamlet's not"—we must also be wary of the sentimental error involved in reversing the terms, which is to excuse the hero and assign the blame entirely to his environment.

An alternative to both positions is to see the dramatic action as a kind of tragic incompatibility between the hero's particular form of greatness and the earthly circumstances that he or she is forced to confront. In Shakespeare's tragic conception of the world, heroic ability becomes a handicap; distinctive talents constitute an ironic form of fallibility. Rather than thinking of the tragic figures as "flawed," we might regard them as gifted, as possessing a surplus of talent that puts them into immediate conflict with a hostile world. So widely credited is the image of the proud, irresponsible, foolish, or doomed protagonist that apparently we need to be reminded that Shakespeare's tragic figures are heroes, and since heroes are out of fashion, we need to put some pressure on the word to make it accessible and meaningful to a contemporary audience. What follows are some guidelines for refreshing our thinking—and that of our students—about these compelling people.

Hamlet, Romeo and Juliet, Brutus, Macbeth—all are exceptional, superhuman, different from the rest of us. A way of putting it that might make them more sympathetic is to say that they are outsiders. We sense this distinction before we arrive at the theater because we know that we are going to see Olivier's Othello or Mel Gibson's Hamlet: casting directors don't give these roles to nobodies. Once the play begins, greatness is signified most obviously by extraordinary patterns of speech: nobody else sounds like Hamlet ("Whether 'tis nobler in the mind to suffer / The slings and arrows of outrageous fortune") or Juliet ("And when I shall die, / Take him and cut him out in little stars") or Macbeth ("The multitudinous seas incarnadine, / Making the green one red"). A primary effect of this brilliant language is to signify exceptional imagination. These men and women speak differently from the rest of us, and from the rest of the cast, because they see differently.

Shakespeare's tragic characters are visionaries, purists, idealists. Believing in a strict correspondence between the way things are and the way things appear to them, they commit themselves imaginatively to the fulfillment of an ideal, whether personal or political or both. This is what Alfred Harbage notices when he remarks on "their *unworldliness*, their incapacity for compromise," and speaks of them as "imperfect ones torn by their dreams of perfection, mortals with immortal longings in them" (*The Complete Pelican Shakespeare*, p. 821). Most of the qualities commonly associated with the Shakespearean tragic figure—pride, solipsism, endurance, nobility, sensitivity—either support or arise from this habit of idealization. Hamlet demands absolute honesty ("I know not seems"); Brutus insists that the assassination of Caesar is not a murder but a noble act of patriotism; King Lear believes that his daughters mean what they say. The action of each of the tragedies represents a heroic attempt to impose this personal vision upon a hostile and recalcitrant world.

Another way of framing these characters' experience is to say that they are like children, for their idealistic conception of the world is usually marked by a radical simplicity or naiveté. Even Hamlet, the most intellectually capable and sophisticated of the lot, displays a youthful confidence and optimism in his capacity to know the truth and by that means to set himself free. That Othello is sometimes thought of as a simpleton is partly a function of his devotion to an elementary and clearly defined sense of honor, honesty, loyalty, and conjugal love. Romeo and Juliet conform well to such a pattern because, relatively speaking, they are children. Brash and independent, the young lovers seek to realize an ideal union in a deceptive and corrupt world. There is, to be sure, haste in their wooing and wedding, not to mention their deaths; and the carelessness with which they act has been taken by some as Shakespeare's indictment of their behavior as thoughtless and foolish. "They stumble that run fast," says Friar Lawrence, a statement often quoted as final evidence of Shakespeare's disapproval. And yet to narrow the meaning of *Romeo and Juliet* to the cliché that "haste makes waste" is surely to misrepresent the destruction of innocence that gives the play its extraordinary poignance. Passionate love, both physical and spiritual, is what destroys them, but it is also what draws us to them. Shakespeare does not present their passion as a flaw.

Macbeth may be difficult to think of as a hero or a visionary, since it is easy to condemn him as ambitious and leave it at that. And it is true that Shakespeare's practice is more complicated here: Macbeth becomes a criminal very early in the play, the shocking nature of his crimes making him much less sympathetic than Hamlet or Romeo. In other words, it is hard to discern idealism in a murderer. Nevertheless, knowing that he should not, Macbeth acts upon a faith in his own strength and privilege. He hopes that by his own will he can transform wish into fact: the great soliloquy delivered during the first banquet reveals a desire for certainty:

> If it were done when 'tis done, then 'twere well
> It were done quickly. If th' assassination
> Could trammel up the consequence and catch
> With his surcease success, that but this blow
> Might be the be-all and the end-all . . .
>
> (1.7.1–5)

If only we could be sure that it would be finished, if only we could control every possibility, if only we could be sure that all the consequences could be accounted for as soon as the deed is done. But such hopes are naive: all the conditionals, the "if"s, remind us that Macbeth's vision of the perfect crime is quixotic. His fantasy is undermined not only morally but also verbally, by the slippage of meaning that we see in the puns. In these few lines alone, the meaning of "done" changes with each of its three uses (and the echoes *Dun*can and *Dun*sinane and "the *dun*nest smoke of hell" are audible in the background). The proximity and similarity of "surcease" and "success," with their equivalent sounds and related meanings, add further complications, since "success" signifies both achievement and continuation (as in "succession"). Macbeth believes erroneously that he can move directly and without resistance from what he calls the "happy prologue" spoken by the witches into the "swelling act," believes that he can exert absolute control over his destiny. If only Fleance had not escaped, Macbeth "had else been perfect" (3.4.23), but evil is never complete, perfection never possible.

But the tragic hero behaves as if it were, as if the world could be remade by strength of will. Coriolanus' mother goes to the heart of the matter when she says to her son, "You are too absolute." The single-mindedness with which the hero pursues the ideal vision produces the central conflict of each play, for the world resists transmutation or control, and this conflict leads to a kind of dislocation, usually geographical (as in Hamlet's trip to England, or Romeo's banishment) but psychological as well. Despite the fierceness of the pressures that frustrate the heroic will, the tragic hero refuses to compromise or to relinquish the object of desire. As Macbeth puts it, in a speech that demonstrates both the power of his will and the tendency of the world to challenge his desire,

> But let the frame of things disjoint, both the worlds suffer,
> Ere we will eat our meal in fear, and sleep
> In the affliction of these terrible dreams
> That shake us nightly.   (3.2.18–22)

The dreams of perfection have become the nightmares that torture Macbeth and Lady Macbeth. Each of the heroes is betrayed by commitment to a vision of perfection and by the force of will dedicated to that commitment. Even when it becomes clear that the ideal vision cannot be sustained, the hero remains faithful to it; and this rigidity is both self-destructive and ennobling.

And what of the world that resists the hero's attempts to change or control it? Shakespeare ensures that our attitude toward that world, like our attitude toward his heroes, is mixed. It is a place of evil, disappointment, and mortality: its characteristics are apparent in the deceptions and illness of the Danish court that frustrate Hamlet, or in the misunderstandings and revenges that Romeo and Juliet attempt to escape. At the same time, however, we recognize it as our own world, the realm of the ordinary, the everyday, the nonheroic. These are the conditions that Malcolm and Macduff manage to restore at the end of *Macbeth*. The tragic figures imagine something extraordinary, seek to transcend the compromises of the familiar, and we both admire that imaginative leap and acknowledge its impossibility. The contest between world and will brings about misery, insanity, and finally death; it also produces meaning and magnificence.

In *Romeo and Juliet* Shakespeare dwells on the attractions of the heroes' dream. Surrounded by an urban environment of hate and violence, the lovers retreat into a nocturnal realm of moonlight and privacy. They create a space free of the restrictions and prejudices implicit in the names Capulet and Montague. In this space, inherited ideas can be discarded ("deny thy name") and feelings truly expressed. Custom requires one kind of behavior; the lovers choose another. As Juliet puts it in the balcony scene:

> Fain would I dwell on form; fain, fain deny
> What I have spoke. But farewell compliment.
> Dost thou love me? . . .
>
> In truth, fair Montague, I am too fond,
> And therefore thou mayst think my havior light.
> But trust me, gentleman, I'll prove more true
> Than those that have more coying to be strange.
>   (2.2.93–95, 103–6)

This innocent appeal to frankness and feeling is surely one source of the play's enduring popularity: in setting the simple candor of youth against the compromises and obstacles of their heritage, present against past, Shakespeare invites the audience to sympathize with the lovers and to wish for a world in which quarreling parents could be brought to their senses, Tybalt could welcome his enemies to the banquet, and Friar John, undeterred by the plague, could have delivered his message to Romeo. "If only" is the persistent theme.

On the other hand, an audience is less inclined to sanction Macbeth's ambitious fantasy of sovereignty than to endorse the young lovers' passionate dreams of fulfillment. Although it is possible early in the play to sense the seductive power of Macbeth's wishes—if only this were a world where desires could be realized by an "easy" act, where "it were done, when 'tis done," where a little water could cleanse us of our wicked deeds—in this tragedy Shakespeare emphasizes the danger of illusion: the ideal itself is associated with murder, the visionary and courageous hero rapidly degenerates into a bloody tyrant, and most of the tragedy is given over to the appalling consequences of Macbeth's wickedness. In this respect *Romeo and Juliet* and *Macbeth* represent the two extremes of the tonal range that Shakespeare draws upon in all the tragedies: in the early play, he concentrates on the loveliness of the ideal, teasing us with the hope of its realization; in the later one, he dwells on the hideous personal and political effects of the hero's subjective view. In both, however, he simultaneously stimulates and deflates our imaginations, teasing us with the promises of illusion and forcing us to feel the pain of disillusionment. The struggle against imperfection is doomed, but to label the heroes as "flawed" is to conclude that the attempt is not worth making, and such a judgment falsifies the balances and paradoxes of Shakespearean tragedy.

One final paradox. Although the tragic hero is dead and the vision dispelled, both visionary and vision are revived every time the play is read or performed. The pessimistic lines about life as a "poor player" should remind us that Macbeth himself survives—in the work of fiction. Shakespeare's tragedies are all to some extent plays about reading and misreading. Macbeth's error is that he misinterprets to his advantage the prophecies and warnings of the witches; he does, in other words, precisely what all of us do every day—he misreads a text, only we do it with literary texts, and so the consequences for us are relatively minor. The text that Macbeth misreads is the text of the world, of the shadowy moral world of good and evil in which misunderstanding can have fatal results. The impulse to dream is safest in the theater, or on the painter's canvas, or in the lyrics of a song. Shakespeare has imagined the stories of heroes and turned those lives into art. The theater is the medium by which we may briefly inhabit a more nearly perfect world, and even though it is transient, our participation in the imaginative world of the tragic hero momentarily enriches our experience of this one.

The King James Version of *Macbeth*

DAVID M. BERGERON

UNIVERSITY OF KANSAS

As I sit to write about *Macbeth*, all around me nature provides a "hurly-burly" of thunder and lightning. "Hurly-burly"— that word I remember from my high-school study of *Macbeth:* I loved the sound of that word. I enjoyed my teacher's evocation of the witches, for which she had particular skill. I reveled in the images of life as a walking shadow or sleep as knitting up the raveled sleave of care. I committed speeches to memory. I liked Banquo, especially his ghost, which haunts Macbeth. As an impressionable teenager I was particularly susceptible to the witches, the ghosts, and the thrilling, if evil, power of Lady Macbeth. I still am. But now I also wonder about Banquo and his purpose in this play: wherefore Banquo? My answer derives in part from this play's presumed connection to King James I, who in 1603 became the first non-English king of England since the eleventh-century invasion of the Normans.

In his 1950 book *The Royal Play of Macbeth,* Henry Paul lays out in some 418 pages his case for Shakespeare's play as conscious flattery of King James. He provides the scene of the first performance of *Macbeth,* presumably at Hampton Court on August 7, 1606, in the presence of King James and his visiting brother-in-law, King Christian IV of Denmark. Paul writes:

> . . . let the enthusiastic Shakespearean picture in his mind's eye the first performance of *Macbeth* in the great hall of Hampton Court. . . . Keeping this picture in mind, he may watch the face of the Scottish king [i.e., James] as he sees his royal ancestors descended in line from Banquo, personated by actors of the King's Company, slowly passing one after the other over the stage as the procession of the kings. (p. 365)

What began in this book as hypothesis has become for Paul apparently established fact. This date of the first performance of *Macbeth* has been accepted by several editors, including Kenneth Muir in the Arden edition. But one fundamental problem remains: lack of evidence. We know from court records that the King's Men performed at court on that day in August; beyond that we know nothing. One could theoretically posit any number of plays as the one performed that August day. On this subject Henry Paul has provided us a rich fantasy: a King James version of *Macbeth.*

If James did not appear at an alleged first performance of the play, what connection, if any, does he have to *Macbeth*? Enter Banquo. Avoiding Paul's excesses and not wanting to push the "topical" nature of the play, I do nevertheless want to offer a kind of "local reading" of *Macbeth.* Such a reading does not deny the possibilities of the "universal" understanding of the play, its grand, seemingly timeless exploration of politics, regicide, and evil. The question of political succession in this play strikes me as both local and universal; it permeates many of Shakespeare's plays, even as it doubtless grows out of immediate concerns about who should succeed the sovereign to the English crown.

When Macbeth first appears, Banquo accompanies him as they encounter the witches (1.3). Just before the witches vanish, the Third Witch says: "So all hail, Macbeth and Banquo!" And the First Witch responds: "Banquo and Macbeth, all hail!" (71–72). For the moment Macbeth and Banquo seem interchangeable, reminiscent of Rosencrantz and Guildenstern. Although friends, Macbeth and Banquo emerge from the prophecies as rivals. The witches assure Macbeth that he shall someday become king. When Banquo, hearing this, presses the witches to look into the seeds of time and enunciate his fate, they respond in riddles:

> FIRST WITCH
> Lesser than Macbeth and greater.
> SECOND WITCH
> Not so happy, yet much happier.
> THIRD WITCH
> Thou shalt get kings, though thou be none.
>
> (68–70)

Macbeth succinctly and correctly interprets Banquo's destiny: "Your children shall be kings" (89). That recognition forms the basis of Banquo's connection to King James, even as it voices what will be the growing theme of the child's place in royal succession. Macbeth and Banquo share a secret; this solidifies their relationship, indicated in part by their speaking "asides" to each other. For example, Macbeth says to Banquo at the close of 1.3: "Think upon what hath chanced, and at more time, / The interim having weighed it, let us speak / Our free hearts each to other" (170–73). No exchange takes place, although Macbeth in 2.1 again suggests such a conversation.

Who was this Banquo, the one who begins to haunt Macbeth, who in turn says of Banquo: "There is none but he / Whose being I do fear . . ." (3.1.59–60)? No evidence survives to suggest that a real Banquo ever existed in Scottish history. Apparently Hector Boece (Boethius) created the myth of Banquo and a son Fleance in his *History of Scotland* (1526). I have no reason to think that Shakespeare read this Scottish chronicle, but he certainly seems to have known that rambling conglomeration of history that we refer to as *Holinshed's Chronicles* (especially the 1587 edition). Holinshed took from Boece the story of Banquo and incorporated it into the history of Macbeth's reign. He underscores the friendship of Banquo and Macbeth. Indeed, we find these disturbing words as Holinshed describes Macbeth's intention to kill Duncan: "At length therefore, communicating his purposed intent with his trustie friends, amongst whome Banquho was the chiefest, vpon confidence of their promised aid, he slue the king at Enuerns . . ." ("The Historie of Scotland," *Chronicles*, p. 171). Holinshed's account implies Banquo's complicity in Duncan's murder. No such idea appears in the play. Although he suspects Macbeth, Banquo has not been involved in the crime. Shakespeare swerves away from what his source indicates. Why?

Enter King James, putative descendant of Banquo. After Macbeth has Banquo killed in 3.3, intending also to have Fleance murdered, he continues to be afflicted emotionally with the ghostly presence of Banquo, as in the banquet scene (3.4), and psychologically and politically by the recognition that Banquo's children would someday rule Scotland. For the childless Macbeth this prophecy especially galls. In his last encounter with the witches his obsession prompts him to ask: "Yet my heart / Throbs to know one thing. Tell me, if your art / Can tell so much: shall Banquo's issue ever / Reign in this kingdom?" (4.1.114–17). In unison they respond: "Seek to know no more" (118). But Macbeth insists. The witches then provide a tableau: "*A show of eight kings, the eighth king with a glass in his hand, and Banquo last*" (126 SD). These kings signify the

Stuart kings who eventually ruled Scotland, King James himself included in that number, this line that seems, in Macbeth's words, to "stretch out to th' crack of doom" (132). The mirror held up to history reveals Banquo's lineage, and this tableau afflicts Macbeth through its art. Assuming that Shakespeare wrote *Macbeth* after James came to the English throne—a relatively safe assumption—he avoids any unflattering portrait of the king's ancestor by changing the historical account found in Holinshed. In this his only exploration of Scottish history, Shakespeare embraces a King James version of Macbeth's story that portrays Banquo in a favorable light. The parade of the kings and Macbeth's interpretation hint at a future that eventually comes to pass with James's successful union of England and Scotland.

Who was this King James whose ancestors Macbeth examines? Having recently written a biography of this king and the immediate members of his family, I have been asked on more than one occasion to explain King James, a man of religious and dramatic as well as political interest. A few people have seriously asked: Was he the one who wrote the Bible? Not quite. In 1604 at the Hampton Court conference of the English church, James tried to reconcile the opposing Catholic and Puritan wings of the church. He had more success in establishing a committee to prepare a new translation of the Bible. Their work culminated in the Authorized Version of the Bible, published in 1611 and familiarly known as the King James Version. For reasons that elude me, we most often refer to the Shakespearean period as the Elizabethan era, when in fact Shakespeare wrote a substantial group of plays after James came to England. The great Folio collection of Shakespeare's plays—which provides the only early text for roughly half of the plays—appeared late in James's reign in 1623. Unlike his predecessor Elizabeth, James put all the principal London acting companies under royal patronage in May 1603. Henceforth Shakespeare's company would be known as the King's Men, servants of the royal household, entitled to wear the king's livery. They regularly performed before the Jacobean court, enjoying the status and protection of royal patronage.

Before he arrived in England to become James I, James had ruled Scotland for thirty-six years with a degree of political success not everyone would have anticipated. Born on June 19, 1566, in Edinburgh Castle as the only child of Mary Queen of Scots and her husband Lord Darnley, the young child found himself thrust inauspiciously into the brutal world of Scottish politics. By the following year James's father had been killed in a mysterious explosion, his mother had remarried, and she and her new husband had been driven into exile in England. Therefore on July 29, 1567, the barely one-year-old infant became James VI, king of Scotland, a position that he would hold for the rest of his life. To assist him in ruling, James had a series of four regents, the first two of whom were assassinated. Violence and cruelty defined his political world. By the late 1570s, however, the teenage king began to rule in his own right; and in October 1579 he received public adulation in a royal civic pageant in Edinburgh's streets. This spectacle marked a rite of passage for the young king, helping define the beginning of his actual rule. In this entertainment James saw, among other things, a tableau that represented all the previous Scottish kings. From early on, then, James manifested a deep interest in and fascination with his lineage—a fact that adds resonance to *Macbeth*, Shakespeare's Scottish play, with its powerful attention to royal genealogy.

The decade of the 1580s may have been one of the most formative and important in James's life. The Scottish lords succeeded in capturing James in 1582 and separating him from his much-loved male cousin, Esmé Stuart. Not until several months later did James escape, never to be reunited with Esmé. If nothing else, the episode illustrates the perilous nature of Scottish politics and the relative power of the nobles: James's authority remained open to serious challenge. Shakespeare's play captures this precarious nature of power in Scotland. If somewhat insecure in Scotland, James also had an uneasy claim to the English throne, a matter of great anxiety to the English people. The topic of succession remained uppermost in everyone's mind as Elizabeth aged without issue. James regularly cast his eye on the English crown, knowing that England would at some moment have to settle the question of the successor to Elizabeth, who steadfastly, if perversely, refused to name or acknowledge an heir. But the two sovereigns reached an agreement in 1586 that tacitly assured James of a claim to the English crown; it also provided him with a much-desired annual pension of £4000.

Only James's mother clearly stood in the way of potentially smooth sailing. But with the trial of Mary in late 1586 and her subsequent execution on February 8, 1587, James gained new confidence about eventual possession of the English crown. It remains difficult to determine who in early 1587 desired Mary's death more, Elizabeth or James. Yes, James showed a few expected signs of grief, but mainly he was enormously relieved; and he did nothing to avenge Mary's execution. Her death removed a rival to the Scottish throne. As long as she lived, James's grasp on the crown could not be secure. Having been separated from Mary as a year-old child, James knew virtually nothing about her as his mother. They kept up a regular correspondence, but much of the writing appears formulaic. Mary indulged in many outbursts at her son, who would not help her, who would not rescue her from English imprisonment, who would not enter an agreement for joint rule of Scotland. James made a calculated decision and abandoned the cause of his Catholic mother: he saw a brighter future in the southern kingdom of England. He tied his political fortunes to his cousin Elizabeth.

In October 1589 James set sail for Denmark to claim the teenage Princess Anne for his bride. Clearly James waited until the fate of his mother had been decided before he focused on marriage. He made it clear in a farewell letter that he wrote before departing that he understood marriage to be his political obligation as king of Scotland. James and Anne even enjoyed some early marital bliss, especially during spring 1590, spent in Denmark.

Although obsessed with problems of succession, James also had a pronounced interest in witches. Shortly after the return to Scotland, James became directly involved in witch trials. He learned to his astonishment and horror that some of the witches had sought to create sea storms during his voyage to Denmark in order to destroy him; only his religious faith, apparently, prevented the success of their efforts. James followed the trials with great attention, even participating in cross-examination. From such experiences and from his own ideas he had no difficulty believing in both the reality and the potentially harmful power of witches. He wrote a pamphlet called *Daemonologie*, first published in 1597, reissued in 1603, and eventually included in the folio collection of his *Workes* in 1616. In this treatise, James outlines his understanding of witches, a view that fits into his theological concepts. If James ever saw a performance of *Macbeth*, he would have found the appearance of witches altogether plausible. He delighted in supernatural explanations of human events.

James's marriage to Anne produced three surviving children from the last decade in Scotland: Henry (1594), Elizabeth (1596), and Charles (1600). Unlike a childless Macbeth or Elizabeth, James now had progeny who could assure a peaceful succession. James had therefore accomplished one of the major tasks of a sovereign. Even though he and Anne fought vigorously over the nurture of Prince Henry, they at least offered the country an heir apparent. Although understanding the political advantages that these children offered, James nevertheless often felt intense jealousy about them. His effort to instruct Henry in the art of governing culminated in his writing *Basilicon Doron,* secretly printed in 1599 but expanded for its official publication in 1603, in time for James's arrival in England. Some scholars have seen in this treatise ideas about government and kingly behavior that find a residue in *Macbeth.* I am less certain of that; but I do know that *Basilicon Doron,* an unusual document because it was written by a reigning monarch, has no immediate precursors in either Scotland or England. Reading this tract filled with sanctimonious idealism, one cannot help but notice finally the ironic gap between James's precepts and his own behavior. James, for example, urges Henry to be frugal, to exercise self-restraint in all matters, and to be especially careful and circumspect in the choice of friends. James himself fails on all counts.

Like his mythical ancestor, Banquo, James knew that his children would be rulers. Their children could expand the Stuart lineage indefinitely. In 1603 English citizens marveled at this Scottish king who had arrived to rule them, complete with a wife and three children. Being at moments politically astute, James emphasized his political advantage as not only father of the country but father of children who could succeed him. The English found this possibility reassuring and in sharp contrast to his three childless predecessors. Macbeth, we recall, stands out because he has no children, a fact that sets him apart from Banquo or Duncan and powerfully emphasizes the crucial importance of progeny.

Because of the plague, James delayed his first speech to Parliament until March 19, 1604, nearly a year after he ascended the English throne. Throughout the address he underscores what he calls his "lineal descent." The peace that he has brought the kingdom derives in part from his "descent lineally out of the loynes of Henry the seventh." Henry's uniting of England "is nothing comparable," James says, "to the Union of two ancient and famous Kingdomes, which is the other inward Peace annexed to my Person." James not only has an illustrious and royal ancestry; he also provides for its continuation, "having healthful and hopeful Issue of my body . . . for continuance and propagation of that undoubted right which is in my Person." Also in 1604 George Owen Harry published *The Genealogy of the High and Mighty Monarch, James.* This curious document starts with Noah, works its way through Brutus, and concentrates on the Welsh lineage of Fleance before finally arriving at James. Obviously, Banquo's legacy has been happier than Macbeth's dead-end lineage.

Civic spectacles of the early years of James's English rule also reinforce concepts of the king's lineage. On March 15, 1604, James witnessed and participated in one of the greatest civic pageants of the Renaissance period. Three major dramatists, Ben Jonson, Thomas Dekker, and Thomas Middleton, devised this London entertainment and wrote the speeches. Shakespeare may also have been present because the King's Men, as servants of the royal household, lined the streets with other groups under royal patronage. Seven triumphal arches, for which the City of London and the guilds spent thousands of pounds and which survive in Stephen Harrison's drawings, rose in London's streets. In a five-hour procession James, Anne, and Henry moved from the Tower through London toward Westminster. The triumphal arch located at Gracious Street contained allusions to James's *Basilicon Doron* and to his poem *Lepanto.* A painting on this arch depicted both Henry VII dressed in imperial robes and James approaching to receive a scepter, thereby highlighting one part of James's genealogy, his lineal descent from the first Tudor that he enunciated four days later in Parliament. Activity at the Soperlane arch underscored James's link to Brutus, mythical founder of Britain. Zeal's speech in Fleet Street noted that, although Brutus divided the kingdoms, James, his heir, had united them. This street pageant fixes in the public mind visual and verbal representations of the new king's heritage.

On a late August afternoon in 1605 James and his family arrived in Oxford. Near St. John's College three sibyls greeted the royal entourage. The first made clear that the three had formerly delivered prophecies in Macbeth's time:

> Fame says the fatal Sisters once foretold
> Power without end, great Monarch, to thy stock.
> One greeted Banquo, proud Lochaber's Thane:
> Not to thee Banquo, but to thy descendants
> Eternal rule was promised by immortals,
> Hid in a glade as Banquo left the Court.
> We three same Fates so chant to thee and thine
> As, watched by all, from fields thou near'st the city. . . .

In the Latin verses written by Matthew Gwinn the sibyls cried all hail to the other members of the royal family and praised James. Without insisting, as some have done, that Shakespeare was present for this occasion in Oxford, we can nevertheless see in a scant few lines the Banquo link to James sung out in a public gathering presumably before Shakespeare wrote *Macbeth*. The first extant Jacobean Lord Mayor's Show, Anthony Munday's *The Triumphes of Re-United Britannia*, took place in London at the end of October 1605. Uncharacteristic of such mayoral pageants, this show emphasizes the king rather than London's new lord mayor. In various ways the drama retells the story of Brutus, thereby making it possible to view James as the second Brutus who has now united the divided kingdoms. Making such a link, the character Brutus says of James: "he is the man / On whose faire birth our elder wits did scan, / Which Prophet-like seventh Henry did forsee, / Of whose faire childe comes *Britanies* unitie." Munday included also a tableau of seven English kings who had been associated with the Merchant Taylors Guild; an eighth place remained vacant for King James—a device analogous to the show of eight kings in *Macbeth*. Both tableaux highlight royal lineage.

The translators of the 1611 Bible dedicated their work to James and noted their relief "when we beheld the Government established in Your Highness, and Your hopeful Seed, by an undoubted Title, and this also accompanied with peace and tranquillity at home and abroad." Royal lineage of the past and the anticipation of the future permeate Shakespeare's concern in *Macbeth*, leading, for example, to decriminalizing Banquo's actions, thereby making him a worthy ancestor of James: "Your children shall be kings." Macbeth understood correctly, and James himself offers valid testimony to that prophecy. Indeed, the current ruling household in Great Britain derives its heritage from James. Without yielding to fantasy, we can accept a local reading of *Macbeth* that provides a King James version of it.

Shakespeare's Clowns and Fools

MEREDITH ANNE SKURA

RICE UNIVERSITY

For a long while Shakespeare's clowns were an embarrassment to everybody, and they were censored from productions. Lear's fool, for example, was left out of every one of the many eighteenth-century performances of *King Lear*. Producers in the nineteenth century kept Macbeth's porter in the play, but they cut his lines to "Knock, knock, knock." Twentieth-century productions have at times imposed their own censorship on Shakespeare, invoking aesthetic if not moral justifications. The clowns in *Romeo and Juliet* and *Othello* are occasionally removed from modern productions, for example. On the whole, however, in our era clowns have been rescued. We find more than random "comic relief" in the clown scenes, and we now see them as part of each play's larger thematic and imagistic design. Macbeth's porter doesn't merely "relieve" us (by slipping comically on a banana peel, for example); he helps create the grotesquely hellish atmosphere created by Macbeth's crime. The rest of this essay explores the clown's function both in Renaissance drama at large and in Shakespeare.

In turning to the fool and the clown we are true to the spirit of the sixteenth and seventeenth centuries. "Everything is full of Fools," said Erasmus—or, as Robin Goodfellow put it in *A Midsummer Night's Dream*, "Lord, what fools these mortals be!" Along with the new sense of individual possibility and the expansion of human horizons in the Renaissance came the continual reminder of the lower side of experience, and the fascination with fools, clowns, and rogues who represent the pure animal existence beneath all our civilized aspirations. They embody the pure life force, as Susanne Langer said appreciatively: "tumbling and stumbling through one disaster and another, the clown shows a brainy opportunism in the face of an essentially dreadful universe."

The clown wasn't invented by dramatists. The fool had always had his role in communal rituals and festivals, the seasonal celebrations that calibrated the agricultural year. And all year round there were real fools or jesters who were permanent representatives of human folly at court and in the great houses; and there were fools in literature, too. Given that comedy in general was part of theater almost from its beginnings, it is no wonder that fools and clowns found their way into plays as well. Even the mystery plays that acted out stories of the Bible for illiterate crowds had their shrewish wives and comic shepherds. The morality plays often starred a comic Vice or Fool who served as master of ceremonies as Everyman made his way between the forces of Good and Evil. Not only was he important to the plot, but he commented on it and interpreted it for the audience, and he occasionally stopped the play to collect ticket money. In the traveling groups who went from town to town putting on outdoor performances, the company clown often had the job of gathering the crowd as well as collecting the money.

By the time Shakespeare started writing plays, clowns were in most of the plays—

even when there were none in the sources for those plays and when none seemed to belong. Preston's *King Cambyses*, for example, was advertised as "a lamentable tragedy," but it was nonetheless "mixed full of pleasant mirth"—just like Bottom's production of *Pyramus and Thisbe* in *A Midsummer Night's Dream*. For the crowds, the clown was the most popular part of the performance. He was the only character identified by role in stage directions, which remained the same from play to play—and from author to author and company to company. Thus Shakespeare's original scripts apparently read "Enter clown"—not "Enter Touchstone"—even though modern editors sometimes substitute the character's name. Audiences knew what to expect from "Clown," just as we know what to expect when we see a Charlie Chaplin film. The clown was usually ugly, wore country clothes with loose pants (called slops), and carried simple instruments like a drum. The clown's role was scattered through the play, but he also had his own skit or jig after the play was over. The jigs were vaudeville routines, the traditional song-and-dance act that was reliably simple, repetitive, funny, and obscene. Even the people who couldn't or wouldn't pay to see the main play waited until the "gatherers" or ticket-takers left their posts at the theater doors, and then sneaked in to see the clowns' jigs. These jigs collected such large and unruly crowds that they were finally outlawed while Shakespeare was still writing.

Some authors actually welcomed the clown's contribution and provided him with stage directions or lines that were in effect temporary licenses to do what he wanted. One stage direction in *The History of the Trial of Chivalry* (1605), for example, reads "Enter Forrester, speak anything, and exit"; and Heywood in *Edward the Fourth* writes that the clown Jocki is to be "led to whipping over the stage, speaking words, but of no importance." But many other authors resisted the clowns. They scorned the "jigging fool," as Brutus called him when he thrust himself head and shoulders into the general's tent during the war in *Julius Caesar*; they looked down on the "jigging veins of rhyming mother wits," as Marlowe called the writing he associated with clowns, and they scorned the audience who called for the clown. They made fun of characters like Polonius, who needed a jig or a tale of bawdry to keep him awake during a performance. Even if the author refused to include any clowning in the main body of his play, often the clown-actor added it himself. The clown was irrepressible—much like the class clown at school, who fills the same needs. Hamlet's warning to the clown among the players who come to Elsinore is typical of many an anticlown playwright's position:

> And let those that play your clowns speak no more than is set down for them, for there be of them that will themselves laugh, to set on some quantity of barren spectators to laugh too, though in the meantime some necessary question of the play be then to be considered. That's villainous and shows a most pitiful ambition in the fool that uses it.
>
> (3.2.40–47)

From Hamlet's lines we can see that clowns often did speak more than was set down for them, and that not only did they speak, they also engaged in attention-getting stage business, like faking a laugh (actors still do this to steal a scene). We can also learn that clowns as characters were considered extra or un-"necessary," and that as actors they seemed "ambitious" to the playwright who was competing for the audience's attention. In the "bad" First Quarto (1603) text of *Hamlet*, Hamlet speaks more than is set down for him in the Folio (1623). Was this a clown's addition? Wherever it originated, this Quarto speech gives Hamlet himself a chance to mimic the popular clown act—probably not very difficult for someone who already has an attitude or, as Hamlet called it, "an antic disposition":

And then you have some again that keeps one suit of jests, as a man is known by one suit of apparel, and gentlemen quotes his jests down in their tables, before they come to the play, as thus:

> "Cannot you stay till I eat my porridge?"
> and: "You owe me a quarter's wages!"
> and: "Your beer is sour!"
> and blabbering with his lips:
> and thus:

—keeping in his cinque-pace of jests, when, God knows, the warm clown cannot make a jest unless by chance, as the blind man catcheth a hare.   (3.2)

We can't reconstruct these skits, which Hamlet thinks weren't very funny anyway, but you get the picture.

Understandably, then, the first theater "stars" in England were the clown actors (or "clowns"), Richard Wilson and Robert Tarlton. Tarlton in particular won the hearts of Londoners. Few Elizabethans were as popular, or simply as well known, as Tarlton. On stage all he had to do was show his face or peep out from behind the curtains and people laughed. But his reputation spread far beyond the walls of the amphitheater. His name was adopted for taverns and for a fighting gamecock. Unlike even Shakespeare's name, Tarlton's name entered the vocabulary—"Tarltonizing" or fooling it; his ghost was resurrected to defend the stage in a pamphlet four years after his death, and collections of his "jests" were still appearing twenty years after he died. When he died, myths grew about a line of successors almost as sacred as the royal line itself. Will Kempe, who followed Tarlton, was known as his "Vice-gerent General," and there are stories of Tarlton adopting Robert Armin, the famous actor of Shakespeare's fools, who followed Kempe. Tarlton's successors were gifted artists in their own right—entertainers, ballad-makers—and were really more like collaborators than scripted actors. Kempe was a dancer, whose marathon nine-days' dance from London to Norwich drew a tremendous crowd and an outpouring of support, if the texts we have are any indication. In plays, Kempe must have improvised his own lines or elaborated on the playwright's text. Kempe was famous for his scenes in *A Knack to Know a Knave,* advertised on the first page as including "Kempe's applauded merriments of the men of Gotham." But the clown's role in that play—at least the part of it that has been recorded in the text—is neither particularly large nor very amusing. It must have depended on Kempe's "extemporal wit." Of course, if for some the clowns were the most popular part of the play, for others in the audience they were also the most mistrusted. The Puritan attack on drama often focused on precisely the sort of outrage the clown was accustomed to perpetrate: "bawdry, wanton shews and uncomely gestures."

Who was this clown, and what did he do that was so terrible—or so wonderful? He simply represented the lowest level of existence in his world. Socially he was an outcast, literally a "rustic" or countryman; "clown" is etymologically related to the words for "clod" or "lump," as in "clod of clay" or "lump of earth." He could also turn up in the form of coal miner, miller, constable, shoemaker, carpenter, or any other form of "rude mechanical," as Shakespeare called Bottom and his friends in *A Midsummer Night's Dream.* Hamlet's speech suggests that the typical clown was a servant, like Macbeth's porter or Capulet's servants. Mentally the clown lived on a lower level, too. While Hamlet might have had his head in the clouds, the "warm clown" had his feet on the ground and was interested in material realities—the bottom line, as we might say. (He was known as a "material fool.") We can also see in Hamlet's speech that the clown's routines included things like porridge and beer: eating and drinking and appetite. Hamlet's clown was above all a physical and passionate creature, and he depended on the kind of humor that Hamlet indicates: blabbering lips and some action even less describable, which Hamlet refers to as "thus." His emotional volatility generated many of his routines. Even as the other players were learning not to out-Herod Herod, the clown howled, yelled, and, in a well-known skit, wept copiously. He made scurvy faces, and he used props (sticks, shoes, animals—Launce comes on with a dog, Launcelot Gobbo's father with a dish of doves, and Cleopatra's servant with a basket of snakes).

Hamlet goes on to describe the clown by using imagery of incompetence—"a blind man catching a hare"—which captures the slapstick nature of many of the clown's familiar routines. Much of the clown's humor consisted of the practical jokes and aggression now relegated to cartoon animals. Also, as Hamlet's lines suggest, the clown, ignorant as he was, was not necessarily stupid; in fact, he was usually something of a trickster or sly fox who was always out for number one ("I pray you, remember the porter" [*Macbeth* 2.3.21]) and not afraid to push others around. The most famous of the three anecdotes about Tarlton's routines tells how, having been boxed on the ear, Tarlton passed the blow on to poor John Cobbler—and called him a "clown" for taking it. A second tells how he was beaten by his fellow actor, and a third how he played the youngest of three sons and insulted his dying father. No wonder that the playwright Fletcher complained, "Just because a player can abuse his fellow," he thinks he's "a first class clown." The rest of the clown's humor depended on scatology and sex, probably in that order. The clown dropped his "slops," farted, pissed, and threw up freely. Macbeth's porter tells us about "urine," "lechery," and having just thrown up; and one clown in Greene's *James IV* provides a graphic description of his diarrhea attack. While the Puritan critic Gosson complained that the players were "uncircumcised philistines," Tarlton told the audience about his troubles with his prepuce.

Finally, as the actual resident clowns in Hamlet's own Elsinore show us, the clown is at home with death as well as dirt. If not always a literal gravedigger, he could collect shoes from dead soldiers, joke about corpses, or pretend to be one himself, always seeming able to rebound into life. His durability is almost mythic. Falstaff, who has much of the clown in him and may have been played by a clown—by Will Kempe—famously revived after being "killed" on the battlefield, all the more remarkably for his great bulk. When Bottom plays the lover in *Pyramus and Thisbe* and kills himself, there is some speculation among the audience that he may "yet recover and prove an ass," that is, he will return to life and be his old self again—which of course he does. In *Merchant of Venice* the clown Launcelot Gobbo stages his own death and rebirth for his father, blind old Gobbo. Those much-ignored clowns in *Romeo and Juliet* are musicians who fiddle while Rome burns, as it were, making music while the tragic world falls apart around them—just as the gravediggers in *Hamlet* make jokes out of death.

Distinctive as all these traits made the clown, however, his attraction—and his uniqueness—came at least as much from his relation to the audience as from the country character he played. He was like a vaudeville act or like one of today's stand-up comedians. In particular his role was to mediate between the play and the audience, whether to gather the crowds and collect money as clowns had done for road shows, or to provide between-act diversions which appealed more directly than the play did to the crowd already gathered. Often he commented on or parodied the action, just the way a spectator might; or he made reference to himself as actor. The character Bubble, played by the clown-actor Greene, makes a point of telling us he is going to see Greene in a play. In this intimate relation to the audience the clown was just as abusive to them as he was to his fellow actors. One spectator recalls that when Tarlton came on stage to hear "no end of hissing" instead of being greeted with the "civil attention" he expected, he broke into "this sarcasticall taunt":

> I liv'd not in the Golden Age,
>> When Jason wonne the fleece,
> But now I am on Gotam's stage,
>> Where fooles do hisse like geese.

If the people threw apples at Tarlton, he rhymed insults back at them. When someone in the gallery pointed at him, Tarlton pretended to take it as an insult, gave the man the horns, and got so much the best of him in the ensuing exchange that "the poore fellow, plucking his hat over his eyes," left the theater. Shakespeare's clowns are not so direct, but both Bottom and the porter are left onstage alone for important speeches, and then their remarks are directed to the audience. When Quince runs away after Bottom is "translated," Bottom reassures *us* that he's not afraid; he assumes we're on his side even if his friends have deserted him:

> I see their knavery. This is to make an ass of me, to fright me. . . . But I will not stir from this place. . . . I will sing, that they shall hear I am not afraid.   (3.1.122–26)

And after the knocking in *Macbeth*, it is the audience whose sympathy the sleepy porter asks for when he enters alone, muttering,

> Here's a knocking indeed! If a man were porter of hell gate, he should have old turning the key.   (2.3.1–3)

He might even wink at us as he exaggerates, to let us in on the joke of saying to his unwelcome but important visitors, in effect, "To hell with you!"

Many observers have emphasized the clown's role as index of social tension outside the theater and even as an ingredient in it. Dario Fo, the Italian director who has made use of the modern clown's comedy for savage political satire, observes that "Clowns always speak of the same thing, they speak of hunger: hunger for food, hunger for sex, but also hunger for dignity, hunger for identity, hunger for power. In fact they introduce questions about who commands, who protests." Scholars of the Renaissance clown do not agree about whether the clown helped work out the social conflicts of the period or helped exacerbate them, but his prominence is important. In any case, Bottom and the rude mechanicals in the palace at "Athens" reflect a version of class structure in Elizabethan England.

Whether for or against the lower classes, Shakespeare seems to have taken to clowns like a duck to water. Some scholars have suggested that Shakespeare was heavily influenced by the clown-actors available to him. Early in his career the company clown was Will Kempe, a dancer and slapstick comedian, so Shakespeare created roles to make use of Kempe's special talents: Bottom, Peter, Dogberry. Then Kempe left and Armin came. Since Armin was a very different kind of actor, Shakespeare created a very different kind of clown: the "wise fool" like Lear's fool and Feste. This may well be true; Shakespeare is just the sort who would make use of the materials at hand. But I think it's also true that Shakespeare would have found his way to the clowns no matter what. His clowns' scenes, as Samuel Johnson said, "seem to be instinct." And even in the very earliest plays (before Kempe's contributions), where we can see signs of awkwardness in many scenes, the clowns (like Jack Cade in *2 Henry VI* or Launce in *Two Gentlemen of Verona*) are often the best part of their play. Then in the middle comedies we find the likes of Bottom, Launcelot Gobbo, and Dogberry (many of whom are much funnier than you'd think just from reading the play). These are the epitome of the Shakespearean clown—physical, fleshly, everything we mean by the bottom. And although they may be ignorant and gauche, they are also savvy, even wise. They know things that the aristocrats have to learn. In *A Midsummer Night's Dream*, for example, although he is silly, Bottom is not merely "a shallow, thick-witted fool." On the contrary, Bottom is deep. He knows that "wisdom and love keep little company" these days. He has something of that other forest actor, Rosalynd:

> O coz, coz, coz, my pretty little coz, that thou didst know how many fathom deep I am in love! But it cannot be sounded; my affection hath an unknown bottom, like the bay of Portugal.
>
> (*As You Like It*, 4.1.205–8)[3]

The clowns know, like Hamlet, that man is neither so noble in reason nor so "infinite in faculty" as he may think. They know that even the loveliest fairy queen has a hairy bottom. And that, in fact, it's not only our lower nature but our very aspirations that make us fools. After all, who is more foolish, Bottom in Titania's arms, or Titania who dotes on him? Shakespeare may have been a clown himself, even before he came to London. We have only one anecdote about Shakespeare's childhood, and—to the degree that one can trust such data at all—it may bear witness to certain tendencies in young William which, with enough hindsight, suggest what was to come later. John Aubrey, one of Shakespeare's earliest biographers, reports that Shakespeare could kill a calf in the high old style. This gave later biographers an interesting clue, and, after much speculation about whether or not Shakespeare had been apprenticed to a butcher, most now agree that "killing a calf" probably refers to playing a role in a comic street play that was still extant in the early twentieth century. The modern version involves several boys to play the butcher and the calf and to catch the calf's blood in a basin. The older version may have been a solo ventriloquist act. Otherwise we do not know much about the show except that it was considered fit entertainment for a five-year-old child—which might explain Hamlet's scornful reference to killing "so capital a calf" when he wants to insult that second-time child, Polonius. Thus Shakespeare, who is said to have played the parts of old men during his acting career, may well have begun—like Mercutio and Hamlet—by playing the fool.

---

[3] *The Riverside Shakespeare*, ed. G. Blakemore Evans (Boston: Houghton Mifflin Company, 1974).

PART TWO

How to Teach
Shakespeare
Through
Performance

·

Michael Tolaydo

EDITOR

Three-Dimensional Shakespeare

MICHAEL TOLAYDO

ST. MARY'S COLLEGE OF MARYLAND

"Shakespeare is hard to understand!"

"They talk funny!"

"The words are archaic!"

"It is written in old English and needs to be translated!"

"Why not read a modernized version!"

"You need to be English to do it!"

"The characters talk too much!"

"The plays are too long!"

When we teach the plays of Shakespeare, we must face our own and our students' baggage. As students ourselves, we have often been confronted with a playtext featuring lines set out in verse form on a page further complicated by a glossary, either beneath or opposite the lines of the text. We are told this page layout is a help to us. We can tell the difference between verse lines and those in prose because verse lines don't go to the edge of the page. We have received a lesson on iambic, trochaic, and other verse forms that, coupled with the number of notes on each page, screams to us that this is very, very complex stuff. For smart people only. As we are made to read the lines out loud, we may be corrected for pronunciation, while the rest of the class following along stops to check the glossary for word meanings. We find ourselves looking up words we already know such as "yea" and "sayest." Some of us have become entirely confused and dejected before we reach the end of the first page. Things plod on. We notice that there are many more pages to go until the end, and at this rate, the task seems impossible.

As teachers, I think we often forget that these plays were created to be heard and seen, and that the text we read—some of it corrupted through time by editors and printers—is actually only an attempt to capture that three-dimensional event which was performed on those old Elizabethan stages where the action often complemented the word. When we read a play, we miss some of what I call the performance language of the play. A line of text on a page does not exist as a piece of theater. A whole play does not come into being when it's in print. It breathes only when it is performed, and for that moment only. When we attend a theatrical performance, the words, pauses, vocal and technical sounds, movement, music, facial expressions, gestures, stage pictures, lighting, actors, costumes, and more are all working together to tell us something.

We know that Shakespeare's plays are not just about plot; many in his audience knew the stories before they saw the plays. They are really more about explorations into human nature, about language, and about the ambiguity that much of the language presents. Without question, some of this language is difficult; however, not all of it is. Each play contains a large amount of material that is easily comprehensible to virtually all age groups. By beginning in the classroom with what is approachable, we can learn—through performance—to take on more complex areas of study and make them absorbing for teachers and students alike.

As a working teacher, I believe that an initial approach to the plays can best be achieved through the performance of an immediately comprehensible scene. This approach generates and puts into play the necessary tools and skills to examine those more difficult and complex portions of the play, while it supplies students with self-esteem and confidence in their own ideas and opinions. A performed scene provides the class with direct experiences and insights into a play, which can be used by the teacher in a variety of ways. The discoveries made during the performance sessions will connect and add information as well as generally resonate throughout further study of the play.

Warning: It is important to note that when I speak of performance, I am not speaking about creating a scene for stage performance, nor am I suggesting that this work involves acting skills. I am rooted in the notion that, in getting up on their feet and doing a scene in the classroom, students will discover that most of the baggage list that begins this chapter is, in fact, myth. This exercise is a learning experience all by itself; in addition, learning in this way can also open up the play and provide the basis for further active exploration of plot, character, structure, language, genre, or What You Will.

The following methodology is one way for students to meet and/or experience Shakespeare through classroom performance. This approach will work with students of any age—elementary school through graduate seminar. Since each class is different and only you know the strengths, weaknesses, and needs of your students, there are sections in the following exercise you may wish to expand, adapt, skip, change, or rearrange.

I begin to teach a new play by arriving in class—well before any assignments or books are distributed—with photocopies of a group scene. Group scenes—those with five or more characters—involve more students, and they are usually easy to understand because they are full of exposition.

I have selected Act 1, scene 2 of *A Midsummer Night's Dream* for this chapter; however, every play you teach contains at least one and usually several scenes you can use in this way. (You will naturally notice that we do not have to begin the study of a play by starting with Act 1, scene 1. Having said that, if you are doing *Romeo and Juliet*, the first scene is an excellent one for this approach.) This particular scene is a perfect choice actually because it shows us a group of people putting on a play.

It's important that the scene be printed in large type and photocopied. There are several ways to achieve this: You can use the cut–paste–enlarge method, or you can use the formatting capabilities of your computer. However, copies should be in **TYPE LIKE THIS** so that everyone can see the words. The page should be free of notes or glossary, and the scene should be spread out over several pages so that many readers may be easily involved. In this case, I have scanned the new Folger edition of *A Midsummer Night's Dream* into my computer and formatted it.

I make sure that there is a copy of the scene for each class member. As I hand them out, I ask that no one look at them until my signal. Naturally, many students do not pay attention to this request. When I have distributed a copy of the scene to each student, I do not ask for volunteers but select my readers. It is very important to stress here that I do not necessarily select my actor-type students or confident readers to read only the good parts. Neither do I ask males to read only the male roles and females to read only female parts. We will be reading this scene several times, and we want to find out what the scene is about rather than who can play a particular part well. I am not casting a play, but involving students in the text and its meanings, and along the way hopefully breaking down a few stereotypical presumptions.

Because the parts of Bottom and Quince are large, I select a different Bottom and Quince for each page, labeling them Bottom and Quince 1, 2, and 3. Each Bottom and Quince begins reading her/his part at the top of the page assigned even if it is in the middle of a speech.

Since any scene you select will contain parts of varying complexity and length—in this scene Starveling and Snout have only one line apiece—your students with reading difficulties can leap into the action immediately.

After assigning parts in this fashion, I request that the rest of the class listen rather than read along. I tell my readers they should not worry about correct pronunciation but do the best they can and pronounce unfamiliar words the way they think they should sound. There are no Elizabethans around to tell us how words were pronounced, and it really does not matter very much; eventually we will collectively come to a pronunciation we feel is right for our scene. I inform them that they should try to read for sense and not to worry about acting the parts; if they want to act, that's fine, but it's not important in this process. Lastly, they need to read loud enough so the rest of the class can hear. I want the class to eventually feel at home with the words.

After they have read through the scene, I praise the readers. I then select ten more readers and ask them to read the scene again. This second reading is not to get a "better" reading but to encourage familiarity with the text. I ask the rest of the class to listen and to note what differences and new information they observe within the scene.

I then begin a discussion with a few questions. I emphasize that, for the purposes of this discussion, the answers to the questions are all contained within the scene and its possibilities, not through a broader knowledge of the play or through fantasy. The photocopied scene is our entire play. *Students must find lines and ideas in the text to support their views.*

In the initial discussion, I ask questions like this:

1. Who are these guys? (Possible answers: a bunch of workmen, a bunch of people putting on a play.)

2. How do you know? (Find the lines in the text that support your argument.)

3. What is going on here? What are these guys up to? How do you know? (Any answer is acceptable as long as it can be supported from the text. Possible answers: "They're putting on a play for the duke's wedding. It says so right here." "They're having trouble casting the parts because one guy wants to play everything. He says . . .")

4. Do these guys know each other? Are they comrades or are they getting together for the first time to put on this play? (Either answer is possible, and can be relatively well supported by the text. Since the class will *direct and enact* this scene, the students must decide—for the purposes of this in-class enactment—whether the characters in the scene are old or new friends. Ask for a hand vote; majority rules.)

5. Who's the boss of this group? How do you know? Who would like to be the boss of this group? How do you know? (Many fine possible answers here about Bottom, who wants to play all the parts and gives his audition piece in the middle of the

scene, and Peter Quince, who has selected the play and will select the cast. How strong or weak can this tension between them be?)

6. Why are they putting on the play?

Sometimes I assign a student to write all the answers on the blackboard or a piece of paper. I then reassign parts and ask the students to read the scene through again. This time I ask students to make notes of what new information they discover and to circle any word or phrase they don't understand. Then we start a second round of discussion:

1. Who wrote this play they are going to do? If Quince wrote it, has he written it all himself? Has he adapted some of it? Is it an original story? What do Snug, Snout, Starveling, and Flute think of the play? What do they think of the tension or lack of tension between Quince and Bottom? Why might they be so quiet during the scene? What are they doing during the scene? Do they want to be in the play? What about their characters? Is Bottom a bully? A loudmouth? An egomaniac? A good actor who wants to help? A leader? Is Snug stupid? Nervous? Slow? A new member of the group? Extremely shy? You can ask similar questions about the other characters in the scene. Is there any poetry in the scene? Is it good or bad poetry? What does it remind you of? While the text does not usually list character specifics or exact place, possible choices can be made if the text and scene context support them. (Possible answers: Quince wrote or organized the play. Snug fits any of the above possibilities. *It is IMPORTANT to note that there are several choices of equal value.* Snug can be shy because he asks for his lines ahead of time. Flute doesn't want to be in the play because he wants to be a hero—"a wand'ring knight"—and not play a woman's part. They are new friends and have never seen the Quince and Bottom show before, so they are stunned into quiet. They are old friends and used to both Bottom and Quince, so they barely react. Robin Starveling, the tailor with one line, knows Quince and is sewing one of the costumes.)

2. Any other comments about anything else that is going on in this scene? (Anything that can be supported by the text is possible.) You may wish to ask students to write down on the board or on paper the acceptable characteristics for each role as they are decided upon by the class.

3. What words do you have circled that you don't understand? (Frequent answers: "Phibbus' car," "Ercles," "a part to tear a cat in," "a lover more condoling," "we will rehearse most obscenely.")

Answers to some questions about meaning can be provided by other members of the class. For the answers to questions that their peers can't answer, direct students to look up the answers after or during class, either in a good text like the new Folger edition, or the *Oxford English Dictionary*, or C. T. Onions's *A Shakespeare Glossary*. I always provide answers to a few questions but not more than a few. I may ask, for example, "Who can think of a name that sounds a little like Ercles?" We may get to Hercules; if not, I will provide the answer and then perhaps ask, "What did Hercules do? What animal family does a lion belong to? What do you think 'a part to tear a cat in' is alluding to?"

Depending on the nature of your class, you may wish to read the scene one more time with another set of readers or, if you have a small group, with previous readers speaking different roles. Ask a few more questions. Ask *them* to ask questions. I sometimes include a fast read-through involving each class member. We form a circle; one student begins to read Quince's first line. As soon as the reader comes to a question mark, a period, a colon, a semicolon, or an exclamation point—commas do *not* count—she stops reading and the next person in the circle picks it up. We want this reading to be smooth and even and to make sense.

The students are now ready to put the scene "on its feet." I select a new cast to act out the parts; this can be anyone who wants to read who hasn't yet had a turn, along with others to complete the cast. *The remainder of the class will direct the scene. No one is uninvolved.* The operating principle here is that there are many different workable ways to stage this scene—not one correct way. Before actual performance work, we need to consider these questions:

1. Where does this scene take place? What time of year is it? (Frequent answers: "a pub," "the back room at Peter Quince's shop," "the town square," "spring," "summer," because the play is called *A Midsummer Night's Dream*.)

The cast and directors check the text to make sure the location "fits." If the forest is suggested, make sure a student searches the text to discover why this scene probably doesn't take place there. Once a location has been agreed upon for this production, talk about what it might look like. Elizabethan? Modern? What does the place have in it? Use chairs and desks and anything else in the room to create the space you want.

2. Entrances and exits: Who should come onstage from where? With whom? Why? Does the text give you a clue?

3. Who's the most important person in the scene? Who *thinks* he's the most important person in the scene? How do you act it out to show this?

4. How does the cast enact the decisions the class made earlier—about the boss, whether these guys have met before this meeting, how Flute, Snug, Snout, and Starveling feel about being in this play at all?

After getting advice from the directors, the cast acts out the scene once. After this first run-through, cast and directors discuss what worked, what changes they would make in the next enactment. The same cast, or a newly selected one, plays the scene again incorporating suggested changes.

Before the end of class, ask for comments on the process of getting a scene on its feet. Is it as complicated as they would have thought? Why? Why not? Point out the advantages of working this way with a group, incorporating many creative viewpoints and many minds working on the same questions. You may wish to assign groups to present the scene at a later class selecting some of the other locations and characteristics mentioned earlier. This introductory session may take two class periods; it is a worthwhile investment. During further study of the play students can use these tools to analyze other more complex scenes.

The students—without the aid of notes, translation, or "helpful" explanatory material from the teacher—have come to understand what's happening in a scene from a Shakespeare play by working through the process of getting the scene from the page into performance. During this process students have acquired important tools and experience: they have acquired Shakespearean language, acted out parts, engaged in literary analysis of a scene, and begun to establish a collaborative and energetic relationship with the playwright.

A Midsummer Night's Dream
ACT 1, SCENE 2

Enter Quince the carpenter, and Snug the joiner, and Bottom the weaver,
and Flute the bellows-mender, and Snout the tinker,
and Starveling the tailor.

QUINCE   Is all our company here?

BOTTOM   You were best to call them generally, man by man, according to the scrip.

QUINCE   Here is the scroll of every man's name which is thought fit, through all Athens, to play in our interlude before the Duke and the Duchess on his wedding day at night.

BOTTOM   First, good Peter Quince, say what the play treats on, then read the names of the actors, and so grow to a point.

QUINCE   Marry, our play is "The most lamentable comedy and most cruel death of Pyramus and Thisbe."

BOTTOM   A very good piece of work, I assure you, and a merry. Now, good Peter Quince, call forth your actors by the scroll. Masters, spread yourselves.

QUINCE   Answer as I call you. Nick Bottom, the weaver.

BOTTOM   Ready. Name what part I am for, and proceed.

QUINCE   You, Nick Bottom, are set down for Pyramus.

BOTTOM   What is Pyramus—a lover or a tyrant?

QUINCE   A lover that kills himself most gallant for love.

BOTTOM   That will ask some tears in the true performing of it. If I do it, let the audience look to their eyes. I will move storms; I will condole in some measure. To the rest.—Yet my chief humor is for a tyrant. I could play Ercles rarely, or a part to tear a cat in, to make all split:

> *The raging rocks*
> *And shivering shocks*
> *Shall break the locks*
>   *Of prison gates.*
> *And Phibbus' car*
> *Shall shine from far*
> *And make or mar*
>   *The foolish Fates.*

BOTTOM 2   This was lofty. Now name the rest of the players. This is Ercles' vein, a tyrant's vein. A lover is more condoling.

QUINCE 2   Francis Flute, the bellows-mender.

FLUTE   Here, Peter Quince.

QUINCE 2   Flute, you must take Thisbe on you.

FLUTE   What is Thisbe—a wand'ring knight?

QUINCE 2   It is the lady that Pyramus must love.

FLUTE   Nay, faith, let not me play a woman. I have a beard coming.

QUINCE 2   That's all one. You shall play it in a mask, and you may speak as small as you will.

BOTTOM 2   An I may hide my face, let me play Thisbe too. I'll speak in a monstrous little voice: "Thisne, Thisne!"—"Ah Pyramus, my lover dear! Thy Thisbe dear and lady dear!"

QUINCE 2   No, no, you must play Pyramus—and, Flute, you Thisbe.

BOTTOM 2   Well, proceed.

QUINCE 2   Robin Starveling, the tailor.

STARVELING   Here, Peter Quince.

QUINCE 2   Robin Starveling, you must play Thisbe's mother.—Tom Snout, the tinker.

SNOUT   Here, Peter Quince.

QUINCE 2   You, Pyramus' father.—Myself, Thisbe's father.—Snug the joiner, you the lion's part.—And I hope here is a play fitted.

SNUG   Have you the lion's part written? Pray you, if it be, give it me, for I am slow of study.

QUINCE 2   You may do it extempore, for it is nothing but roaring.

BOTTOM 2   Let me play the lion too. I will roar that I will do any man's heart good to hear me. I will roar that I will make the Duke say "Let him roar again. Let him roar again!"

QUINCE 2   An you should do it too terribly, you would fright the Duchess and the ladies that they would shriek, and that were enough to hang us all.

ALL   That would hang us, every mother's son.

BOTTOM 2   I grant you, friends, if you should fright the ladies out of their wits, they would have no more discretion but to hang us.

BOTTOM 3   But I will aggravate my voice so that I will roar you as gently as any sucking dove. I will roar you an 'twere any nightingale.

QUINCE 3   You can play no part but Pyramus, for Pyramus is a sweet-faced man, a proper man as one shall see in a summer's day, a most lovely gentlemanlike man. Therefore you must needs play Pyramus.

BOTTOM 3   Well, I will undertake it. What beard were I best to play it in?

QUINCE 3   Why, what you will.

BOTTOM 3   I will discharge it in either your straw-color beard, your orange-tawny beard, your purple-in-grain beard, or your French-crown-color beard, your perfit yellow.

QUINCE 3   Some of your French crowns have no hair at all, and then you will play barefaced. But, masters, here are your parts, and I am to entreat you, request you, and desire you, to con them by tomorrow night and meet me in the palace wood, a mile without the town, by moonlight. There will we rehearse, for if we meet in the city, we shall be dogged with company and our devices known. In the meantime I will draw a bill of properties such as our play wants. I pray you fail me not.

BOTTOM 3   We will meet, and there we may rehearse most ob-scenely and courageously. Take pains. Be perfit. Adieu.

QUINCE 3   At the Duke's Oak we meet.

BOTTOM 3   Enough. Hold, or cut bowstrings.

PART THREE

In the Classroom

•

Nancy Goodwin
EDITOR

A Midsummer Night's Dream

•

Elstein

TOR

ny students and probably most of yours have
e they heard Theo doing a rap version of Julius
ere was an answer on *Jeopardy*, but somehow,
in that name: Shakespeare. In fact, to many
art of high-school education, and they expect
ve them that exposure, they feel vaguely cheated
nt to meet the challenge of something important.
t comes and the teenage eye actually meets the
words—

blyta, our nuptial hour
e. Four happy days bring in
. But, O, methinks how slow
wanes! She lingers my desires
dame or a dowager
ng out a young man's revenue.

interest too often is followed by:

is this? Why are we reading this?")
o boring.")
locker.")
ff is dumb. I'm not doing it.")

And, dear teacher, ... , of our careful summary of action, meticulous explication of text, creative explanation of symbols, thorough analysis of meter, and, most dishearteningly, despite our own honest enthusiasm, in this classroom equation, *B*, *C*, and *D* all equal *A*:

"HUH? WHAT IS THIS? WHY ARE WE READING THIS?"

The faces of the bored and defiant can make the best of us dread going into the classroom. It's happened to me, and maybe it's happened to you, but it doesn't have to be that way.

Incredibly, teaching Shakespeare can actually invigorate both your class and you. In the following pages you will see a student-centered, dynamic approach to *A Midsummer Night's Dream* that stresses language and performance as the essential elements for success.

This unit emphasizes the importance of preparing students to use Shakespearean language while reading the play and continues to address language as well as content throughout the exploration of the comedy. Working on rhyme and meter in conjunction with performance activities will develop in students a sense of the underpinnings of the play and build the confidence they need to work with language that is initially intimidating.

The ideas in the unit grew out of work done at the Teaching Shakespeare's Language Institute at the Folger Library in Washington, D.C. All the activities were developed, reality-tested, and revised by Martha Christian, Ellen Diem, and Judith Elstein in suburban, rural, and urban English classrooms in Massachusetts, Oklahoma, and New Jersey.

Keeping in mind that learning styles vary, we have included activities for visual, aural, and kinesthetic learners. Language is seductive, and delight in sound, rhythm, and words can seduce students from reluctant participation to ultimate comprehension.

Getting students comfortable with that language is essential. They need practice and preparation to deal with inverted word order ("Thou hast by moonlight at her window sung") and obsolete words ("methinks," "doth") that are strange to adolescent ears. Lessons, therefore, consistently stress reading, writing, speaking, and responding to Shakespearean/Elizabethan language.

Shakespeare's plays are public productions and are at their best when seen and heard rather than read in silence. Student actors bring life to the plays and zest to your classroom; therefore, becoming familiar with performance techniques is also essential to the Folger approach to *A Midsummer Night's Dream*.

Our goal as teachers is to get everyone in the class to employ acting skills that will take the play from the page to the stage. You do not have to have a background in drama to accomplish this goal. This unit will help you to help your students overcome their fears of breaking the basic teenage commandment: "Thou shalt not look foolish." The confidence-building exercises move students gradually from very brief, one-line, in-seat readings to on-their-feet acting-company presentations.

A Midsummer Night's Dream is a delightful play to teach because it has characters and plot lines that appeal to kids: mismatched and quarrelsome lovers, foolish stooges, powerful spirits, and magical transformations. When you help kids unlock the language so they can hear and see and understand this romantic comedy, you allow them to participate in a timeless play.

In planning this unit, we have imagined a target class of twenty to thirty high-school students of average ability (which, of course, means some work diligently, most work sporadically, and some look out the windows). All these techniques can be and have been adapted successfully for a broad spectrum of students. One of the most important concepts we have learned from studying at the Folger is that Shakespeare is not just for college-bound secondary-school students. Any group of students can become involved in this play if the presentation is inviting and expectations are high.

The amount of time you spend on the play or on an individual exercise will vary according to your curricular needs, your students' prior exposure to Shakespeare, and their ability level. The unit is flexible. You can do more or fewer activities on a given day, change board work to handouts or homework assignments. To provide choice and to keep your teaching fresh, there are many activities, perhaps more than you can comfortably use in the unit. (One snare that has caught some of us in the past is overteaching. *Keep in mind that our goal is not to turn out Shakespeare scholars, but Shake-*

speare enthusiasts.) Involve your students in the decision-making process when possible. Would they prefer to keep journals? Write literary letters? Or create promptbooks?

Knowing your targeted audience, what are your own preferences? Would you prefer to do selected scenes from the play rather than read it in its entirety? Do you have an itchy group of sophomores who, you know, would love acting out the quarrels and the chases in the forest scene? Would you like to fill in the gaps with taped or recorded versions? You are the authority on what works best in your classroom.

There are twenty-two lessons in this language and performance unit, but you may prefer to move more quickly or more slowly. We realize that teaching, like poetry, has its own rhythm and every class its own pace. You have an intimate knowledge of your teaching style and of the workings of your class. Use that knowledge to select those exercises that you think will provoke excitement, enhance learning, and help ease your students past the language barrier and into the wonder of the play.

Here's to the magic in the play and to the magic in your classroom.

Judith Elstein

Judith Elstein
Atlantic City High School
Atlantic City, New Jersey

UNIT CALENDAR FOR
A Midsummer Night's Dream

❧ 1	❧ 2	❧ 3	❧ 4	❧ 5
LESSON 1	LESSON 1	LESSON 2	LESSON 3	LESSON 4
An Actor's Approach	An Actor's Approach *(cont.)*	Taking on Shakespeare's Language	Living Pictures	Acting Companies
Text: 1.2	Text: 1.2	Text: 1.1.21–129	Text: 1.1.1–182	Text: 1.1.183–257
❧ 6	❧ 7	❧ 8	❧ 9	❧ 10
LESSON 5	LESSON 6	LESSON 7	LESSON 8	LESSON 9
Finding Shakespeare's Beat	Comparative Film Production	Close Reading	Stressing the Subtext	Shakespearean Subtext
Text: 2.1.1–61	Text: 2.1.62–194	Text: 2.1.125–142	Text: 2.1.125–276	Text: 2.2.33–89
❧ 11	❧ 12	❧ 13	❧ 14	❧ 15
LESSON 10	LESSON 11	LESSON 12	LESSON 13	LESSON 14
Acting Scenes from Act 2	3.1 in Film	Three Scenes from Act 3	Memorization Recital	Three More from Act 3
Text: 2.2.90–163	Text: 3.1	Text: 3.2.1–180	Text: 2.1.125–142	Text: 3.2.181–365
❧ 16	❧ 17	❧ 18	❧ 19	❧ 20
LESSON 14	LESSON 15	LESSON 16	LESSON 17	LESSON 17
Three More from Act 3 *(cont.)*	Insults	Taking Liberties with the Script	Character Committees	Character Committees *(cont.)*
Text: 3.2.181–365	Text: 3.2.181–365	Text: 3.2.366–4.1.106	Text: 4.1.107–4.2	Text: 4.1.107–4.2
❧ 21	❧ 22	❧ 23	❧ 24	❧ 25
LESSON 18	LESSON 19	LESSON 20	LESSON 21	LESSON 21
Introduction to Final Performances	Planning for Performance	The Play Within the Play	Rehearsal	Rehearsal *(cont.)*
Text: 5.1.1–113	Text: 5.1.114–387	Text: 5.1.388–455		
❧ 26				
LESSON 22				
Performance				

LESSON 1 "Is All Our Company Here?"

An Actor's Approach to *A Midsummer Night's Dream*

ॐ

PLAY SECTION COVERED IN THIS LESSON

1.2. Quince assembles some workingmen to plan a performance of a play for the duke's wedding celebration.

LINES: Quince, 46; Bottom, 52; Flute, 4; Starveling, 1; Snout, 1; Snug, 2

ॐ

WHAT'S ON FOR TODAY AND WHY

Today we'll give the class an overview of the four intertwined plots of *A Midsummer Night's Dream*—the royal couple, the tangled lovers, the mechanicals, and the fairies—by showing and discussing a play map. We'll temporarily bypass the complex first scene of the play and go for the poetic rightness of starting with a scene about a group of amateurs—not unlike our students—who are going to put on a play. From the first day, we want students involved in the performance and doing their own paraphrasing and visualizing of the language.

Because it's important to be successful with this first acting assignment, we will follow all the steps and allow ourselves all the time we need. Squeezing this lesson into one class just doesn't work. It needs and deserves two class periods.

WHAT TO DO

1. Play Map

Distribute and briefly discuss the play map (following this lesson), which introduces the characters and gives students a visual overview of the relationships in the play. Encourage students to use the map for reference throughout the unit, keeping it in a notebook or (folded) as a bookmark.

2. Actors' Circle (Day 1)

Following the instructions laid down by Michael Tolaydo (see page 28), ask students to move their desks to form a large circle. Pass out copies of Act 1, scene 2 (1.2) with no notes, just as Michael prescribes. Follow his instructions until the period ends—there will probably be time for students to read the entire scene sentence by sentence, circle the words they don't understand, discuss the circled words, and reach consensus about meaning. You may have time to read this scene again, stopping to paraphrase into modern English the phrases that are hard to understand.

3. Actors' Circle (Day 2)

Picking up where we left off, continue to follow Michael Tolaydo's instructions for 1.2. Start by reviewing the scene, then letting the class decide where it is taking place. (Students' suggestions might include "in a bar or pub," "in the city park," "in the woods," etc.) Continue to move through the scene as Michael describes—using classroom furniture to suggest a set, assigning parts, getting students on their feet, letting students decide where and when characters should enter, changing casts, etc. Throughout this exercise the most important task the teacher has is to ask questions: Should Bottom and Quince come in together? Who should come in first? What's a joiner? What sort of personality does Snug have? Work with this scene as long as time permits. After the last run-through, ask students to predict what the mechanicals will be doing the next time we see them.

4. Homework

Ask students to write, relying on memory alone, a summary of *A Midsummer Night's Dream* (henceforth abbreviated *Midsummer*), Act 1, scene 2 (1.2).

HOW DID IT GO?

If everyone got a few moments of on-their-feet acting and directing, and if students made some good suggestions about staging, we know that they're beginning to see Shakespeare's play as a play, a three-dimensional space in which they move and speak the words Shakespeare penned some 400 years ago. Count the lesson successful if students see themselves *in* the play as well as outside analyzing it.

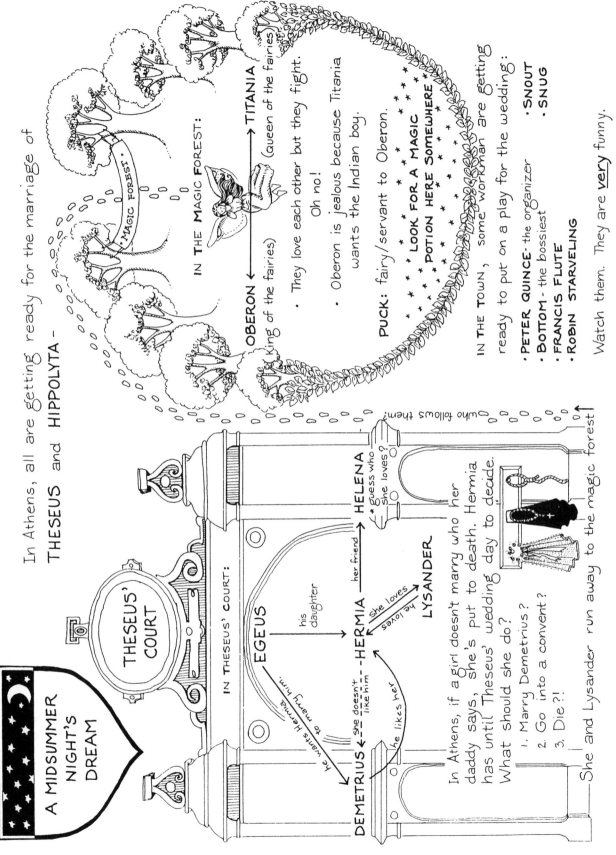

In Athens, all are getting ready for the marriage of
THESEUS and HIPPOLYTA -

·MAGIC FOREST·

IN THE MAGIC FOREST:

OBERON → TITANIA
(King of the fairies) (Queen of the fairies)

• They love each other but they fight. Oh no!

• Oberon is jealous because Titania wants the Indian boy.

PUCK: fairy/servant to Oberon.

★ LOOK FOR A MAGIC POTION HERE SOMEWHERE

IN THE TOWN, some workman are getting ready to put on a play for the wedding:

• PETER QUINCE - the organizer   • SNOUT
• BOTTOM - the bossiest   • SNUG
• FRANCIS FLUTE
• ROBIN STARVELING

Watch them. They are <u>very</u> funny.

A MIDSUMMER NIGHT'S DREAM

THESEUS' COURT

IN THESEUS' COURT:

EGEUS
his daughter →
HERMIA ← her friend → HELENA
★ guess who she loves?

She loves
he loves
LYSANDER

DEMETRIUS ← she doesn't like him -- HERMIA
he wants Hermia
he likes her

...who follows them?

In Athens, if a girl doesn't marry who her daddy says, she's put to death. Hermia has until Theseus' wedding day to decide. What should she do?

1. Marry Demetrius?
2. Go into a convent?
3. Die ?!

She and Lysander run away to the magic forest

LESSON **2** "Full of Vexation Come I . . ."

Taking on Shakespeare's Language

ë

PLAY SECTION COVERED IN THIS LESSON

1.1.21–129 Egeus is angry because his daughter Hermia will not marry Demetrius. Theseus, the duke, offers her three choices: marry, become a nun, or die.

LINES: Egeus, 30; Theseus, 50; Hermia, 13; Demetrius, 2; Lysander, 14

ë

WHAT'S ON FOR TODAY AND WHY

To facilitate the transition from one lesson to the next, to remind teacher and students of anything left unfinished or unanswered, to provide practice for careful note-taking, to give students an audience for their writing, and to inform absentees what went on while they were away, we will set up a class log and maintain it throughout the unit.

To enable students to use lines from *Midsummer* in short segments immediately, and to demonstrate that complex material can be remembered through repetition, we will engage students in a game, "tossing lines." Then we will ask them to make suppositions about plot, setting, and character based on the lines they hear and say. Teachers will need to prepare index cards for this game.

Tonight's homework, like most until Act 3, is a reading assignment that *reviews the passage we cover in class today.* Later we will ask students to preview text as well.

WHAT TO DO

1. Class Log

Each day a different student will be responsible for taking careful notes about what we do in class. Today we will establish the procedure: assigning days to each student, telling how to get the form, how to fill it out, when and where to turn it in. Have available a stack of class-log forms (see sample at the end of this lesson). In the section for notes, students describe all classroom activities, including notes from the board as well as their own. Ask them to attach any handouts or questions from the acting companies.

Logkeepers turn in the class log at the end of the period. At the beginning of class the next day, they must read it aloud, then post it on the bulletin board.

2. Homework Review

Collect the summaries from yesterday. If time permits, read one or two aloud.

3. Tossing Lines

Because this game works best with a group of 15 or fewer, divide the class in half. Tell the class they are going to read some lines concerning an argument between a father and daughter. Distribute, one per student, index cards, each with a different line:

> "Thanks, good Egeus. What's the news with thee?"
> "Against my child, my daughter Hermia."
> "This man hath my consent to marry her."
> "This man hath bewitched the bosom of my child."
> "thou hast given her rhymes"
> "Thou hast by moonlight at her window sung"
> "thou filched my daughter's heart"
> "I beg the ancient privilege of Athens"
> "As she is mine, I may dispose of her"
> "either to this gentleman / Or to her death"
> "What say you, Hermia?"
> "To you, your father should be as a god"
> "Demetrius is a worthy gentleman."
> "So is Lysander."
> "I would my father looked but with my eyes."

Ask: Who has a card with a word you don't know? Who has a card with words you can't pronounce? List the words students don't know, along with brief definitions, on the board. Agree on pronunciations for the words in question. (Note: Coming to a consensus on pronunciation is more important than struggling to be "right.")

Ask students in the first group to study their cards and stand in a circle. Produce an object for tossing, ideally something symbolic of the play—a magic wand, a small heart-shaped pillow, a "Shakesbear" would all be suitable. To play the game, a student reads aloud the line on her card, then tosses or passes the object to another student, who reads a line and tosses to another student. Students continue until all the lines have been read several times and the lines come quickly and naturally. Then ask everyone in group 1 to sit and write down as many lines as they can remember. (Although there will be incorrect quotes, it is surprising how much students retain.)

Repeat the game with group 2, using these lines:

> "Rather your eyes must with his judgment look."
> "I do entreat your Grace to pardon me."
> "But I beseech your Grace"
> "The worst that may befall me"
> "If I refuse to wed Demetrius"
> "to die the death"
> "question your desires"
> "the livery of a nun"
> "Relent, sweet Hermia"
> "You have her father's love, Demetrius"
> "My love is more than his"
> "I am beloved of beauteous Hermia"

"There, gentle Hermia, may I marry thee"
"And in the wood"
"There will I stay for thee."

Ask students to use these lines as clues to figure out what is happening in this passage. Where does the scene occur? Who is involved? What is the problem? What is the threatened punishment? Why do some lines start with capital letters? Why do some lines start with lower-case letters? Some inferences will be correct and some not, but this is a natural way to lead to a reading of 1.1 to see what actually occurred.

4. Books in Their Hands

It's time to distribute the texts. Discuss the format of the book. Juniors and seniors will be familiar with textual notes or glosses and line numbers, but inexperienced students can be confused by these references. Give students some practice by having them quickly find line references and definitions: Who can find line 1.1.25? Line 1.1.42? Line 1.1.34 refers to a "gaud"; what is it?

5. Read Around

Read 1.1.21–129. A straightforward reading of these lines, going around the room with each student reading to an end stop or colon (as we did in Lesson 1), is in order. Afterward, ask questions about the plot: What is Hermia's problem? Egeus' request? The duke's solution?

Ask students to compare the language in this scene with that in the mechanicals' acting practice. What do they notice about formality, line length, vocabulary, etc.? Follow up with a short clarification of prose vs. verse.

6. Homework

Assign 1.1.1–129 for reading. Ask the students to make a list of the characters in this passage and, as specifically as possible, tell what each character wants. They should support their analyses with quotes from the play. Example: Egeus—wants his daughter to marry Demetrius. "As she is mine, I may dispose of her, / Which shall be either to this gentleman / Or to her death . . ." (1.1.43–45).

HOW DID IT GO?

If all, even the shy ones, read their lines several times in the tossing-lines game, if they applied listening skills and began to make some sense of these lines, if they recalled some lines and had a reasonable understanding of the plot, and if the magic wand was not broken by frantic tossing as kids cried "Faster," then the lesson went well.

By looking over the summaries students did for homework, you can evaluate their level of comprehension. It is not necessary to grade the summaries, but for teachers who want to reinforce student work, here is a suggested marking system:

- a check-plus for papers that are both complete and accurate
- a check for papers that are fairly complete and accurate
- a check-minus for papers that are incomplete or inaccurate

In the same way, teachers can give marks for participation in the tossing-lines game and/or the reading aloud and discussion.

CLASS LOG

TO THE LOGKEEPER: You are to show the utmost commitment to accuracy and thoroughness as you take notes today. At the end of the period, give this log to your teacher. Retrieve it at the beginning of the next class. Read it aloud to your classmates. Then post it on the bulletin board.

LOGKEEPER'S NAME: _____ DATE: _____

ABSENTEES: _____

_____

TARDY STUDENTS: _____

_____

DESCRIBE ALL CLASSROOM ACTIVITIES. (Include notes from the board as well as your own. Continue on the back of this sheet if needed. Clip any handouts or questions from acting companies to this sheet.)

ASSIGNMENTS OR ACTIVITIES COMING UP: _____

HOMEWORK FOR NEXT CLASS: _____

LESSON **3** "The Course of True Love Never Did Run Smooth"

Living Pictures

ॐ _____

PLAY SECTIONS COVERED IN THIS LESSON

1.1.1–20 Duke, Theseus and Hippolyta await their wedding day.

LINES: Theseus, 15; Hippolyta, 5

1.1.21–129 Egeus is angry because his daughter, Hermia, will not marry Demetrius. Theseus offers her three choices: marry, become a nun, or die.

LINES: Egeus, 30; Theseus, 50; Hermia, 13; Demetrius, 2; Lysander, 14

1.1.130–182 Hermia and Lysander plan to elope.

LINES: Lysander, 31; Hermia, 22

ॐ _____

WHAT'S ON FOR TODAY AND WHY

In this lesson, we will help students feel more comfortable with Elizabethan pronoun and verb forms. They will conduct a silent, written conversation with a partner in modern English, then rewrite it in a later lesson using Elizabethan forms.

Also, we will work hard to help students identify two sets of lovers in *Midsummer*. Students will use their eyes, ears, and whole bodies as they arrange living pictures in *tableaux vivants* to reflect the relationships described in 1.1.

To help students recognize characters, it would be fun, though not absolutely necessary, to make available to them a collection of hats and props garnered from yard sales or thrift shops: baseball hats, hats with veils, children's hats, silly hats, crowns, whatever. Even minimal costuming enhances students' enjoyment of the play. In addition to hats, teachers can put out a general call for: wands, crowns, wings, flowers, netting, tinsel, donkey's ears (they can be paper), glitter, gold and silver paper, capes, flashlights, a tree, and a tape of Mendelssohn's music for *A Midsummer Night's Dream*. If you have such a collection, bring it out during this lesson. If not, write the name of each character in large letters on a paper heart and pin it on the actor during the living-pictures activity.

WHAT TO DO

1. Log/Homework Review

As per the daily routine, ask the logkeeper to read the log and then post it on the bulletin board. Collect the homework papers. Hear one or two read aloud or discuss the students' findings.

2. Silent Conversation 1

Divide the students into pairs and give each pair a sheet of paper. Give students five minutes to conduct a silent, *written* conversation. This will be natural for them, as students will pass the paper back and forth like passing notes in class. In this conversation they can "talk" about anything on the play map or about the previous lessons. They can write questions and answers, or make comments on plot or characters, or ask about anything they don't understand. Enforce the silence. When the five minutes are up, file the sheets for follow-up in the next lesson.

3. Living Pictures 1: "Our Nuptial Hour Draws on Apace"

To clarify the court relationships in 1.1, let students use each other to create living pictures—what audiences in earlier centuries called tableaux vivants. Pick two students; one will be Theseus and one Hippolyta. Let the other students arrange them in poses suggesting romantic longing. For example, they might stand a bit apart and gaze at each other with arms outstretched. Then ask two other students to read lines 1–20 while the picture figures hold their poses.

4. Adding Hats and Props

To help identify characters throughout the unit, use emblematic hats and props that suggest something about the personality or status of the character. Pull out the costume/prop box (or the duffle or garbage bag as the case may be) and select permanent hats for Theseus and Hippolyta, something in keeping with their royal status. Try on several hats and/or scarves or capes. Ask the tableaux vivants figures to model the final selections.

5. Living Pictures 2: "And She Is Mine, and All My Right of Her I Do Estate unto Demetrius"

Ask the students to choose four people to illustrate the mixed-up lovers, one to represent the stern father, Egeus, and one to represent the duke. Then let the students arrange the living pictures. For example, Demetrius might kneel behind Hermia tugging at her, but Hermia might be pushing him away with one hand while holding Lysander's hand with the other. Helena might be behind Demetrius trying to capture his attention. A few feet away, Egeus might be pointing to the four with one hand while gesturing emphatically to Theseus with the other.

Again, assign permanent hats to Egeus and the lovers, let the figures wear the hats and assume their poses, and then ask other class members to read lines 21–129.

6. Living Pictures 3: "How Now, My Love?"

Clear the stage of all but Hermia and Lysander, who assume a new pose but continue to gaze adoringly at each other. Ask all the males to read aloud in unison Lysander's lines and the females to read Hermia's responses, 130–142. The teacher may need to read aloud with each group to set the rhythm. Finish by having the Lysander and Hermia pictures read 158–181. Ask the class members to paraphrase the lovers' speeches.

7. Homework

Assign 1.1.130–257 for reading.

Writing assignment: Egeus, Hermia's father, does not like Lysander and tries to stop him from seeing Hermia. If you had a friend of whom your parents did not approve, what arguments would you present to change their minds? Explain.

HOW DID IT GO?

Our main objective in this lesson was to solidify in the students' minds the relationships of the two sets of lovers: the royal couple, Hippolyta and Theseus; the tangled foursome. If through the visual and oral display students comprehended these relationships, breathe a sigh of relief and smile smugly. If, in addition, the students remembered that they had heard of Hermia and Egeus before, if the first student in the alphabet stopped grumbling about how unfair it is to be born with a last name that starts with *A* and starts to keep the log, if everyone participated in the silent conversation, if Theseus, Lysander, and Demetrius told you they weren't going to gaze longingly at any girl in *this* room, and if everyone had a fit of the giggles when you brought out the hats, things were swell.

As with all writing assignments, the evaluation of written student homework from Lesson 2 is optional. Going through the thinking process the assignment requires is valuable in itself, but you may want to do more. If your students need immediate rewards for their writing, perhaps the check method described in Lesson 2 would be an expedient way to accomplish this. Formal evaluation will, of course, be according to methods you are currently practicing. Perhaps you would want to ask students at the end of the unit to choose one writing assignment to revise and polish for assessment.

LESSON 4 "Love Looks Not with the Eyes but with the Mind"

Acting Companies

❧

PLAY SECTION COVERED IN THIS LESSON

1.1.183–257 Helena thinks that, if she were more like Hermia, Demetrius would love her. She plans to buy his favor by telling him about the elopement.

LINES: Hermia, 21; Helena, 45; Lysander, 9

❧

WHAT'S ON FOR TODAY AND WHY

In this lesson we will establish acting companies, groups of four or five students that will meet throughout the unit to:

- help each other paraphrase and comprehend scenes
- plan and perform scenes
- discuss issues in the play

Because so much of the work of this unit depends on these collaborative activities, we will give careful thought to the makeup of the groups, balancing each acting company as evenly as possible for gender, race/ethnicity, and ability. We will have the roster of company members and company folders ready for students at the beginning of this lesson, and we will do all that is possible to foster in students a sense of belonging and enthusiasm in the groups.

Also in this lesson, students will rewrite yesterday's silent conversation, this time using Elizabethan forms of verbs and pronouns. Our chief concern with this activity is not that students use these forms with absolute correctness, but that they understand the rules about them well enough to remove some of the stumbling blocks in reading Shakespearean language.

WHAT TO DO

1. Log/Homework Review

Hear the logkeeper's notes and post them. If you made a writing assignment, collect it.

2. Using Elizabethan Forms

On the board, write two sentences containing second-person pronouns and the verbs *are*, *does*, and *has*. Example: Why do you have a pumpkin in your locker? Ask students to make these sentences sound Shakespearean. (They may respond with something like "Oh, Romeo, I do entreat you—why doth you have a golden pumpkin in your—er—satchel?") Distribute Handout 1, "The Second Person Familiar/Verb Inflections," an efficient chart devised by South Pasadena High School teacher and Folger teacher Skip Nicholson. Review the handout with the students; then ask them to revise the sentences on the board, concentrating on the pronouns and verbs. (This time they may come up with "Why dost thou have a pumpkin in thy locker?" If so, praise them liberally.)

3. Silent Conversation 2

With the help of Handout 1, ask students to rewrite the silent conversations they did in Lesson 3, this time using Elizabethan pronoun and verb forms. Ask the pairs to read aloud their revised conversations.

4. Establishing Acting Companies

Announce that, like the mechanicals in *Midsummer*, each student in the class will become a member of an acting company. Read the group rosters. Ask each group to select:

- a name
- a regular meeting place—e.g., the Cool Four always meet next to the filing cabinet, the Wise Fools sit near the front door, Lord Chamberlain's Women meet in the center of the room
- a rotation order for directors—each time the group meets, one member acts as the director, who is responsible for:
  (1) picking up the company folder
  (2) taking notes on company activities and filing them in the folder
  (3) writing down any unanswered questions the company might have
  (4) keeping the company on task

Give each company a folder and send them off to meet. Ask each group to write on its folder the group and member names. Show them where the folder is stored when not in company meetings.

During the company meetings, the teacher walks from group to group, listening and observing, asking questions, and serving as a resource person. On your rounds today, make sure that everyone is following instructions.

Post the names of acting companies, accompanied by a list of members and meeting places, on the bulletin board for easy reference.

To expedite the logistics of group movement, and to encourage groups to work efficiently, tell students that they will get regular grades on their ability to set up and disband their acting groups quickly and on their willingness to use their time together productively. As adults, we all know that changing one's seat is not a hard thing to do, but as teachers we also know that practice and reinforcement are necessary to establish even the simplest classroom procedure.

5. Acting Companies at Work

To develop cohesiveness, ask company members to spend five minutes going around their circle and sharing any comments they wish about the play.

Ask the companies to review the scene work we did in getting ready to act out the mechanicals' play-rehearsal scene (perhaps you will want to have this procedure outlined on the board):

- round-robin reading to a period, semicolon, colon, or question mark
- circling words we don't know and coming to consensus about definitions
- paraphrasing hard-to-understand phrases into modern English
- making sense of the scene

Ask each company to go through the same procedure for a shortened scene, 1.1.230 ("Helena, adieu") to 257 ("To have his sight thither and back again"). This is a critical moment, the moment when students take over, relying on themselves and each other rather than the teacher to understand Shakespeare's language. Allow about 20 minutes.

Remind company directors to write down questions the group could not answer and hand them in to the logkeeper or teacher at the end of the period.

6. Acting Company Follow-up and Evaluation

Reconvene the whole class and ask for their questions. To encourage students to ask questions, ask them to read them aloud, giving others in the room a chance to supply an answer when they can. Follow up by asking for a summary of the action in the scene they read.

Collect each company's folder.

Give a check to each acting company that moved from individual seats to group meeting and back again with reasonable speed and minimal disruption. Give an extra-credit point to the group that did the best. Give similar on-the-spot grades to groups for staying on topic. Announce the grades for swift positive reinforcement.

HOW DID IT GO?   To evaluate the activities of this lesson, answer these questions:

- Did students absorb and use some Elizabethan pronoun and verb forms?
- Did students organize themselves into acting companies and complete the tasks assigned to them?
- Did the directors take notes?
- Did the logkeeper keep taking notes?
- Did the directors write down questions?
- And, the most important question of all, did the groups work out together what Shakespeare was saying in the passage?

If your answers are mostly yes, consider this—you have set up the mechanism whereby students will grapple with Shakespeare's language on their own and with their fellow students.

If that thought is not compensation enough, consider this—today you finished the first act.

ॐ

HANDOUT 1

THE SECOND PERSON FAMILIAR / VERB INFLECTIONS

Modern English has dropped a set of pronouns and verbs called the "familiar" or *thee* and *thou* forms once used among close friends and family and to children, inferiors, animals, and inanimate objects. These old forms did, though, survive into Elizabethan England, and they appear frequently in Shakespeare. They correspond roughly to the *tu* forms of the Romance languages, the *ty* forms of the Slavic languages, the *su* forms of Greek, and the *kimi* forms of Japanese.

Familiar Pronouns

	SINGULAR PRONOUNS			PLURAL PRONOUNS		
	1st	2nd	3rd	1st	2nd	3rd
Subject	*I*	*thou*	*he/she/it*	*we*	*ye*	*they*
Object	*me*	*thee*	*him/her/it*	*us*	*you*	*them*
Possessive Adjective	*my mine**	*thy thine**	*his/her/ its*	*our*	*your*	*their*
Possessive Noun	*mine*	*thine*	*his/hers/ its*	*ours*	*yours*	*theirs*

*Substitute forms used before a noun beginning with a vowel

Verb Inflections

2ND PERSON FAMILIAR
  Adds the ending *-est, -'st,* or *st*
  Example: *thou givest, thou sing'st*

SOME IRREGULAR VERBS
Present:	*you*	*are*	*have*	*will*	*can*	*shall*	*do*
Present:	*thou*	*art*	*hast*	*wilt*	*canst*	*shalt*	*dost*
Past:	*thou*	*wast*	*hadst*	*wouldst*	*couldst*	*shouldst*	*didst*

THIRD PERSON SINGULAR
  Often substitutes *-th* for *-s*
  Example: *she giveth* (for *she gives*)

ॐ

LESSON **5** "Over Hill, Over Dale"

Finding Shakespeare's Beat

PLAY SECTION COVERED IN THIS LESSON

2.1.1–61 Puck (called "Robin Goodfellow" in the Folger edition) talks about the quarrel between Oberon and Titania over her ward, a little Indian boy, and Robin describes his mischievous spirit.

LINES: Fairy, 28; Robin, 33

WHAT'S ON FOR TODAY AND WHY

The rhymes and rhythms of children's verse, rap, and rock music comprise the poetry with which our students are most familiar. We will use them as springboards to the teaching objective of this lesson: Shakespeare has a beat. To feel and distinguish distinctive rhythms in *Midsummer*, students will do exercises that kinesthetically teach them the connection between the word and the beat.

If your school has a large open area, the children's-poem exercise will be well placed there. If not, tell the other teachers in the corridor to keep their doors closed and apologize in advance for the noise. Yes, the exercise does seem chaotic, but this engagement of speech, sound, and movement is an important element in the play, and students love discovering it.

WHAT TO DO

1. Class Log

Hear the logkeeper's report and post it.

2. Remember That Song

Give students a few minutes to recall and write down the lyrics of a song—most students have a huge storehouse from which to choose. Follow with a brief discussion about the songs students remember: How long have you had this song in your memory? What is the song about? Why did you remember it? What helped you remember it—the subject? the singer? the rhymes? Lead the students to consider the part rhythm (the beat) played in remembering the song. Did any student sing silently or tap out the beat to recall the words?

These comments will be useful for the memorization activity later on, but for now make the point that in Shakespeare's plays we see distinctive verse (rhyme) and repetitive beats (rhythm) in regular patterns (meter).

3. Children's Poem

Read aloud any short children's poem with strong meter and rhyme. For example, A. A. Milne's "Christopher Robin / Had wheezles / And sneezles, / They bundled him / Into / His bed. / They gave him what goes / With a cold in the nose, / And some more for a cold / In the head." Or try a section from Dr. Seuss's *Green Eggs and Ham*, "I am Sam. Sam I am. Do you like green eggs and ham?" This will bring nostalgic smiles to many in the class.

Put a few lines of the poem you selected on the chalkboard. Ask students to read the lines in unison several times. Reassure them that you know you're not teaching second grade. Ask students to tap out the rhythm on their desks by using the eraser end of pencils. Repeat several times until everyone is keeping time to the beat and reading with gusto.

4. Group Rhythm: Tetrameter

Using a passage from the last speech of *Midsummer*, 5.1.440–447, repeat the exercise above, but this time, in addition to choral reading and rhythm tapping, add one more step (literally)—movement. Push the desks back to create an open area. Give students a script, or have them open their books to 5.1.440. Tell them to walk around the room reciting, taking one step per beat, and stamping on the stressed syllables:

> *If* we *sha-*dows *have* of-*fend*-ed,
> *Think* but *this* and *all* is *mend*-ed:
> *That* you *have* but *slum*-bered *here*
> *While* these *vi*-sions *did* ap-*pear.*
> *And* this *weak* and *i*-dle *theme,*
> *No* more *yield*-ing *but* a *dream,*
> *Gent*-les, *do* not *re*-pre-*hend.*
> *If* you *par*-don, *we* will *mend.*

This may take a couple of starts, and teachers may need to be aggressive leaders, but once you get students into the rhythm, the beat takes over and they naturally scan the passage. Try it several times.

Then ask students what they noticed about the rhythm. How many strong beats to the line? What is the pattern for weak beats to strong beats? Is that true for every line? If you like, label the passage *tetrameter* (four beats to the line).

Tell the students that, although their eyes cannot always recognize the rhythm pattern, their bodies can.

5. Group Rhythm: Pentameter

Contrast the tetrameter passage above with a passage of plot-advancing pentameter, 2.1.18–32. Again, have the group walk and stamp.

> The *King* doth *keep* his *re*-vels *here* to-*night.*
> Take *heed* the *Queen* come *not* with-*in* his *sight,*
> For *O*-ber-*on* is *pass*-ing *fell* and *wrath*
> Be-*cause* that *she,* as *her* at-*tend*-ant, *hath*
> A *love*-ly *boy* stol-*en* from *an* In-dian *king;*
> She *nev*-er *had* so *sweet* a *chan*-ge-*ling.*

> And *jeal*-ous *O*-ber-*on* would *have* the *child*
> Knight *of* his *train*, to *trace* the *for*-ests *wild*.
> But *she* per-*force* with-*holds* the *lov*-èd *boy*,
> Crowns *him* with *flow*-ers, and *makes* him *all* her *joy*.
> And *now* they *nev*-er *meet* in *grove* or *green*,
> By *foun*-tain *clear*, or *span*-gled *star*-light *sheen*,
> But *they* do *square*, that *all* their *elves* for *fear*
> Creep *in*-to *a*-corn *cups* and *hide* them *there*.

Ask students to note the differences in length of line, number of strong beats, pattern of weak to strong beats. (If you like, review with students the term *iambic pentameter*—five beats to the line, light heavy, light heavy, etc.)

6. No Rhythm: Prose

To emphasize the way in which sound and rhythm affect a line, have students read aloud and try to stamp to Bottom's comment, 1.2.76–80: "I grant you friends. . . ." This will seem leaden and slow compared to the poetic lines just read. Have students consider why prose is an appropriate vehicle for Bottom and the other mechanicals, and why poetry is appropriate for the fairies and other mortals.

7. Follow-up: Acting Companies

Send students to their acting companies to do three tasks:

- read aloud 2.1.33–61 *stressing rhythm*
- review 2.1.1–61, piecing out who are the new characters, what is the new setting, how is it different from Athens, and what is the new mood
- paraphrase the entire scene so far, 2.1.1–61

8. Homework

Assign 2.1.1–61 for reading. Ask the students to list, in their own words, the mischievous tricks played by Robin as well as the kindnesses he performs for humans (2.1.33–59).

HOW DID IT GO?

If the other teachers on your floor want to know what *was* that noise, you achieved the right volume. If students now "understand" the rhythm in Shakespeare's language, if they know it in their bones, if they recognize that they can discover the rhythm of verse by letting their bodies help them, you have accomplished the lesson's objective. If students remembered how to convene into groups and how to work cooperatively there, you are progressing in the arena of peer teaching. If not, stop and work on it because group work is critical to the dynamics of this unit.

LESSON **6** **"Ill Met by Moonlight, Proud Titania"**

Comparative Film Production

ે‌હ‌

PLAY SECTIONS COVERED IN THIS LESSON

2.1.62–124 Oberon and Titania quarrel, accusing each other of infidelity.

LINES: Oberon, 14; Titania, 49

2.1.125–150 Titania refuses to hand over the little Indian boy to be Oberon's page.

LINES: Titania, 24; Oberon, 2

2.1.151–194 Oberon sends Robin for a magic flower with which to punish Titania.

LINES: Oberon, 41; Robin, 3

ે‌હ‌

WHAT'S ON FOR TODAY AND WHY

Yesterday we concentrated on how Shakespeare used rhythm to enhance language. In this lesson, we are going to discuss some of his other language tricks. Our goal is to help students see that he *does* use tricks, that he uses *many* tricks, and that he uses them *well*. To help students appreciate Shakespeare's rich language, we will review a list of unusual usages.

Then we will add a visual dimension to the words by viewing two film versions of the same scene. By watching professionals stage a scene, we will also prepare students for the time when they will mount a production, and we will let them know that there are many ways to interpret a play—all are "correct" as long as the choices can be justified by the text.

Comparative film will take considerable preparation on the teacher's part. First, before you start the unit, locate two productions of *Midsummer*. All of the films have strong and weak points.

- The 1935 Warner Brothers USA production directed by Max Reinhardt and starring James Cagney as Bottom, Olivia de Haviland as Hermia, Mickey Rooney as Robin, and Dick Powell as Lysander is currently out of print but shown often on late-night television. It uses Mendelssohn's music and is very *Wizard of Oz*-ish.
- The 1964 Rediffusion Network production stars Benny Hill. It is available from The Writing Company (1-800-421-4246).
- The 1982 Joseph Papp's New York Shakespeare Festival production directed by James Lapine was made in Central Park. The plus for this film is that it features multicultural casting; the negative is that William Hurt is a whining Oberon. It is available from Film for the Humanities (1-800-257-5126).

- The 1982 BBC production directed by Elijah Moshinsky is available from Ambrose Video (1-800-526-4663). It is very expensive, but sometimes available through college or public libraries.
- The Royal Shakespeare Company's 1996 film, directed by Adrian Noble, was originally conceived as a Stratford-upon-Avon stage production. After a season in London and a world tour, the RSC decided to turn it into a film. It stars Alex Jennings as Theseus/Oberon and Lindsay Duncan as Hippolyta/Titania, as well as Desmond Barrit as Bottom.
- The 1999 Michael Hoffman film was set in nineteenth-century Tuscany and stars Kevin Kline as Bottom, Michelle Pfeiffer as Titania, Rupert Everett as Oberon, Stanley Tucci as Puck, Calista Flockhart as Helena, and David Strathairn as Theseus. It even features Bottom's wife, played by Robin Wright Penn.

On the day before this lesson, cue up the films you selected to 2.1.62, "Ill met by moonlight, proud Titania." Preview the scene so you know where to stop. Go from 2.1.193, "I am invisible, / And I will overhear their conference," up to Demetrius' entrance.

On presentation day, in the best of all possible worlds, you will have at least two versions of *Midsummer*. In real life, even if you have only one, students will be informed and delighted by the presentation.

WHAT TO DO

1. Log/Homework

Hear the logkeeper's report and post. Ask students to identify the purpose of yesterday's exercises. Review the terms *rhythm, iambic, tetrameter, pentameter, verse,* and *prose.* Collect the homework.

2. "I Can Gleek upon Occasion": Shakespeare's Unusual Usage

Remind students that Shakespeare's language is dense and luxurious, rich with unusual words, filled with metaphor, and poetically arranged for maximum effect. Distribute copies of Handout 2: "Shakespeare's Unusual Usage" (at the end of this lesson). Read and discuss the items, with emphasis on the various language tricks (unusual word order, ellipsis, etc.) and how to translate them so students comprehend. When, in Sonnet 18, Shakespeare says "So long lives this, and this gives life to thee," he speaks the truth, but we later-than-Elizabethans need to do a little work on usage to get the full message.

3. Play/Pause/Rewind

Now that students have absorbed, vocalized, paraphrased, and decoded Shakespeare's words, they will see how professional actors handle the language. Show two film versions of the same scene and ask them to observe how the actors in each production speak, interpret, and move to the language.

As you show the film, use the pause button so you can ask the class: What's going on? What's his complaint? What's hers? What is he saying? What examples of unusual usage did you catch? How do the actors convey the meaning of the words? How do costumes add to the atmosphere? How does the lighting make a difference (especially notable in the RSC version)? Are the gestures justified by the text? What directions do you think the actors were given?

Rewind and watch again, this time without interruptions.
Repeat the process with the second film.

4. Homework

Assign 2.1.62–194 for reading. Tell the students to pay particular attention to lines 125–142; then write out this passage exactly as it appears in the text.

**HOW DID
IT GO?**

If you, nontechnical teacher of the humanities, figured out how to play the film without embarrassing yourself in front of the children of the media age, be proud.

To evaluate the success of the film presentations, ask yourself: Did students figure out what was going on in the scene? To what extent was the language a stumbling block?

If students commented on the lines left out or argued that Titania should not have moved in a particular way on a particular line because "that's not what the words are saying," you stimulated some very high reading skills.

To evaluate the homework from yesterday's lesson, give checks, check-minuses, and check-pluses depending on completeness.

HANDOUT 2

SHAKESPEARE'S UNUSUAL USAGE

Unusual Word Order
  "Call you me 'fair'? That 'fair' again unsay." (1.1.184)
  "Helen, to you our minds we will unfold." (1.1.213)
  "Wherefore speaks he this / To her he hates?" (3.2.232–233)
  "Sleep thou, and I will wind thee in my arms." (4.1.41)
Ellipsis (Omission of Words)
  "Godspeed, fair Helena. Whither away?" (1.1.183)
  "As you on him, Demetrius dote on you!" (1.1.231)
  "Thou shalt not from this grove . . ." (2.1.151)
Archaic Words and Idioms
  "For aye to be in shady cloister mewed . . ." (1.1.73)
  "Nay, I can gleek upon occasion." (3.1.148–149)
  "To what, my love, shall I compare thine eyne?" (3.2.141)
Words with Old Meanings
  "And she respects me as her only son." (1.1.162)
  "To bait me with this foul derision?" (3.2.202)
  "But soft! What nymphs are these?" (4.1.131–132)
Familiar Pronouns and Verb Inflections
  "This man hath bewitched the bosom of my child." (1.1.28)
  "If thou lovest me, then . . ." (1.1.165)
  "Hast thou slain him, then?" (3.2.68)
Old Verb Inflections
  "Thou told'st me they were stol'n unto this wood . . ." (2.1.198)
  "Be as thou wast wont to be." (4.1.72)

LESSON **7** **"Set Your Heart at Rest"**

Close Reading

&

PLAY SECTION COVERED IN THIS LESSON

2.1.125–142, "Set your heart at rest" (memorization passage)

&

WHAT'S ON FOR TODAY AND WHY

In this lesson, we will present a challenge to students: memorizing a speech from *Midsummer*. This is an exciting and personal way for students to make a piece of the play their own. And it is an effective way to get Shakespeare's language deep into students' thinking processes. Initially, some students will say they cannot possibly succeed at this assignment, but with encouragement not only will they succeed, they will feel positively triumphant.

To further strengthen their ability to recognize language tricks and patterns, students will do a close reading of the memorization passage.

WHAT TO DO

1. Log/Homework Review

Hear the logkeeper's report and post. Give checks to everyone who completed the homework assignment.

2. Memorization

Tell students that one of the best ways to become comfortable with poetic language is to learn it "by heart." Ask them to memorize a passage from the scene they just watched. "Set your heart at rest . . ." (2.1.125–142) is a moving excerpt from Titania's speech. It is a separate narrative within the larger story, rich in visual images, evoking the friendship between two women.

Announce the due date for having the passage memorized, and tell students that they will receive much practice and help for this assignment in class.

3. Getting the Passage Between the Teeth

Ask the class to read the targeted passage several times, once all together, once with single voices, once all together but with variations called out by the teacher—whisper, roar, speed up, slow down, talk in a high voice, talk in a low voice, etc.

4. Close Reading: Companies

Send the students to their acting companies with copies of the passage and one very emphatic instruction: make a list of what you notice in the language of the passage. Tell them to write down any idea that comes to them—if they notice a funny spelling, a repeated word, a recurring image, a coffee stain on the page, *anything*, add it to their list. Give them 15 minutes.

5. Close Reading: Whole Class

Call the class together. Hear the reports of the company directors. Using the company findings as a springboard, lead a discussion in which you help the students to see more language tricks in this passage:

- *Images.* Ask a student to read the passage slowly and the rest of the class to wave their hands any time pictures pop into their heads. (Words like *heart, fairyland, child, Indian air by night* evoke pictures in the mind.) What can you say about these images? Is there a pattern, a theme? Are the pictures peaceful or violent, hot or cool? What are the most memorable mental pictures produced in this passage?
- *Metaphors.* Look for places in which one thing is described in terms of another ("to see the sails conceive / And grow big-bellied with the wanton wind," "with swimming gait").
- *Smells.* Look for words that evoke smells ("spicèd Indian air").
- *Sounds.* Look for words that evoke sounds ("gossiped by my side," "we have laughed").
- *Alliteration.* Look for repeated consonant sounds ("big-bellied," "wanton wind").
- *Assonance.* Look for repeated vowel sounds (as in "S*et* your heart at r*e*st.").
- *Repeated syllables.* "M*ar*king th' emb*ar*kèd," "*in* the spicèd *In*dian air."
- *Repeated words.* "Rich," "she," "I."
- *Repeated phrases.* "And for her sake."

Talk about and define words that you don't know: *vot'ress, wanton*. What kind of *Indian*?

Refer to Handout 2 and look for unusual usages in this passage.

Talk about the overall mood of the piece, if the mood changes, and if so where.

Notice the switch to one-syllable words in the last two lines.

Come to conclusions about the overall effect of the piece, and the part played by all of the above in achieving this effect.

6. Memorization Practice 1

Give students 10 minutes to practice memorizing the passage. Then hand out Memorization Practice 1 and ask them to write as much of the passage as they can. Let them check to see how well they did.

MEMORIZATION PRACTICE 1

Set your . . .
The Fairyland buys . . .
His mother was . . .
And in the spicèd . . .
Full often hath she . . .
And sat with me . . .
Marking th' . . .   on the . . .
When we have . . .   to see . . .
And grow . . .   with the . . .
Which she, with pretty . . .
Following (her . . .   with my . . .
Would imitate and . . .
To fetch me . . .   and . . .
As from a . . .
But she, being . . .
And for her sake do . . .
And for her sake I will not . . .

7. Homework

Ask the students to read aloud the memorization passage three times.

HOW DID IT GO?

If no one fainted on being told of the memorization assignment, and if voices got stronger on repeated recitations, students are on their way to folding this passage into their brains. It is too soon to mark their written attempts at memorization; at this point, liberal praise is the most effective reinforcement.

If students noticed the subtle blend of sounds and images in "Set your heart at rest," if their awareness increased as the discussion progressed, if they were able to talk about the patterns of pictures and sounds, congratulate yourself. You have helped humans to open the channels and tune in to some of the most beautiful language ever written in English.

LESSON 8 "And for Her Sake Do I Rear Up Her Boy"

Stressing the Subtext

ஐ _____

PLAY SECTIONS COVERED IN THIS LESSON

2.1.125–150 Titania refuses to hand over the little Indian boy to be Oberon's page.

LINES: Titania, 24; Oberon, 2

2.1.195–253 Helena pursues Demetrius through the forest; they quarrel.

LINES: Demetrius, 23; Helena, 34; Oberon, 2

2.1.254–276 Oberon gets the flower, plans his revenge on Titania, and seeks to help Helena

LINES: Oberon, 21; Robin, 2

ஐ _____

WHAT'S ON FOR TODAY AND WHY

Acting and memorizing require active comprehension and oral interpretation of the text. Today students will practice their oral skills in inflection exercises and their thinking skills in subtext exercises.

Understanding the subtext—thoughts that we imagine characters to have as they speak—affects the actor's interpretation of a role and enhances students' ability to read the character's lines. For example, when Oberon greets Titania with the words "Ill met by moonlight, proud Titania," he might be thinking, "I'm sorry I ran into you," or "I may be mad at you, but you still look good to me," or "I'll pretend to be angry so she'll know she can't butter me up." Thus we have vocalized three possible subtexts to the same line. We have no idea what Shakespeare had in mind when he wrote the line, so we guess, and our guess affects the way we read the line. To determine subtext, students need to consider:

- the context of the lines (Continuing with "Ill met by moonlight," it's the first thing Oberon says to Titania.)
- what the character wants in this particular scene (Oberon wants the little Indian boy for a page.)
- what the character's ultimate objective is (Oberon wants to have life running smoothly with himself in power.)
- what obstacles prevent the character from attaining his goals (The little Indian boy is in Titania's possession.)

To sharpen students' ability to focus on subtext and its relation to inflection, they will do several acting exercises crafted by Folger teacher Paul Cartier from Classical High School, Providence, Rhode Island.

WHAT TO DO

1. Log/Homework

Hear the logkeeper's report and post. Have students recite "Set your heart at rest" while looking at the text.

2. Acting Exercises: Stressing the Subtext

Write the following sentence on the chalkboard:

"I'm glad you're here this evening."

Ask students what the sentence means. After a brief discussion, ask six students to read the line, stressing a different word each time:

- With *I'm* the subtext becomes "even though nobody else is."
- *Glad* indicates that you haven't always felt this way.
- *You're* makes the subtext "Frankly, the others bore me."
- *Here* implies "It's so reassuring to see you right here."
- With *evening* the subtext becomes "This is much better than any other time of day."

Now try the same exercise with the line "The Fairyland buys not the child of me."

- Stressing *Fairyland* insults Oberon.
- Stressing *buys* emphasizes Titania's principles.
- And so forth.

Introduce the term *subtext* to the students and convey to them the information in the "What's On for Today" section above. (Enjoy this moment, teachers. This is as close to a lecture as this unit gets.)

3. Acting Exercises: Inflection

Tell students that the way in which our voices go up or down on a word or phrase influences the oral interpretation of the written word. Ask two students to say "Joe didn't steal the book, did he?" Have one student's voice go up in pitch on "did he." Have the other student's voice go down in pitch on "did he." Ask the listeners what beliefs about Joe are implied by each speaker.

Give five students index cards with one of the following subtexts written on each one: "How lovely!," "So what?," "Look out!," "Don't be so rude!," and "I don't believe it." Ask the five students to say "Oh!" while conveying the thoughts on their cards, and ask the listeners to guess the subtexts.

Do the same thing with the word "Well" to express contempt, surprise, indignation, love, confusion, condescension, coquetry, or other subtexts.

Do the same thing with the phrase "Good morning" to imply "Let's chat," "Please be brief," "Don't say a word," and "I'm just being polite."

4. Shakespearean Subtexts: I Love Thee, I Love Thee Not

Now have the class apply what they have learned about subtext and inflection to the passage in which Helena pursues Demetrius, 2.1.195–253. First, ask students to identify each character's objective. Next, keeping the objective in mind, have them read the lines adding stress and inflection to reflect subtext. Break this scene into small sections. Change casts and elicit subtexts often.

5. Subtext in Acting Companies

Finish the lesson by having the acting companies work in the same manner as in section 4 above on Oberon's speech, "Hast thou the flower there?" (2.1.254–276). Every now and again, review the procedure for the acting companies. Continue to give points to groups who meet, engage, and disband efficiently. Make sure that the director rotation is going smoothly and that directors write into their notes any questions about the passage at hand.

6. Homework

Assign 2.1.125–276 for reading. Ask the students to rewrite the memorization passage in their own words, phrase by phrase, sentence by sentence.

HOW DID IT GO?

Did students participate in the acting exercises? Did they pick up the nuances of meaning as related to inflection? Could they change implication by changing diction? Could they "read" implication in another's diction? If so, they are doing very sophisticated work in two areas:

- that of the professional actor (Classes at the Royal Shakespeare Company and other professional acting companies do the same sort of work your students did today.)
- that of irony (One of the most difficult literary conventions to teach, irony requires humans to hold in their minds simultaneously two conflicting lines of thought. Although students didn't analyze this convention today, they enacted it in subtext exercises.)

How is the confidence level in your classroom? If you saw more and more hands go up as students volunteered to participate in the exercises today, you know that you've got actors whose trust is building.

LESSON 9 "What Thou Seest When Thou Dost Wake"

Shakespearean Subtext

ঌ _____

PLAY SECTIONS COVERED IN THIS LESSON

2.2.33–40 Oberon squeezes the juice of the magic flower on Titania's eyes.

LINES: Oberon, 8

2.2.41–71 Lysander and Hermia fall asleep in the forest.

LINES: Lysander, 17; Hermia, 14

2.2.72–89 Robin mistakes Lysander for Demetrius and puts the potion on the wrong eyes.

LINES: Robin, 18

ঌ _____

WHAT'S ON FOR TODAY AND WHY

To keep students engaged with Shakespeare's language in the most active way, we will continue with more work on inflection and stress, then get students on their feet blocking a scene.

Actors do not stand like inanimate blocks of clay and recite their lines, but unless students think about context and meaning and receive some direction, they may turn into talking lumps. When students incorporate movement appropriately, we see that they are comprehending the play, and we see the characters come to life; therefore, in this lesson we will focus on blocking entrances, exits, and movements appropriate to the text. But what will be the authority for choices about movement? We are uncertain about Shakespeare's original stage directions. Most stage directions in modern editions have been added by modern editors. The wisest plan, therefore, is to do what professional directors and actors do—look closely at Shakespeare's lines to figure out how to move.

Because the writing assignment in the homework section of this lesson involves lengthy instructions, it needs to be given to students in written form; therefore, we will need either to prepare handouts or to write the instructions on the board.

Note: From now on, teachers, you'll frequently be choosing students to perform in front of the room. Experiment with choices in actors. As Michael Tolaydo urges (pages 28–29), don't be restricted by physical type; casting against type often produces new insights and reactions. Having a tall, mature Helena pursue a smaller Demetrius can make students rethink the relationship. Try having two males or two females play the roles and note the very different movements and gestures each will use and the different subtexts that the actors will find. And, of course, remember to call on those students whose hands aren't frantically waving. They're often dying to be discovered by you but are too shy to enter the fun unasked.

WHAT TO DO

1. Log/Homework Review

Hear the logkeeper's report and post. Discuss yesterday's paraphrasing of "Set your heart at rest." Do a choral reading of the memorization passage, asking everyone to read together the opening and closing sections, 2.1.125–126 and 2.1.141–142, and select different speakers for lines 127–140.

2. Warm-up Acting Exercises: Inflection and Stress

To review and connect with yesterday's work, pass out cards with these messages: "I command you to stay!," "Please stay around if you care for me," "It's not safe out there," and "I warn you—you'll be sorry if you go." Ask each of the five students to say the line "Don't go!" stressing the subtext on his card. Let the listeners guess the subtext.

Ask three pairs of students to deliver the following lines: "What time is it?" "It's eleven o'clock." Again, write various subtexts on index cards and give to the performing pairs. Let the class guess the subtext.

- Pair 1 subtext:
  Q: How much longer do I have to live?
  A: Exactly one hour; you'll be executed at midnight.
- Pair 2 subtext:
  Q: When is this class going to end?
  A: Thank goodness the bell is about to ring.
- Pair 3 subtext:
  Q: We've completely lost track of time.
  A: We're already late for class.

3. Oberon's Subtext

Ask two students to read Oberon's speech 2.2.33–40 ("What thou seest when thou dost wake . . ."), each with a different subtext.

- The first: "I will have my revenge."
- The second: "The joke that I play on you will really be funny."

Set up the scene with a sleeping Titania, and be sure to have Oberon squeeze the juice on her eyes. A real flower or a plastic one will serve as a good prop here.

4. Shakespearean Subtext: Wandering in the Woods

Cast 2.2.41–71 ("Fair love, you faint with wand'ring in the wood"). Ask students to suggest various subtexts for Lysander and Hermia:

- Lysander could be macho and Hermia sarcastic.
- Lysander could be innocent and Hermia seductive.

- Lysander could be seductive and Hermia cold.
- Lysander could be genuinely smitten and Hermia could say no but be tempted all the same.

Select a subtext and ask the actors to act the scene accordingly for a few lines. Then change subtexts and casts and continue.

5. Student Directors

Choose three students for Robin, Lysander, and Hermia. Tell students to scan 2.2.72–89 ("Through the forest have I gone . . .") intently looking for clues regarding the staging and possible movements. *Insist that students cite the line(s) that suggest the movement.* Initially you may get suggestions like:

- Hermia is on the ground (2.2.80–81).
- Hermia is not near Lysander (2.2.82–83).
- Robin has something in his hands (2.2.84–85).
- Robin leaves the stage (2.2.89).

Follow up by asking students to look closer. Do Hermia and Lysander sleep restfully? Does either move? Does Robin come close to them? Does he touch them? (Remind students that Robin is invisible. Even if they wake, the lovers do not see him.) What would be the effect on the audience if Hermia woke, stared at Robin but saw nothing, frowned, and went to sleep? Consider how such an action would tie in with Hermia's last speech in the scene.

6. Homework

Assign 2.2.1–163 for reading.

Tell students to practice the memorization passage.

Writing assignment: (Teachers should give this to the students in written form.) *Midsummer* has several references to dreams; the word itself appears in the play 16 times. In the homework passage for tonight, Hermia dreams of a snake, then wakens to find that Lysander has abandoned her. Strange dreams can be the most profound, predictive, or helpful when they seem most bizarre. Describe a weird dream you've had. Did this dream become useful or predictive in your life? Could you relate the dream to anything that happened in your life?

HOW DID IT GO?   If students are beginning to think of the text as something with which they can interact, something on which they can speak authoritatively when they justify their positions by referring to lines, they are taking ownership of the play.

LESSON **10** "Night and Silence! Who Is Here?"

Acting Scenes from Act 2

🐚 _____

PLAY SECTIONS COVERED IN THIS LESSON

2.2.90–151 Abandoned by Demetrius, Helena finds Lysander sleeping in the woods. On waking, he falls instantly in love with her and deserts Hermia.

LINES: Helena, 33; Demetrius, 2; Lysander, 27

2.2.152–163 Hermia awakes from a nightmare and discovers Lysander gone.

LINES: Hermia, 12

🐚 _____

WHAT'S ON FOR TODAY AND WHY

Again we will ask the acting companies to work with scenes. Our objective is to have students practice and increase their abilities to read a scene, determine subtext, and add appropriate movements.

For the first time, students will encounter a homework assignment (in day 2 of this lesson) in which they will be asked to *preview* material rather than review what we did in class.

WHAT TO DO

1. Log/Homework Review/Memorization Practice

Hear the logkeeper's report and post. Collect the homework. Recite the memorization passage twice, each time having half the class recite and the other half listen. Call on students to complete the following sentences eliciting sensory details about the passage: "I see . . . ," "I hear . . . ," "I touch . . . ," "I smell . . . ," supporting each answer with a phrase from the text.

2. Student Directors: Waking Up

Building on the work we did yesterday, review with students the principles of subtext and movement, stressing the importance of looking to the text for clues. If weather permits and if there is a suitable setting, today would be a great time to take students outside to work on two more forest scenes.

Assign each acting company 2.2.90–151 ("Stay, though thou kill me, . . .") or 2.2.152–163 ("Help me, Lysander . . .").

Depending on the number of companies, you will see each scene interpreted in two or three ways before the day is out. Give the students 20 minutes to plan and rehearse their scene. Tell them that along with the performance they will present the objective and subtext for each character. As each group performs, build their confidence with praise.

3. Homework

Assign 3.1 for reading.

Ask students to practice "Set your heart at rest." Tell them to do Memorization Practice 2:

MEMORIZATION PRACTICE 2

Set_____rest:

The Fairyland_____me.

His mother_____order,

And_____night

Full often_____side

And sat_____sands,

Marking th'_____flood,

When we_____conceive

And grow_____wind;

Which she, with_____gait,

Following (her_____squire),

Would imitate_____land

To fetch me_____again,

As from_____merchandise.

But she, being_____die,

And for her sake_____boy,

And for_____him.

Optional writing assignment: In Act 1, Helena says, "Love looks not with the eyes but with the mind; / And therefore is winged Cupid painted blind." We have seen several examples of blind love in *Midsummer.* List as many examples as you can.

HOW DID IT GO?

To evaluate this lesson, answer these questions:

- Do students show comprehension of subtext?
- Did they apply the principles of subtext and inflection to their performances?
- Did students look to the text to determine blocking?
- Did students take initiative in directing and planning scenes both in the class as a whole and in companies?

To take stock of where we are with student accomplishments at the end of Act 2, ask yourself:

· Do the logkeepers take notes and make helpful reports?
· Do the companies continue to function?
· Do all of the students participate in the work of the companies? Are students being responsible about doing their homework?
· Do the students show comprehension of the plot?

If any of these areas need additional attention, work on them before going on to the next lesson.

At this point in the unit, the end of Act 2, we assume that students have become more accomplished at reading new material. If students are having a difficult time comprehending the reading assigned for homework, remind them to read aloud and paraphrase as they go along. If students are neglecting the reading assigned for homework, consider giving a short three-question comprehension quiz at the beginning of class.

If students need more work in paraphrase, stop and do the paraphrase test that follows this lesson.

ટ્રે

PRONOUN / VERB / PARAPHRASE TEST, ACTS 1 AND 2

The purpose of the test is to give you practice at decoding Shakespeare's language. This is an open-book test. To see where the lines fit into the play, use the citation numbers. You may also refer to Handout 1: Second Person Familiar / Verb Inflections.

Directions: As accurately as possible, rewrite the following lines in modern English.

1. Hippolyta, I wooed thee with my sword
   And won thy love doing thee injuries . . . (1.1.17–18)

2. Stand forth, Demetrius.—My noble lord,
   This man hath my consent to marry her. (1.1.25–26)

3. Thou, thou, Lysander, thou hast given her rhymes
   And interchanged love tokens with my child. (1.1.29–30)

4.   If thou lovest me, then
   Steal forth thy father's house tomorrow night . . . (1.1.165–166)

5. O, teach me how you look and with what art
   You sway the motion of Demetrius' heart! (1.1.196–197)

6.   Pray thou for us,
   And good luck grant thee thy Demetrius. (1.1.225–226)

7. Love looks not with the eyes but with the mind;
   And therefore is winged Cupid painted blind. (1.1.240–241)

8. A very good piece of work, I assure you, and a merry. Now, good Peter Quince, call forth your actors by the scroll. Masters, spread yourselves. (1.2.14–16)

9. An I may hide my face, let me play Thisbe too. I'll speak in a monstrous little voice: "Thisne, Thisne!" (1.2.49–51)

10. How now, spirit? Whither wander you? (2.1.1)

11. The King doth keep his revels here tonight.
    Take heed the Queen come not within his sight . . . (2.1.18–19)

12. Either I mistake your shape and making quite,
    Or else you are that shrewd and knavish sprite
    Called Robin Goodfellow. (2.1.33–35)

13. Do you amend it, then. It lies in you.
    Why should Titania cross her Oberon?
    I do but beg a little changeling boy
    To be my henchman. (2.1.121–124)

14. Fetch me that flower; the herb I showed thee once.
    The juice of it on sleeping eyelids laid
    Will make or man or woman madly dote
    Upon the next live creature that it sees. (2.1.175–178)

15. I am your spaniel, and, Demetrius,
    The more you beat me I will fawn on you.
    Use me but as your spaniel: spurn me, strike me,
    Neglect me, lose me; only give me leave
    (Unworthy as I am) to follow you. (2.1.210–214)

LESSON **11** **"What Sayest Thou, Bully Bottom?"**

3.1 in Film

❧ _____

PLAY SECTIONS COVERED IN THIS LESSON

3.1.1–130 Near the sleeping Titania, the mechanicals, observed by Robin, begin to rehearse.

LINES: Bottom, 59; Quince, 37; Snout, 10; Starveling, 3; Robin, 12; Flute, 9

3.1.131–208 Titania wakes, spots Bottom, and falls in love.

LINES: Titania, 34; Bottom, 32; Peaseblossom, 4; Cobweb, 4; Mote, 3; Mustardseed, 4

❧ _____

WHAT'S ON FOR TODAY AND WHY

To demonstrate the differences between live theater and film, and to continue to help students see that there are many ways of interpreting a Shakespearean text, we will present film productions of two scenes, Bottom's transformation into a donkey and Titania's awakening. Any of the productions described on pages 58 and 59 would work well for this scene. The 1935 Warner Brothers USA production features Jimmy Cagney as Bottom and vaudeville actors as the mechanicals. In the 1964 British TV production Benny Hill appears as Bottom.

Have the scenes cued up before class begins.

WHAT TO DO

1. Log/Homework Review/Memorization Practice

Hear the logkeeper's report and post. Collect last night's homework. Lead the class through Memorization Practice 2, with the teacher saying the printed words and the students filling in the blanks in unison. Ask students to go "off book" and say the passage in unison without looking at books. Ask for a student to pantomime the actions while another student slowly reads the passage aloud.

2. Play/Pause/Rewind: Bottom's Transformation

Present a film production of 3.1, at least two different versions if you can locate them. Pause after showing each and ask students to write down as many details of the production as they can remember.

Discuss: Why did Shakespeare have Bottom's metamorphosis occur off stage yet in many of the filmed versions it occurs onstage? Did any of the directors take liberties with the text? Did the changes enhance or detract from the plot? What did you notice about the productions you saw? (For example, if students watched the 1968 Royal Shakespeare Company version, they might have noticed the unusual lighting, quick cuts between characters, speeded-up action, or the opening up of the forest to include different locations.)

3. Contest: An Angel Sings, Hee Haw

For a stress-breaker, stage a donkey-braying contest. Then fish out the donkey ears or silly hat from the prop box and let the winner play Bottom in 3.1.131–208 ("What angel wakes me from my flow'ry bed?"). With the help of student directors, stage this scene, then view it in one or more of the productions you used in the activity above.

4. Homework

Assign 3.2.1–180 for reading.

Ask students to practice the memorization passage and do Memorization Practice 3.

MEMORIZATION PRACTICE 3

Set ＿＿＿＿＿＿＿ rest:

The ＿＿＿＿＿＿＿ me.

His mother ＿＿＿＿＿＿＿ order,

And, in ＿＿＿＿＿＿＿ by ＿＿＿＿＿＿＿

Full ＿＿＿＿＿＿＿ she ＿＿＿＿＿＿＿

And ＿＿＿＿＿＿＿ on ＿＿＿＿＿＿＿ ,

Marking ＿＿＿＿＿＿＿ on the ＿＿＿＿＿＿＿ ,

When ＿＿＿＿＿＿＿ to see ＿＿＿＿＿＿＿

And ＿＿＿＿＿＿＿ wanton ＿＿＿＿＿＿＿ ;

Which ＿＿＿＿＿＿＿ and with ＿＿＿＿＿＿＿ ,

Following ＿＿＿＿＿＿＿ rich with ＿＿＿＿＿＿＿ ,

Would ＿＿＿＿＿＿＿ and ＿＿＿＿＿＿＿

To fetch ＿＿＿＿＿＿＿ and ＿＿＿＿＿＿＿ ,

As from ＿＿＿＿＿＿＿ rich ＿＿＿＿＿＿＿ .

But she, ＿＿＿＿＿＿＿ that boy ＿＿＿＿＿＿＿ ,

And ＿＿＿＿＿＿＿ do I ＿＿＿＿＿＿＿ ,

And ＿＿＿＿＿＿＿ I ＿＿＿＿＿＿＿ .

HOW DID IT GO? Did students hold the film directors accountable for variations based on the text? Did students act/direct with an eye on Shakespeare's words? Do students continue to comprehend the plotline and character relationships? Do students recognize and respond to Shakespeare's language tricks? Did students who had never heard a real donkey bray loudly? Did your ears hurt? Success.

If you assigned the dream papers, read them and comment. If you like, evaluate them as you do other essays, according to the standards you have established.

12 "Lord, What Fools These Mortals Be!"

Three Scenes from Act 3

&❧

PLAY SECTIONS COVERED IN THIS LESSON

3.2.1–42 Robin reports to Oberon that Titania is in love with Bottom and that Robin has put a spell on an Athenian man.

LINES: Oberon, 8; Robin, 34

3.2.90–123 Oberon and Robin attempt to rectify the spell that was placed on the wrong lover.

LINES: Oberon, 20; Robin, 14

3.2.124–180 Lysander, enchanted, pursues Helena. Demetrius, under the spell of the magic flower, wakes and also falls in love with Helena.

LINES: Lysander, 15; Helena, 26; Demetrius, 16

&❧

WHAT'S ON FOR TODAY AND WHY

Because 3.2 is long, and because we want to maintain student interest, we will extract three short subscenes and perform them over several days. The teacher can provide the transitions between these scenes by giving brief summaries.

First, to review the most recent plot developments, students will enact pantomimes. Second, they'll consider the characterization of Robin and Oberon. Third, they will try a modern-day improvisation to identify Helena's amazement and anger at her friends.

WHAT TO DO

1. Log/Homework Review/Memorization Practice

Hear the logkeeper's report and post. Collect yesterday's homework, or give check marks for completing. Since this is the practice for the memorization before graded recitals tomorrow, ask several volunteers to recite for the class without using notes. Conclude with an "off book" choral reading.

2. Pantomime: The Mistress and the Monster

Robin summarizes the events of the previous scene in his speech to Oberon, 3.2.6–36 ("My mistress with a monster is in love"). Divide the lines of this speech among the acting companies and give them a few minutes to prepare a pantomime of their passage. Some of the lines are quite direct and will present no problem. The challenge comes in lines like 3.2.19–25 ("When they him spy . . ."), but our previous work on unusual usages should help. Students will ask questions about language: "What's a fowler?" "A chough?" Refer them to the notes, to a dictionary, or to a Shakespeare glossary. During the presentations, you, teachers, might be the best narrators because you can pace the lines to the action at hand.

3. Oberon and Robin: Lord, What Fools

The line that for some epitomizes the major theme of this play is "Lord, what fools these mortals be!" We will hear it in this exchange. Choose two students to read Oberon and Robin, the invisible but very present observers of the action on stage in 3.2.90–123 ("What hast thou done?"). Don't forget the hats. Ask students to consider why the meter and poetic form change so abruptly in the last 20 lines of the dialogue. How many beats to these lines?

This is also a good time to address the characterizations of Oberon and Robin and the relationship between the two. Ask students to characterize Oberon. Is he tyrannical? Paternal? Mean-spirited? What about Robin? Is he servile? Mischievous? Idiotic? Do these members of the fairy world share a common attitude toward the humans? As always, have students support answers with textual references.

4. Improvisation: Disbelief

Define the term *improvisation:* a brief skit in which the context is given but the dialogue is up to the participants. Ask for volunteers to improvise the following situations:

- Person A is in the school library. Person B, the sweetheart of Person A's best friend (C), arrives and suddenly confesses that he or she loves Person A and despises C.
  B's objective: to get A to believe him/her
  A's objective: to prove he or she cannot be fooled and to show loyalty to his or her best friend
- The situation above still exists, but Person D now enters the scene. A has long adored D, but D has always ignored A and pined for C. Suddenly D approaches A and confesses undying love.
  D's objective: to get A to go out with him or her
  A's objective: to keep from getting hurt

Discuss the two improvisations. What was the primary emotion expressed by A in scene 1? In scene 2?

5. Text: Disbelief

Have students act out 3.2.124–180 ("Why should you think that I should woo in scorn?"). As you did in the previous scene, pause periodically to get directorial suggestions from the class on setting, inflection, pauses, movements, and tone.

Discuss Helena's reaction in this passage. What is her primary emotion? Is it justified? Compare this passage with Helena's soliloquized complaint at the end of 1.1. Tie this exchange in with Robin's comment, "Lord, what fools these mortals be!"

6. Homework

Do Memorization Practice 4. After reading the passage aloud several times, fill in the blanks.

MEMORIZATION PRACTICE 4

Set_____

The_____

His mother_____

And in_____

Full_____

And_____

Marking_____

When_____

And_____

Which_____

Following_____

Would_____

To fetch_____

As from_____

But she,_____

And_____

And_____

HOW DID IT GO?

If students are making informed comments on blocking, characters, setting, and props, then you have successfully established your role as facilitator, not lecturer. If students are becoming their own authorities on Shakespeare, they are acquiring the skills to read his work for the rest of their lives.

To ascertain how far students have progressed along these lines, ask yourself:

- When students speak the words, do they know what they are saying?
- When students speak the words, do they have in mind a particular objective and/or subtext?
- Do students move? If so, do they base their movements on clues in the text?
- Do students demonstrate knowledge of character motives and relationships?
- Do students keep in mind the four groups of people (the royal couple,

the tangled lovers, the mechanicals, and the fairies) and the plot situations that surround them?

- Do students show knowledge of how the four groups intertwine?
- Do students show that they have grown in their ability to paraphrase Shakespeare's language?
- Do students demonstrate willingness to deal with the more complex aspects of Shakespeare's language—reversals, Elizabethan forms, iambic pentameter, et al.?

LESSON 13 "Full Often Hath She Gossiped by My Side"

Memorization Recital

WHAT'S ON FOR TODAY AND WHY

It's memorization day. To minimize nervousness and fear of failure in front of the class, students will recite privately at the teacher's desk.

To keep the quiet mood needed for concentration, and to increase their storehouse of Shakespearean words still current today, students will do vocabulary exercises. When students first start reading Shakespeare, they sometimes assume that words will be old-fashioned. Certainly, there are some archaic words in the text, but on the other hand Shakespeare used (and sometimes created) many words that are still with us. If the educated person of today has a vocabulary of 15,000 words, then Shakespeare's vocabulary, at 30,000, is twice as great. So we'll let students borrow a few of his words to add to their own supply.

WHAT TO DO

1. Log/Homework Review/Memorization Practice

Hear the logkeeper's report and post. For one last practice, have students recite "Set your heart at rest" to their acting groups.

2. Vocabulary: Words Still With Us

Give students Handout 3: Vocabulary in Context. Ask them to complete it during this class period.

3. Recitation: "Set Your Heart at Rest . . ."

Call students up to your desk, one at a time, to hear their memorizations. To expedite the process, ask each of the first four students who've done perfect recitations to listen to four other students. They will be punctilious about reporting the results, and you'll finish up the grading handily.

4. Homework/Evaluation

Assign 3.2.181–365 for reading.

Writing assignment: Lysander flipflops in his affections as a result of the magic flower. Compare his earlier loving statements to Hermia (1.1.130–170 and 2.2.41–70) with his current vows to Helena. What conclusions can you draw about Lysander from this comparison? Cite specific lines to support your comments.

HOW DID IT GO?

In evaluating student recitations, keep in mind your goals and your announced intentions. If indeed you wish to fold these words permanently into the brains of your students, try this grading method:

- On the due date, give 1 point for every line the student recited correctly.
- To foster longer-term retention, give 5 extra-credit points for reciting all the lines one week later and 10 extra-credit points for reciting all the lines correctly one month later.

If you were pleasantly surprised by how many students did letter-perfect recitations, you know you've been effective.

HANDOUT 3

VOCABULARY IN CONTEXT

Directions: Study the following lines. Carefully examine the way in which the underlined word is used in each sentence, then write out the meaning in your own words. In some sentences there is a change in the part of speech of the underlined words. Finally, write an original sentence for each underlined word.

1. a. "Now, fair Hippolyta, our nuptial hour draws on apace."
   b. The members of the court will attend the nuptials of Theseus and Hippolyta.
   c. A member of the clergy can perform nuptials.

Nuptials means:

2. a. "But, O, methinks how slow / This old moon wanes!"
   b. The moon wanes at the end of the month and gets harder to see.
   c. Demetrius' love for Helena has waned.

Wane means:

3. a. "Thou hast by moonlight at her window sung / With feigning voice verses of feigning love . . ."
   b. First Demetrius loves Helena, and then he hates her. When he tells her that he loves her again, she thinks he is feigning.
   c. The children feigned surprise at the presents, but, in fact, they already knew what they were getting.

Feign means:

4. a. ". . . and she, sweet lady, dotes, / Devoutly dotes, dotes in idolatry, / Upon this spotted and inconstant man."
   b. Helena dotes upon Demetrius; Demetrius dotes upon Hermia; Hermia dotes upon Lysander, who also dotes upon her.
   c. Some people dote upon dessert.

Dote means:

5. a. "But I <u>beseech</u> your Grace that I may know / The worst that may befall me in this case / If I refuse to wed Demetrius."
   b. Hermia <u>beseeches</u> her father to let her marry Lysander.
   c. The Student Council decided to <u>beseech</u> the administration for permission to have another dance.

Beseech means:

6. a. "What is Pyramus—a lover or a <u>tyrant</u>?"
   b. Hermia's father acts like a <u>tyrant</u> when he forces her to choose between marrying Demetrius or going to a convent.
   c. The citizens overthrew the <u>tyrant</u> who was ruthlessly ruling their country.

Tyrant means:

7. a. "Our play is 'The most <u>lamentable</u> comedy and most cruel death of Pyramus and Thisbe.'"
   b. To Helena, it is <u>lamentable</u> that Demetrius does not love her.
   c. A <u>lamentable</u> story may make the reader cry.

Lamentable means:

8. a. "For Oberon is passing fell and <u>wrath</u> / Because that she, as her attendant, hath / A lovely boy . . ."
   b. Oberon is full of <u>wrath</u> because Titania will not give him the Indian boy.
   c. When the sheriff discovered the prisoner had escaped, his <u>wrath</u> was great.

Wrath means:

9. a. "And this same <u>progeny</u> of evils comes / From our debate, from our dissension; / We are their parents and original."
   b. Egeus is Hermia's father; she is his <u>progeny</u>.
   c. Parents want to be proud of their <u>progeny</u>.

Progeny means:

10. a. "Lord, what fools these <u>mortals</u> be!"
    b. "But she, being <u>mortal</u>, of that boy did die."
    c. Helena, Hermia, and their suitors are <u>mortal</u>, but Oberon and Titania are immortal and live forever.

Mortal means:

11. a. "We'll rest us, Hermia, if you think it good, / And tarry for the comfort of the day."
    b. Tired out by their walk through the forest, Lysander and Hermia decide to tarry in the woods.
    c. If you tarry at breakfast, you may be late for school.

   Tarry means:

12. a. "The more you beat me I will fawn on you."
    b. Although Demetrius is unkind to Helena, she fawns on him and gives him compliments.
    c. Sometimes people fawn on others to get money or approval.

   Fawn means:

13. a. "Content with Hermia? No, I do repent / The tedious minutes I with her have spent."
    b. Once Lysander falls out of love with Hermia, he finds her tedious and he leaves her.
    c. A tedious task may make you fall asleep.

   Tedious means:

14. a. ". . . a surfeit of the sweetest things / The deepest loathing to the stomach brings . . ."
    b. Lysander has had a surfeit of Hermia's company and wants to leave her.
    c. A surfeit of food can cause a stomachache.

   Surfeit means:

   DIRECTIONS: First, write a brief definition of the italicized word. Second, answer the text question.

   1. Why is it ironic that "Pyramus and Thisbe" is a *lamentable* comedy?

   2. Hermia *flouts* her father's wishes. How?

   3. When does Hermia become *odious* to Lysander?

   4. Name one mortal who is *doted* upon by a fairy and explain how that happens.

   5. Three *nuptials* are planned in the play. Whose?

   6. Explain this statement: In the play, the moon *wanes* and so does the love of certain characters.

   7. At times, two characters in this play *fawn* on two others. Who are they and why do they do so?

   8. Oberon feels *wrath* toward Titania; Egeus feels *wrath* for Lysander. Why?

   9. Why does Helena feel that the men's love for her is *feigned*?

   10. Explain what causes each of these situations: Helena *entreats* Demetrius; Demetrius *entreats* Hermia; Hermia *entreats* Lysander, and Lysander *entreats* Helena.

LESSON 14   "O, Is All Forgot?"

Three More from Act 3

ॐ _____

PLAY SECTIONS COVERED IN THIS LESSON

3.2.181–249 When Hermia finds the other young people, Helena accuses them all of teasing and humiliating her. She reminds Hermia of their long-standing friendship and appeals to her to stop the cruel joke.

LINES: Hermia, 12; Lysander, 7; Helena, 50

3.2.250–295 Swearing that they love Helena, the men insult Hermia.

LINES: Lysander, 22; Helena, 2; Hermia, 13; Demetrius, 9

3.2.296–365 Hermia accuses Helena of stealing Lysander from her.

LINES: Hermia, 22; Helena, 33; Lysander, 7; Demetrius, 8

ॐ _____

WHAT'S ON FOR TODAY AND WHY

In yesterday's homework, students previewed the quarrels and insults that they will work on today. To interpret and visualize these passages, we'll turn to the acting companies. Increasingly, we will give students larger sections of the play to read.

This lesson will take two days, one for planning, one for performance and evaluation.

WHAT TO DO

1. Log/Homework Review

Hear the logkeeper's report and post. Collect last night's comparison papers.

2. Paraphrase/Act: Planning

If you have six acting companies, this assignment will fall right into place. If you have more, you may want to divide the longer passages. Make the following assignments:

- Company 1: Paraphrase, phrase by phrase, 3.2.181–249.
- Company 2: Plan and present a performance of 3.2.181–249.
- Company 3: Paraphrase, phrase by phrase, 3.2.250–295.
- Company 4: Plan and present a performance of 3.2.250–295.
- Company 5: Paraphrase, phrase by phrase, 3.2.296–365.
- Company 6: Plan and present a performance of 3.2.296–365.

Tell the companies that are paraphrasing to translate the scene into modern vernacular and current slang and then plan a staged reading of their new version. Tell the other companies to dramatize the passage considering subtext, blocking, and setting. Have each company follow these special instructions:

- Companies 1 and 2: Incorporate pantomime to clarify the double cherry speech.
- Companies 3 and 4: Emphasize rapid use of language and block very carefully.
- Companies 5 and 6: Do a very physical interpretation.

Allow a good amount of time for students to work, perhaps the rest of the class period.

3. Presentations (Day 2)

Have companies make their presentations alternating paraphrase and dramatization. The paraphrase groups can read (in hats, in chairs, on stools, whatever style they or the teacher prefer) or improvise movements. The acting groups will have had more time to work on staging.

4. Evaluation

Ask groups to quickly review their performances. What did they do well? What could have been better? Did they use their time wisely?

5. Homework

Assign 3.2.366–493 for reading.

Writing assignment: Think about your company's presentation today. If you were going to do it again, what changes would you make in preparation and presentation? Write a memo to your company about your suggestions.

HOW DID IT GO?

To evaluate the comparison papers, see if students presented both cases—Lysander's wooing of Hermia and Lysander's wooing of Helena. Reward students for supporting their comments with lines from the text.

To evaluate this lesson, answer these questions:

- What percentage of the companies' planning time was spent productively?
- How often did problems with Shakespeare's language arise?
- How often did students solve these problems in their groups?
- To what extent did students paraphrase or perform Shakespeare's lines as if they knew what they were saying?
- Did students display more confidence and comprehension than when they did similar exercises in Act 2?

Another gauge of the success of this lesson is the amount of time the teacher had for other business during the planning sessions. If students solved their own problems while the teacher read the comparison papers, we know that they are becoming their own Shakespeare experts. If the teacher, looking up from checking papers, saw students writing and gesturing, arguing and persuading each other, then they've been getting good directions and are incorporating them into their work.

As for the quality of the presentations, they will be far from polished, but for our purposes they will be perfect if students showed through their work an increased knowledge of character, plot, and language. If you can see a difference between this lesson's performance and earlier performances, and if students are saying "We could've done it better if we had more time," you have evidence of engagement.

LESSON **15**

"You Juggler, You Cankerblossom, You Thief of Love!"

Insults

ॐ

PLAY SECTION COVERED IN THIS LESSON

3.2.181–365 When Hermia finds the other young people, Helena accuses them all of teasing and humiliating her. She reminds Hermia of their long-standing friendship and appeals to her to stop. Swearing that they love Helena, the men insult Hermia. Hermia accuses Helena of stealing Lysander from her.

LINES: Hermia, 47; Helena, 85; Lysander, 36; Demetrius, 17

ॐ

WHAT'S ON FOR TODAY AND WHY

Today students will focus on the insults they heard in the scenes yesterday and consider the craft of Shakespearean name-calling. Once again we want students to absorb and vocalize Shakespeare's language, this time with words propelled by malice.

WHAT TO DO

1. Log/Homework Review

Hear the logkeeper's report and post it. Collect the memos.

2. Insults from *Midsummer*

Ask students to quote, without using their texts, some memorable insults from the material presented yesterday. Why did these insults stand out? (Students may say that a good insult is clever or funny.) Tell students that Shakespeare is famous for his insults, that he uses them in many of his plays. To demonstrate, give cards to six students, each with one of the following insults from *Midsummer* written on it:

> "Get you gone, you dwarf, / You minimus of hind'ring knotgrass made . . ."
> —Lysander, 3.2.346–47

> "I will not trust you, I, / Nor longer stay in your curst company."
> —Helena, 3.2.361–62

> "Out, tawny Tartar, out! / Out, loathèd medicine! O, hated potion, hence!"
> —Lysander, 3.2.274–75

> "You juggler, you cankerblossom, / You thief of love! What, have you come by night / And stol'n my love's heart from him?"
> —Hermia, 3.2.296–98

"Fie, fie, you counterfeit, you puppet, you!"

—Helena, 3.2.303

"Tempt not too much the hatred of my spirit, / For I am sick when I do look on thee."

—Demetrius, 2.2.218–19

Ask all the students to stand in a circle. Ask the students with cards to go around the circle, choose a student, and deliver the insult. Do the insults one at a time so that everybody can react. Talk about the insults. What rude names does Shakespeare use? What's a Tartar? What's a cankerblossom?

Remind students that all of these insults came from *Midsummer.* Ask: How do these insults propel 3.2.181–365? Notice how many of these emphasize a person's physical attributes. Do we do the same when we insult people?

3. Other Shakespearean Insults

Give the rest of the students cards with quotes from other plays:

"Why you bald-pated, lying rascal . . ."

—Lucia, *Measure for Measure*

"Oh you beast!
O faithless coward! O dishonest wretch!"

—Isabella, *Measure for Measure*

"Come; you are a tedious fool."

—Escalus, *Measure for Measure*

"Vile worm, thou wast o'erlook'd even in thy birth."

—Pistol, *Merry Wives of Windsor*

"Out of my door, you witch, you rag, you baggage, you poulcat, you runnion!"

—Ford, *Merry Wives of Windsor*

"Let vultures gripe thy guts!"

—Pistol, *Merry Wives of Windsor*

"Thou monstrous slanderer of heaven and earth!"

—Elinor, *King John*

"Go thou and fill another room in hell."

—King Richard, *Richard II*

"Hence, villain! never more come in my sight."

—Duchess of York, *Richard II*

"Avaunt, thou witch!"

—Antipholus of Syracuse, *Comedy of Errors*

"A pox o' your throat, you bawling, blasphemous, incharitable dog!"

—Sebastian, *The Tempest*

"Hang, cur! hang, you whoreson, insolent noisemaker!"

—Antonio, *The Tempest*

"Villain, thou shalt fast for thy offenses ere thou be pardoned."
—Armado, *Love's Labors Lost*

"Thou art too wild, too rude, and bold of voice . . ."
—Bassanio, *Merchant of Venice*

"Turn, hell-hound, turn!"
—Macduff, *Macbeth*

"What, you egg!
Young fry of treachery!"
—Murderer, *Macbeth*

"You, minion, are too saucy."
—Julia, *Two Gentlemen of Verona*

"Ruffian! let go that rude, uncivil touch . . ."
—Valentine, *Two Gentlemen of Verona*

Go around the circle. Let each student hurl his insult. Then ask the students to move around exchanging insults with at least three other people. When time is up, talk about the language. What did you notice about the words? What is there to admire—or condemn—in Shakespeare's insults?

4. Homework

Assign 3.2.366–493 and 4.1.1–106 for reading.

Since the homework assignment is long, if there is time left in class, let the students read what they can in their companies.

HOW DID IT GO?

The supreme reward for this lesson is to overhear students hurling Shakespearean insults at McDonald's or in the parking lot.

LESSON 16 "Jack Shall Have Jill"

Taking Liberties with the Script

ॐ _____

PLAY SECTIONS COVERED IN THIS LESSON

3.2.366-417 To resolve all the mortals' problems, Oberon tells Robin to befog the night, separate the lovers, and undo the charm on Lysander. Meanwhile, Oberon will get the Indian boy from Titania.

LINES: Oberon, 34; Robin, 18

3.2.418-493 Robin follows Oberon's orders and confuses the lovers. Exhausted, all fall on the ground and sleep.

LINES: Robin, 39; Lysander, 10; Demetrius, 15; Helena, 6; Hermia, 6

4.1.1-46 Titania and her fairies wait on Bottom.

LINES: Titania, 14; Bottom, 28; Peaseblossom, 1; Cobweb, 1; Mustardseed, 2

4.1.47-106 Oberon takes pity on Titania. The spell is undone and their quarrel is over.

LINES: Oberon, 47; Titania, 9; Robin, 4

ॐ _____

WHAT'S ON FOR TODAY AND WHY

As we look at films today to see how filmmakers concluded Act 3 and began Act 4, we will be laying the groundwork for the rest of the play in which acting-company activity will dominate.

Practically since the moment Shakespeare's plays were written, producers and directors have often taken liberties with them, cutting and moving speeches, changing words or phrases (usually to make the production easier to understand). An uncut *Hamlet*, for instance, runs about four hours, but scholars tell us that in Shakespeare's day a production of *Hamlet* probably ran closer to two; therefore, it is likely that the author himself cut the script for performance. Besides cutting the script, there is also a long Shakespearean stage tradition of adding instrumental music, songs, and dances. In this lesson, students will examine directors' changes, consider the rationale for them, and decide what the production gains or loses as a result of the changes.

As in the two previous lessons using film productions of *Midsummer*, we will select at least two productions and cue them up to the beginning of the scene. We will start at 3.2.366 (Oberon: "This is thy negligence") and end at 4.1.103 (Titania: "Come, my lord, and in our flight / Tell me how it came this night / That I sleeping here was found / With these mortals on the ground").

WHAT TO DO

1. Log/Homework Review

Hear the logkeeper's report and post. Collect last night's homework. Give students checks for doing it. Then put the memos from Lesson 14 in the company folders.

2. Film Liberties

On the chalkboard, list each film that you will show. Tell students to turn to 3.2.366 in their books. Tell them that they will watch several versions of a scene and to look for places where the director made changes in the script as Shakespeare wrote it. Ask them to raise their hands when they find a variance.

Play the first film. As students' hands go up, pause and note the change. List each change on the board. At the conclusion of the film excerpt, ask the students to consider:

· What was the effect of the changes?
· Why do you think they were made?
· Considering the language and the plot, did the changes enhance the production?
· Did they damage it?
· What—if anything—was lost?

Repeat for the second film production. Students may not agree on answers. Some may like the simplification; some may find the omissions confusing; some may find the effect funnier; some may be outraged at any change.

As they attack and defend various approaches, students are also focusing on the language and objectives of the play.

Students will find that the BBC and Royal Shakespeare Company productions are the most faithful to the text. There are a few word changes, some words are eliminated, and there is no music; but this is almost exactly the text that the class has been studying. The 1935 Max Reinhardt version is the most altered. Parts of 3.1 and 4.1 are combined; many words, lines, and speeches are omitted; some words are changed and visual spectacle lengthens the scenes. The New York Shakespeare Festival version cuts lines, changes the sequence of action, and rearranges 3.2.387–417, moving it to the end of the act.

3. Homework

Assign 4.1.107–229 and 4.2 for reading.

Writing assignment: Bottom is stubborn, bossy, and vain, but he is valued by his friends. Describe the "Bottom" in your life. Draw parallels between the person you know and Bottom in *Midsummer.*

HOW DID IT GO?

If students had surprisingly strong, even vociferous opinions about what could and couldn't be done to the play, you have confirmation of their involvement and their expertise with *A Midsummer Night's Dream.*

LESSON 17 "Are You Sure That We Are Awake?"

Character Committees

ƻ _____

PLAY SECTIONS COVERED IN THIS LESSON

4.1.107–209 Theseus, Hippolyta, and Egeus find the lovers sleeping. Egeus asks Theseus to punish Lysander, but Demetrius confesses that he no longer loves Hermia; he loves Helena. The lovers return to Athens to discuss their dreams and to join in a triple wedding ceremony.

LINES: Theseus, 42; Hippolyta, 7; Egeus, 12; Lysander, 10; Demetrius, 24; Hermia, 3; Helena, 4

4.1.210–229 Bottom wakes from his dream and resolves to go to town.

LINES: Bottom, 20

4.2. The mechanicals worry about Bottom and praise his acting. Bottom returns and urges them to get ready for the play.

LINES: Quince, 9; Flute, 12; Starveling, 2; Snug, 4; Bottom, 18

ƻ _____

WHAT'S ON FOR TODAY AND WHY

Completing Act 4, we will look briefly at the scenes in which the mortals wake and leave the enchanted forest. Because some students are still getting the characters mixed up, and because this is a natural place in the unit to solidify our understanding of the four intertwined character groups—the royal couple, the lovers, the mechanicals, and the fairies—we will concentrate on characters and consider what we have learned about them.

Students will split into small groups, each focusing on a different character. They will collect essential information about a character, then report to the class as a whole. Our goal is for students to leave the classroom with clearer pictures of each character in their minds.

This lesson will take two days.

WHAT TO DO

1. Log/Homework Review

Hear the logkeeper's report and post. Let students keep their writing assignments, as you may wish to call on students to read their essays during the character discussion on Bottom.

2. Reading: Two Voices

Have students read 4.1.144–209. To emphasize the confused response of Lysander, have two students read 152–159 in alternate lines.

3. Reading: Echoes

Bottom's prose soliloquy (4.1.210–229) demonstrates his preoccupation with himself and his response to his experience. To make this clear to students:

· Have them circle every use of the pronouns *I* and *me.*
· Have them search for the two nouns most repeated and circle them (*man* and *dream*).
· Tell them that you are going to read Bottom's soliloquy (4.1.210–229) slowly and they will echo the key words. (Exaggerate the pauses to emphasize his wondering state of mind.)
· Divide the class in half.
· Have one half of the class echo the words *I* and *me.*
· Have the other half echo the word *man.*
· Have everyone echo the word *dream.*
· Discuss the effect of this repetition.

4. Character Discussion: Bottom

Bottom appears as a blowhard, a bully, and a fool, yet the other workmen genuinely admire him. What makes him a sympathetic character? Refer to the information in 4.2, the information in previous scenes, and to students' homework essays, as you discuss his character traits.

5. Formalization of Character Notes

Ask students to begin a collection of notes on each character. For now, they will work only on Bottom, and they will work together under the teacher's guidance. (The teacher can work on an overhead transparency or on the board while students work on paper.)

· Under the title "Bottom," list three to five character traits. (Students may suggest several, then agree on a few—perhaps "bossy," "over-achieving," "gullible.")
· Ask the students to find the scenes where Bottom appears (1.2, 3.1, and 4.1 so far). Look in each scene for examples and/or lines that prove each of the three character traits. For example, for "bossy," students may note that, although Peter Quince is in charge of the first rehearsal, Bottom wants to run the show: "First, good Peter Quince, say what the play treats on, then read the names of the actors, and so grow to a point" (1.2.8–10). By the second rehearsal, his every speech contains an order: "Write me a prologue . . . No, make it two more . . . bring in (God shield us) a lion . . . you must name his name . . . Look in the almanac . . ." (3.1). In 4.1, he is giving orders to the fairies: "Scratch my head, Peaseblossom . . . Monsieur Cobweb, get you your weapons in your hand and kill me a red-hipped humble-bee on the top of a thistle. . . ." Make sure that students take careful notes, getting the quotes and line numbers right.

- Ask the students what Bottom's objectives are. What does he want? Does this change in the course of the play? Make a list of his objectives. Find an example and/or line to prove each one. For example, if students think that one of Bottom's objectives is to enjoy creature comforts, they might say that in 4.1 all the things that Bottom asks for—to have his head scratched, to send out for honey and oats, to hear music, to take a nap—have to do with physical pleasures.
- Ask the students to look at *how* Bottom talks. Does he talk in verse, prose, or what? If verse, what form—tetrameter, pentameter, or what? Is he consistent, or does he change verse forms in certain situations? Make a note of your conclusions. In what style does he talk—simple, fancy, or what? Write down a line that is a good example.

6. Character Committees

Break students into nine groups of two or three. Assign to one group all the rest of the mechanicals. Give them the special task of distinguishing the various personalities and of completing as much of the general directions as possible. To another group assign the three high-ranking court figures: Theseus, Hippolyta, and Egeus. As with group 1, give this group the task of distinguishing the various personalities and completing as much of the general directions as possible. To each of the other groups, assign one of these characters: Lysander, Demetrius, Helena, Hermia, Oberon, Titania, and Robin.

Ask each group to prepare a formal character report for the character(s) they were assigned by repeating the formal character-analysis process we went through with Bottom, above. It would help if you listed the steps on the board:

- List three to five character traits.
- Find examples and quotes from the play to prove each character trait.
- List the character's main objectives. Find examples and quotes to support each objective.
- Describe how the character talks—in what verse pattern, in what style. Find a sentence that demonstrates the style.

Students will need plenty of time for this activity, probably the rest of the period for day 1 and the first 15 minutes of the period for day 2. Ask that the reports be written in dark ink or pencil so you can run their papers through a copying machine.

7. Character Committee Reports (Day 2)

Ask committees to present their reports. Collect the papers and duplicate later for distribution.

8. Character Discussion: The Four Plots

Referring to the play map (Lesson 1), ask students to sort the characters into four groups. (Students will probably suggest: the royal couple, the lovers, the mechanicals, the fairies.) Where do they put Egeus? Do they need to change one of the categories?

9. Character Discussion: The Young Lovers

Some critics claim that the lovers are virtually identical. Do students agree? Can they find any significant differences in personality? Refer to character experts and have students cite lines from the text to support their ideas.

10. Homework

Assign 5.1.1–113 for reading.

Writing assignment: Hippolyta appears in 1.1, 4.1, and 5.1, but she says very little. From reviewing the text and considering what she does and doesn't say, what conclusions can you reach about her?

HOW DID IT GO?

The character work students did in this lesson is not easy. It calls for both precise detail and intuitive reading. Considering both, to what extent did students increase their understanding of each character? To what extent did students increase their understanding of the network of characters? How successful were students in finding texts to support their ideas about character?

The information students assembled today could be the foundation for a well-researched paper on a *Midsummer* character, but we will leave that option for teachers to use later if they like. For this unit, we will continue to do what Peggy O'Brien calls "vertical close reading," approaching the play as actors, using this rich and specific information to make choices in performance.

Don't forget to send character committee reports to the copy machine so students can have them for Lesson 20.

LESSON 18 "Lovers and Madmen"

Introduction to Final Performances

è&
_____

PLAY SECTIONS COVERED IN THIS LESSON

5.1.1–33 Theseus attributes the young lovers' stories to the delusions of love.

LINES: Hippolyta, 6; Theseus, 25

5.1.34–113 Philostrate announces the revels planned and derides the mechanicals' play, but Theseus insists on seeing it.

LINES: Lysander, 2; Theseus, 53; Philostrate, 24; Hippolyta, 3

è&
_____

WHAT'S ON FOR TODAY AND WHY

Rather than the traditional test or paper, we will use a performance to draw together students' energies and information for a conclusion. From the beginning, we have asked students to understand *Midsummer* as a play and to convey Shakespeare's words to an audience of their classmates. We ask the same for the final performances; however, we will give students more time to plan and rehearse, and we will ask more in the way of set, costuming, and character study.

To inform students of our expectations for this project, we will prepare and pass out Handout 4: Scenes for Final Performance and Handout 5: Acting Companies—Performance Preparation.

Teachers may choose to have the final performances in the classroom or in a larger setting. If at all possible, arrange to videotape the companies' performances. The students will get great pleasure out of seeing themselves on tape, and many will want to share the tape with family members.

WHAT TO DO

1. Log/Homework Review

Hear the logkeeper's report and post. Collect the writing assignment due today.

As promised in Lesson 13, give students the opportunity to earn five extra credit points for reciting or writing "Set your heart at rest." Ask them to write the passage from memory.

2. The Power of Imagination: The Lunatic, the Lover, and the Poet

As we did at the outset of the play, go around the room reading 5.1.1–33. Change readers at each semicolon or end punctuation. Stop as needed to paraphrase or clear up comprehension problems.

When the reading is completed, ask students to consider why the description of the poet, who does not appear in the play, should be so much longer than that of the lover, who does. (Some in the class may make a connection with Shakespeare the poet/playwright whose imagination produced this play.)

3. Irony: A Tedious, Brief Scene

The conversation between Theseus and Philostrate sets the ironic tone for the play that will follow. Because identifying irony is sometimes difficult for students, have them:

- summarize what they know of the players and predict the kind of performance they will give
- find the contradictions within the phrases in 5.1.34–113 (tedious brief, tragical mirth, etc.)
- find the contradictions within speeches—e.g., "And tragical, my noble lord, it is" (5.1.70); ". . . but more merry tears / The passion of loud laughter never shed" (5.1.73–74)
- talk about the nature of irony, how when irony occurs people who "get it" have to hold in their minds at once two strands of thought, one contradicting the other

4. Acting Companies: Introduction to the Presentation

Tell students that the culminating activity for this unit will be a performance, that each acting company will present a five- to ten-minute scene.

Explain the basic requirements:

- Each acting company will perform a different scene.
- Students may do parts of scenes or cut speeches to facilitate comprehension or to fit within the time allotted, but they may not modernize language.
- Everyone should be on stage at least some of the time, and every actor must say at least one line. Sharing roles or doubling (playing two roles) is acceptable.
- Actors should have movements blocked out and know their blocking.
- Actors are strongly encouraged to memorize their lines, but may use scripts; if so, they should be familiar enough with them to look at the audience frequently and to be convincing. (Encourage actors to write or type out their scripts on notecards.)
- Casts should supply themselves with some rudimentary costumes and props. (They can borrow from the class box if necessary.)
- Some class time will be set aside for organization and rehearsals, but, for best results, groups will also get together outside of class.

5. Acting Companies: Scene Choices

Give students Handout 4: Scenes for Final Performance. Give students a few minutes to review them. Send students to their acting companies to discuss their preferences. Ask each group to write down first, second, and third choices and submit them to the teacher.

Teachers will be the ultimate arbiters of scene assignments. The plan is to present some scenes from earlier acts and to complete the play by having three acting companies perform all of the fifth act. If students are reluctant to tackle scenes that have not been covered in class, sharpen their interest by offering extra points for those who undertake the new.

The eight scenes on the handout work well, but there are many other choices that you may wish to make. Ideally, scenes should be long enough to develop characterization and to give students an opportunity to grapple with language and presentation.

Point out the particular challenge of each scene. Encourage students to be creative in all aspects of their productions.

To give the teacher time to make the assignments, pass out Handout 5: Acting Companies—Performance Preparation. Ask students to discuss this in groups. Then, when your calculations are complete, announce scene assignments.

6. Homework

Assign 5.1.114–417 for reading.

Ask students to review the scenes they will act.

Ask them to review the handouts they received today.

HOW DID IT GO?   If all is well, two essential events occurred today:

• Students came to a minimal understanding of what is expected of them in the final performance project.
• Students accepted the assignment with grace and joy.

♪

HANDOUT 4

SCENES FOR FINAL PERFORMANCE

3.1.76–208   Titania falls for Bottom.
Lines: Robin, 12; Quince, 13; Bottom, 51; Flute, 8; Titania, 34; Fairies, 12
(Challenge: emphasize the difference between the exquisite language of Titania and the earth-bound responses of Bottom.)

3.2.181–365   The lovers quarrel.
Lines: Lysander, 34; Helena, 84; Demetrius, 17; Hermia, 47
(Challenge: maintain audience interest and comprehension in long speeches, carefully planning interpretation and blocking, and short exchanges, which need crisp, rapid-fire dialogue.)

3.2.375–493   Oberon instructs Robin to undo the spell on the lovers.
Lines: Oberon, 32; Robin, 50; Lysander, 10; Demetrius, 15; Helena, 6; Hermia, 6
(Challenge: interpret, orally and physically, the change of mood from the fairies' conversation to Robin's mischief-making.)

4.1.1–106   Titania waits on Bottom; Oberon and Robin undo the spell.
Lines: Titania, 23; Bottom, 28; Fairies, 4; Oberon, 47; Robin, 4
(The challenge is similar to that in choice A. Students also are challenged to include music and a dance.)

5.1.1–133   Theseus and Hippolyta welcome the lovers and preview the nuptial entertainment.
Lines: Hippolyta, 12; Theseus, 81; Lysander, 5; Philostrate, 24; Prologue, 11
(Challenge: create a connection between Theseus' speech to Hippolyta at the beginning of the act and the transition to the conversation between him and Philostrate.)

5.1.134–231   The mechanicals present "Pyramus and Thisbe" (Part 1).
Lines: Quince (Prologue), 27; Theseus, 14; Snout (Wall), 12; Bottom (Pyramus), 27; Flute (Thisbe), 9; Demetrius, 4
(Challenge: contrast the naive acting of the workmen with the polished sarcasm of audience members.)

5.1.232–371   The mechanicals present "Pyramus and Thisbe" (Part 2).
Lines: Snug (Lion), 10; Theseus, 24; Demetrius, 20; Lysander, 7; Starveling (Moonshine), 7; Flute (Thisbe), 25; Bottom (Pyramus), 37; Hippolyta, 9
(Challenge: same as above)

5.1.372–455   The duke and the fairies leave their parting thoughts.
Lines: Theseus, 16; Robin, 36; Oberon, 28; Titania, 4
(Challenge: interpret and stage a series of monologues and a song and dance so as to maintain audience interest.)

♪

HANDOUT 5

ACTING COMPANIES—PERFORMANCE PREPARATION

1. Editing

a. Make copies of the scene for everyone in the group.

b. Read the scene aloud going around the group. As you read, circle any words and phrases you don't understand.

c. Get definitions for those words from notes, dictionary, or teacher.

d. Read again, deciding together what each speech means.

e. Read again, deciding on the objective of each character.

f. Decide how your passage fits into the context of the act and the whole play.

g. Read again to edit out lines that could be omitted without damaging the meaning. Remember that performance time should not exceed 10 minutes.

h. Read again to check your editing.

2. Casting

a. When everyone has a comfortable understanding of the scene, cast parts.

b. If you don't have enough people in your group, you may have members "double" (play two parts—use a prop or sign to indicate each character) or, if the extra characters have only one or two lines, you may draft people from other acting companies.

c. If you have too many people, you may split larger parts (have two Oberons) or consider including choral reading.

d. Appoint a director to oversee the whole production.

3. Blocking

a. Read through the scene, locating character entrances and exits.

b. Decide on appropriate placement and movements for the characters and write them into your script.

c. Move through the blocking several times. Talking about what to do is not the same!

4. Characterization

a. Read through your lines silently and aloud many times until you're sure you understand every word, phrase, and sentence.

b. Identify your objective in the passage.

c. Decide what words, phrases, or ideas need to be stressed and indicate that on your script.

d. Decide where pauses are appropriate and indicate them on your script.

e. Identify your movements.

f. Read your part aloud many times. You do not have to fully memorize the part, but you should feel completely comfortable with it when you perform it in front of the class.

5. Furniture, Props, Costumes

a. Decide if you need furniture. Remember that classroom desks can be trees, walls, etc.

b. Decide what props you need and who will bring them.

c. Decide on costumes. These don't need to be elaborate, but you will feel more like a performer if you change your appearance to look somewhat like the character you are portraying.

6. Performance Worksheet

Fill out this form (at the end of this handout) so that all members of your company know their responsibilities.

7. Rehearse! Rehearse Again! More!

Rehearse your scene several times. Remember, the more you practice, the more relaxed you will be in front of the class.

a. Get on your feet and go through the scene acting out the parts.

b. Use your notes on blocking to help you decide where to come in, where to stand, which direction to turn while speaking, where to exit, etc.

c. Listen to your director. She may have suggestions about changes in blocking, movement, inflection, pauses, characterization, etc.

ACTING COMPANY PERFORMANCE WORKSHEET

ACTING COMPANY: _____

SCENE TO BE PERFORMED: (List act, scene, and lines)

CHARACTER:	PLAYED BY:	COSTUME DESCRIPTION:
1. _____	_____	_____
2. _____	_____	_____
3. _____	_____	_____
4. _____	_____	_____
5. _____	_____	_____
6. _____	_____	_____

PROPS: (List all needed; include those borrowed from class prop box.)

WHO IS RESPONSIBLE FOR BRINGING WHAT?

_____ will bring her/himself and _____
_____ will bring her/himself and _____
_____ will bring her/himself and _____
_____ will bring her/himself and _____
_____ will bring her/himself and _____
_____ will bring her/himself and _____

NOTES AND REMINDERS:

LESSON **19** "For Your Play Needs No Excuse"

Planning for Performance

ᘏᕤ _____

PLAY SECTION COVERED IN THIS LESSON

5.1.114-367 As the mechanicals present "Pyramus and Thisbe," Theseus, Hippolyta, Lysander and Demetrius critique the play and the actors.

LINES: Prologue, 11; Theseus, 42; Lysander, 10; Hippolyta, 15; Quince, 27; Demetrius, 26; Snout, 12; Bottom, 60; Flute, 34; Snug, 10; Starveling, 7

ᘏᕤ _____

WHAT'S ON FOR TODAY AND WHY

To give students a sense of how the play within the play is performed, we're going to view one or two (depending on time and availability) productions of 5.1.112–364, the mechanicals' performance of "Pyramus and Thisbe." Both the Max Reinhardt and the New York Shakespeare Festival versions are very broadly acted; students will want to discuss the liberties taken with the text and decide whether or not they are effective. The version by the Royal Shakespeare Company is extremely low key and should give rise to a discussion of the directors' objectives.

A rare but interesting production that a student found in a Cambridge, Massachusetts, bookstore is "Meet the Beatles," a set of black and white short film clips made for fan clubs. A brief segment features the erstwhile Fab Four and friends enacting the mechanicals' play. The clip is more interesting for the celebrity cast than for the quality of the work, but it offers a look at famous amateur actors enacting a group of amateur actors putting on a play.

After a brief discussion comparing and contrasting the different conceptions of the play, students will meet in acting companies to continue to plan their performances.

WHAT TO DO

1. Log/Homework Review

Hear the logkeeper's report and post. Ask and answer questions students have about Handout 5: Acting Companies—Performance Preparation. Make sure they know the expectations for this project.

2. Play/Pause/Rewind: "Pyramus and Thisbe"

Show students one or two film productions of 5.1.112-364. (It begins with Philostrate, the master of ceremonies, introducing the play,

"So please your Grace, the Prologue is addressed.") Enjoy. Discuss. As always, discuss the directors' choices.

3. Acting Companies: Planning

For the balance of the period, circulate, listen in, answer questions, give advice when asked and reassurance when needed as acting companies continue to plan their projects. Make sure that each group has cast roles and selected a director before class finishes today. Ask each group to fill out the "Performance Worksheet" at end of Handout 5 and turn it in.

4. Homework/Evaluation

Assign 5.1.367–439 for reading.

Optional writing assignment: With "Pyramus and Thisbe," Shakespeare wrote a funny "bad" tragedy within a well-written romantic comedy. What makes "Pyramus and Thisbe" bad and *Midsummer* good? Consider characterization, plot, and language in your essay. Do whatever assignments are decided upon by individual acting companies.

HOW DID IT GO?   If you noticed a businesslike, let's-get-down-to-it tone to the group meetings today, it's because students understand what they're doing. You've done a good job.

LESSON **20** "Following Darkness Like a Dream"

The Play Within the Play

✌ _____

PLAY SECTIONS COVERED IN THIS LESSON

5.1.388–407 When the play is over and the mortals have retired to bed, Robin announces that now it is the fairies' hour.

LINES: Robin, 20

5.1.408–439 Oberon and Titania bestow blessings on the newly wedded couples.

LINES: Oberon, 28; Titania, 4

5.1.440–455 Robin bids a final farewell to the audience.

LINES: Robin, 16

✌ _____

WHAT'S ON FOR TODAY AND WHY

The last three passages in the play, which students read for homework last night, are spoken by the fairies. One reminds us of magic, one of romance, and one of the art of the play. Students will read these passages in class and place them in the larger context of the play as a whole. If time permits, and if teachers can locate it, students may enjoy seeing a brief clip from *Dead Poets Society*. In this movie, one of Robin Williams's students plays Robin in a school production of *Midsummer*, and we see his rendition of the final speech, "If we shadows have offended . . ." (5.1.440–455).

Option: If students did last night's writing assignment, their papers can serve as an effective review of the play. To reinforce earlier discussions of irony in Lesson 17, contrast the mechanicals' play and *Midsummer*. After all, Shakespeare wrote both plays. In "Pyramus and Thisbe" he deliberately and amusingly incorporated the mistakes of amateur playwrights in constructing a wooden plot relying on ridiculous coincidence, inadequate characterization, and inane, trite, and forced language and rhyme—and thereby highlighted the strengths and beauty of the larger play and poetry. Furthermore, Shakespeare wrote *Midsummer* and *Romeo and Juliet*, a tragedy similar in its bare plot to "Pyramus and Thisbe," at about the same time.

Again, students will spend most of the period preparing for their performances. To aid them in their homework assignment, distribute copies of the character committee reports you copied after Lesson 6.

If your school's Audio-Visual Department has a video camera, be sure to reserve it today. If none is available, ask your students. Taping is fun for actors, allows parents to share some enjoyable moments, and provides a record for you.

WHAT TO DO

1. Log/Homework Review

Hear the logkeeper's report and post. Field questions about performances. Collect performance sheets from each group and keep on file.

2. Good and Bad: *A Midsummer Night's Dream* and "Pyramus and Thisbe"

(Optional) Call on several students to read their essays or comments from them, and compile a cumulative list of contrasts on the chalkboard under the headings *Midsummer* and P&T. Talk about the differences in characters, plots, visual effects, and particularly discuss differences in the ways people talk—vocabulary, style, language tricks.

3. Happily Ever After: Farewells

Ask a student to read Robin's speech, "Now the hungry lion roars . . ." (5.1.388–407). Compare it with his speech in 3.2.399–409. What's the purpose of each? Does the second add something new, or is it a reminder of what has passed?

Ask two student volunteers to read Oberon's and Titania's speeches, "Through the house give glimmering light . . ." (5.1.408–439). Consider the purpose of the speeches. Can students relate them to the happily-ever-after ending of fairy tales?

Ask another volunteer to read Robin's last speech, "If we shadows have offended . . ." (5.1.440–455). Or show the video clip described in the What's On for Today and Why section above. Ask students to consider the context. Where else have we seen the theme of plays and players? What does this speech have to do with the rest of the play? In what ways is it a satisfactory conclusion to the play?

4. Acting Companies: Planning

Again, allow a good part of the period for acting companies to continue to plan their projects. Today as you circulate, encourage companies to stand up and rehearse on their feet. Keep an eye and ear out for students whose planning has hit a snag or is becoming so elaborate that they will have a hard time getting it together.

5. Homework/Evaluation

Ask the students to make a copy of their scene and paste each page on a larger piece of plain paper so they will have large margins for notes.

Writing assignment: Think about the character you will play. Review the notes you took in class on Bottom and the work we did in class and in character committees (Lesson 17). If one of the committees did a sheet on your character, consult it. (Teachers, at this point, distribute the reports done by the character committees.) After serious review, write a short essay discussing the essential personality of your character, citing examples from the text to support your views. Then list the objectives your character has in the scene your company will present.

Do whatever assignments are decided upon by individual acting companies.

HOW DID IT GO?   If you hear a constant buzz punctuated by occasional shrieks as companies rehearse, and if a few students each period rush up to you anxiously asking for your approval of an interpretation, a reading, or creative approach, independent learning is occurring.

If you resisted the urge to direct every scene and let the students make their own mistakes, you are a master teacher.

If there was only a small amount of blood spilled during "collaborative learning," students are learning the art of negotiation.

LESSON 21   "'Tis Almost Fairy Time"

Rehearsal

The unit is almost over, and still there is no final exam. No bubble sheets. No blue books. From the beginning, we have said that performance makes the language come alive, so ending with dramatic presentations by acting companies seems most appropriate.

We do, however, want to evaluate the students' achievements in the areas we set out to work on: language acquisition, comprehension of plot and character networks, communication of subtext and objective, knowledge of the play as a play. The "Performance Evaluation" sheet (Lesson 22) is based on these goals, and on a demonstration of student responsibility as a group member. In this lesson, students will receive and review the evaluation form upon which they will be graded.

In preparation for well-planned performances, students will design a set and costumes for their scene, and they will mark their scripts with notes about movement, objectives, subtext, pauses, stresses, and inflections.

Again, students rehearse, probably for two days; teachers will decide at the end of the first day of this two-day lesson.

WHAT TO DO

1. Log/Homework Review

Hear the logkeeper's report and post. Collect character essays. Check and return since students will use them later.

Check to see that each student has copied the play script and pasted the pages on larger plain paper.

2. Putting Thoughts on Paper

Guide the first part of rehearsal time:

- Ask the companies to conduct a five-minute discussion of what their set would look like if this were a full-blown production. Have one of the company members sketch it—no fancy artwork required, just indications of what is where.
- Ask students to take the playscripts and character papers they did for homework and merge them. In a margin of the script, each student should write his character's objective in the scene; if that objective changes in the course of the scene, the student should write the new objective in the margin at the point of change.
- Ask students to mark on their scripts any cuts the group has agreed on.
- Ask students to mark their lines for inflections, pauses, and stresses.
- Ask students to note on their scripts every move they will make in the

course of the scene. (Later units get into formal stage directions; use them if you like, but for now improvised directions will do.)

3. Rehearsal

Give students time to rehearse their scene with their newly annotated scripts in hand.

4. Homework (Day 1)

Plan a costume for your character and draw it or describe it.

5. Log/Homework Review (Day 2)

Hear the logkeeper's report and post. Collect costume sketches/descriptions. Exclaim over them. Hang the sketches.

6. Preparation Miscellany: Students

Remind students:

- If they are bringing music, they must also bring a machine on which to play it.
- If they are bringing props or costumes that must be stored, they need to make arrangements with the teacher in advance.
- If they will be moving furniture around the room, they will also be responsible for restoring the room to order.
- If they become ill the night before the performance and will be absent the next day, they need to alert their company members. (Have them exchange phone numbers in advance.)

7. Preparation Miscellany: Teachers

Here is a list of things to do to facilitate the performance day:

- Post a schedule listing day and order of performances.
- Decide how you want to handle absenteeism if it should occur the day of performance. Will you postpone the scene? Will you have another company or class member fill in for the absentee? Will you require a makeup assignment from the absentee?
- Distribute the Performance Evaluation form during rehearsals so students will know in advance what you are looking for. Decide how many points you want to allot for performance. (Because you appreciate the time, work, courage, and ego involvement of students in doing a presentation before the class, you will probably want to give favorable grades to all who worked.)
- Remember that no matter how hard students worked, they are students, not professionals. Smile, laugh, and applaud their big moments even if they miss cues, nervously gulp lines, or drop props.

8. Rehearsal (Day 2)

Keep students on their feet working. Keep spirits high.

HOW DID IT GO?

At this point you must decide if students need an additional day to rehearse their scenes. They should be ready by now, but who knows how many interruptions you have had, or how many students have been absent.

The work students did annotating their scripts should strengthen their performances. In order to gauge the accuracy and thoroughness of their work, go from group to group on day 2 of rehearsals checking scripts and asking questions about student choices.

LESSON 22 "A Play There Is, My Lord"

Performance

WHAT'S ON FOR TODAY AND WHY

Today students will show their stuff. If they acquired Shakespeare's language and understood his characters, they will show it today.

Because there will be a storm of questions and costumes and misplaced scripts, the teacher's role today is that of organizer: get the video set up, the stage arranged, the actors in their places. The teacher, if desired, could also fancify the room, dress up, play music, publish programs, do what is possible to create a festive theater space.

If there are more than five acting companies, performances will take more than one day. Students and teachers alike should be prepared to keep up the enthusiasm and decorum for those later performances.

WHAT TO DO

1. Call the Companies One by One

Present the scenes in the order in which they appear in the play. Ask each group to introduce the scene by:

· telling what the set would look like if it existed
· introducing the players and naming their parts
· commenting on the scene they will present

As the students perform, teachers fill out the evaluation sheets. Pass them out at the end of class.

2. The Very End

When all the groups are done, when the books have been collected, go around the room and ask students to recall favorite lines. Then do the memorization—one last time.

HOW DID IT GO?

If there were boisterous laughs and quiet surprises, boys playing girls and girls playing boys, lines said imperfectly and speeches that unexpectedly soared, props that fell apart and blocking that didn't quite work, difficult passages creatively bridged, inappropriate music that was oddly right, leaden-footed dances hysterically performed, rushed rhythms and perfect moments, you've taught a play that students will remember. You've given them an opportunity to work together, to bring their own breath of life to timeless lines. You've given them the skills and confidence to read difficult material. You've given them Shakespeare.

PERFORMANCE EVALUATION

ACTING COMPANY NAME:

SCENE PERFORMED:

CHARACTER	PLAYED BY	COMMENTS

POINTS POSSIBLE	POINTS AWARDED	TO WHAT EXTENT DOES THE PERFORMANCE SHOW:
15		Careful Reading and Rehearsal
15		Understanding of Characters
15		Understanding of Plot
20		Understanding of Language
15		Ability to Use Language to Portray Character
10		Well Planned Movements
10		Well Planned Use of Props and Costumes
(BONUS)		Something Extra
100 TOTAL (+ BONUS)		

COMMENTS:

Romeo and Juliet

•

Susan C. Biondo-Hench

EDITOR

Dear Colleagues,

Shakespeare. Mere mention of his name is likely to make a class of freshmen panic, so it is important that a student's first encounter with Shakespeare's plays be dynamic and engaging. A starting point for this encounter is the very heart of Shakespeare's work—his language. Shakespeare enthusiasts may love its rich complexity, but teachers know that this same language can be a barrier for students. Once students can make the language work for them, they have access to the pleasures of the play—the jokes, the heart tugs, the fear, the anger, the thousands of problems humans create for themselves, and the one or two problems created by outside forces. It is language, therefore, that is the focus of this *Romeo and Juliet* unit, and those lessons that don't focus directly on language help to pave the way.

The following pages provide a six-week working outline of lessons based on strategies such as choral reading, performance, and word study. Representing the combined efforts of Susan Cahill, Whippany Park High School in Whippany, New Jersey; Robin Tatu, National Cathedral School for Girls in Washington, D.C.; and myself, these activities are varied and fresh, designed to bring a distant relationship between students and blocks of intimidating lines into a meaningful dialogue.

What is needed to make this unit a success?

A spirit of flexibility and adventure is a key requirement.

For which teaching situation is this unit best suited?

Although traditionally taught to ninth graders, the unit is designed to be adapted to many teaching situations. Too long? Cut out some of the optional activities and/or combine some of the lessons. Too difficult? Assign less reading for homework and allow the students to work with partners or in groups when tackling tricky sections. Too easy? Give the students more independence and have them complete the optional lessons. Customize.

What about the need to cover everything?

Less is more. There are so many layers and facets in *Romeo and Juliet* that it is best to help the students sample a little and to leave them wanting to discover more on their own.

What about tests and quizzes?

There are no tests and quizzes to accompany this unit. Participation and involvement are the goals, and plenty of assignments—individual and group, written and oral—are provided to keep this goal in sight.

What is the first step?

Read on. And as Juliet says, "Hie to high fortune!"

Susan C. Biondo-Hench

Susan Biondo-Hench
Carlisle High School
Carlisle, Pennsylvania

UNIT CALENDAR FOR
Romeo and Juliet

❧ 1	❧ 2	❧ 3	❧ 4	❧ 5
LESSON 1	LESSON 2	LESSON 3	LESSON 4	LESSON 4
An Introduction	A Choral Reading of the Act 1 Prologue	Barbs from the Bard	Acting 1.1	Acting 1.1 *(cont.)*
	Text: 1. Prologue		Text: 1.1.1–105	Text: 1.1.1–105
❧ 6	❧ 7	❧ 8	❧ 9	❧ 10
LESSON 5	LESSON 6	LESSON 7	LESSON 8	LESSON 8
Viewpoints on Love and Marriage	Mercutio's Queen Mab	Elizabethan Dance	A Performance of 1.5	A Performance of 1.5 *(cont.)*
Text: 1.2–3	Text: 1.4		Text: 1.5	Text: 1.5
❧ 11	❧ 12	❧ 13	❧ 14	❧ 15
LESSON 9	LESSON 9	LESSON 10	LESSON 10	LESSON 11
Act 2 Prologue	Act 2 Prologue *(cont.)*	Praiseworthy Promptbooks	Praiseworthy Promptbooks *(cont.)*	The Balcony Scene in Film
Text: 2.1.1–14	Text: 2.1.1–14	Text: 2.1–2	Text: 2.1–2	Text: 2.2
❧ 16	❧ 17	❧ 18	❧ 19	❧ 20
LESSON 12	LESSON 13	LESSON 14	LESSON 14	LESSON 15
Language Tricks	More Language Tricks	Tableaux Vivants for 3.1	Tableaux Vivants for 3.1 *(cont.)*	A Word Study of 3.2
Text: 2.3.1–93	Text: 2.4–6	Text: 3.1	Text: 3.1	Text: 3.2
❧ 21	❧ 22	❧ 23	❧ 24	❧ 25
LESSON 16	LESSON 17	LESSON 18	LESSON 19	LESSON 20
Cutting the Script	Subtext, Stress, and Inflection	Shakespearean Subtext	Imagery in 4.3	Looking for Multiple Causes
Text: 3.3–5		Text: 4.1–2	Text: 4.3	Text: 4.4–5
❧ 26	❧ 27	❧ 28	❧ 29	❧ 30
LESSON 21	LESSON 22	LESSON 23	LESSON 23	LESSON 23
The Fate Debate	A Close Study of Romeo's Last Speech	Acting Companies	Acting Companies *(cont.)*	Acting Companies *(cont.)*
Text: 5.1–3	Text: 5.3.88–120			
❧ 31				
LESSON 23				
Acting Companies *(cont.)*				

LESSON 1 "In Fair Verona"

An Introduction to *Romeo and Juliet*

WHAT'S ON FOR TODAY AND WHY

To provide a colorful opening to the unit and to help students envision the main characters and their relationships, reveal and discuss a *Romeo and Juliet* bulletin board. Like a travel agent, display pictures that will entice the student travelers to explore the play and to find their own souvenirs.

WHAT TO DO

1. Whetting Interest with a Bulletin Board

Before the unit, layer the background of a bulletin board with overlapping magazine pictures to create a mood. Use cutouts such as a full moon, water, night sky, and cobblestone passages to establish the setting of Verona. (*National Geographic* and *Travel and Leisure* are good resources.)

On top of this setting, layer pictures of key characters and label the pictures with appropriate names. For impact, choose provocative character pictures—Montague as a CEO, Mercutio as a motorcycle-gang leader.

Staple a "Coming Attractions" banner on the upper corner of the board and then abandon the display to speculation and wonder.

2. Overview via Discussion

Use the display as a storyboard at the beginning of the *Romeo and Juliet* unit. Before the students actually start reading, give a brief synopsis of the story and its conflicts. Introduce and identify each character on the board. The pictures provide a quick, effective way to help students visualize the characters, and because of the magazine format, students seldom get locked into a single visual interpretation.

As the students study the play, let them refer to the board if they become confused about characters and relationships. Continue to develop the board throughout the unit with student drawings, quotations, favorite lines, special words, articles about *Romeo and Juliet*, and trivia questions. Some lively discussions will take place as students argue over why their Neiman Marcus Juliet is better than the one from the Gap ad.

HOW DID IT GO?

For immediate evaluation of this lesson, ask yourself:

- Did the bulletin board capture the students' attention?
- Did the discussion prepare students for the plot and characters of *Romeo and Juliet?*

For end-of-unit evaluation, ask:

- Was the bulletin board used as a resource throughout the unit?
- Did the pictures generate discussion and encourage the students to visualize the characters and settings?
- Did the students add to the bulletin board during the unit?

LESSON 2 "Traffic of Our Stage"

A Choral Reading of the Act 1 Prologue

WHAT'S ON FOR TODAY AND WHY

Students will find themselves immersed in a concert of sound, rhythm, and movement as they read the opening prologue aloud in a variety of ways. The goal for this lesson is simple—to get Shakespeare's language flowing from the students' mouths.

Before class, teachers will prepare copies of Handout 1: The Prologue to Act 1.

WHAT TO DO

1. Reading the Prologue

Have the class sit in a large circle. Distribute Handout 1: The Prologue to Act 1 (at the end of this lesson). Have the students read the prologue several times. Choose from among these variations:

Reading 1: Have the students read the prologue aloud in unison. After the reading, discuss and define together any words the students don't recognize.

Reading 2: Going around the circle, have the students read the prologue one word at a time—
  First student: "Two"
  Second student: "households"
  Third student: "both"
  And so on . . .
This reading will help the students recognize the importance of the individual words.

Reading 3: Have the students repeat Reading 2. This time ask them to try to read as if the words were all spoken by one voice, without lengthy pauses between readers and with some expression.

Reading 4: For this reading, each student takes a half-line, reading to the pause in the line (see Handout) or to the line end. Again, the group should attempt to create a single voice.
An ensemble effect may be added to this reading in several ways:

• Have the boys read the first half of each line and the girls read the second half.
• Double up voices on some of the lines.

Reading 5: Have the students take turns reading to the punctuation stops—semicolons and periods, not commas. Notice how this reading helps clarify the meaning of the passage and allows for more natural stress.

Reading 6: Have the students repeat Reading 5, this time vocally emphasizing the word before the stop.

Reading 7: (Whatever you do, don't skip this reading.) Have the students walk and read the prologue, stamping one foot and changing direction on the final word before each full stop.

The last two readings help demonstrate how rhythm propels speech.

2. Analyzing the Effects

Discuss the approaches to the reading and their differences. This dialogue may help to emphasize the power of a single word, the value of the meter, or the correct way to read iambic pentameter. Point out that the prologue is a sonnet.

Discuss the story that Shakespeare tells in the passage. Clarify any words or sections that are still unclear. Ask which words, ideas, and images seem important and why. The bulletin board may be helpful during this discussion. Use the pictures to clarify the plot and character relationships.

Highlight words and phrases such as *civil blood* and *star-crossed lovers* by adding them to the board.

3. Focusing on "Two"

Give attention to the word *two*. Ask the students to circle the word each time it occurs in the prologue. Have the students identify any ways in which the concept of "two" is reinforced: What twosomes do we have in this passage? (Students will find the obvious ones like "two households" and "two foes." Help them to find twosomes in repeated words like "civil," in echoing concepts like grudge and mutiny, and in sounds like "*d*oth with their *d*eath" or "*f*orth the *f*atal.") Discuss the effects of this repetition.

4. One More Reading

Ask for a volunteer to read the entire prologue or read it together as a class. This final reading will provide a sense of closure for the discussion and direct the students' attention to 1.1.

HOW DID IT GO?

Evaluation of this activity is based on your answers to the following questions:

• Did everyone participate in the various readings?
• As students read the prologue several times, did their fluency and comprehension increase?
• Did students show comprehension of basic plot and character elements?
• Did the students consider ideas and images?

HANDOUT 1

THE PROLOGUE TO ACT ONE

Two households,   both alike in dignity

(In fair Verona,   where we lay our scene),

From ancient grudge   break to new mutiny,

Where civil blood makes civil hands   unclean.

From forth the fatal loins   of these two foes

A pair of star-crossed lovers   take their life;

Whose misadventured   piteous overthrows

Doth with their death   bury their parents' strife.

The fearful passage   of their death-marked love

And the continuance   of their parents' rage,

Which, but their children's end,   naught could remove,

Is now the two hours' traffic   of our stage;

The which, if you   with patient ears attend,

What here shall miss,   our toil shall strive to mend.

LESSON 3 "I Strike Quickly"

Barbs from the Bard

WHAT'S ON FOR TODAY AND WHY

Students will have an opportunity to see the power and variety of Shakespeare's language when they create, deliver, and receive their own Shakespearean insults in an energetic activity designed by Folger teacher Jerry Maguire from Center Grove High School in Greenwood, Indiana.

To prepare for this activity, make copies of Handout 2: Shakespearean Insult Sheet, found at the end of this lesson.

WHAT TO DO

1. Feuding Families, Gangs, and Clans

Ask students: What is a feud? Who were the Hatfields and the McCoys? Are there any feuds going on with people you know? Do you know any other stories that might be based on feuds? What do these feuds seem to have in common? What does it usually take to resolve a feud?

What's the difference between an argument and a feud?

A component of any feud—and sometimes a part of our own teasing and arguing—is the insult. What kinds of insults might be exchanged during a feud?

2. Hurling Insults

Tell the students that Shakespeare designed insults that really sizzled. Then let the students create and hurl Shakespearean insults of their own:

- Pass out Handout 2: Shakespearean Insult Sheet
- Have each student create and memorize an insult by combining one word from each column.
- Have students use the *Oxford English Dictionary* or C. T. Onions's *A Shakespeare Glossary* (Oxford University Press, 1986) to define each part of the insult.
- Divide the students into pairs or triads and have them practice delivering their insults to each other. Get them on their feet for this event.

3. Montagues vs. Capulets

Regroup the students into two families, the Montagues and the Capulets, for a verbal duel.

- Let the students warm up by having the Montagues boo the Capulets and the Capulets hiss the Montagues.
- Then have the opposing families take turns hurling insults from across the room. Let the activity continue for a few minutes, giving everyone a chance to participate.

This activity is a high-spirited one, and for best results let the students express themselves loudly and enthusiastically.

Discuss the verbal duel. Which age has the most deliciously vile words for insults—Shakespeare's or ours? Explain your answer. Which insult was the best? Who was the most effective insult-hurler? There is the potential for both fun and danger in an insult. How can play quickly lead to injury?

Explain that feuding is a focal point of *Romeo and Juliet* and encourage the students to listen to the way Shakespeare develops the feud through verbal dueling.

4. Barbs from the Bard Variation

Give each student one word from the insult sheet to look up for homework the night before the lesson. Don't tell the students why they are defining these words and don't let them see the sheet in advance. Just give them *waggish* or *motley* or *rampallion*. The students will be interested in these funny words and eager to see what their next lesson is all about.

HOW DID IT GO?

Evaluation of this activity is based on your answers to the following questions:

• Did the students participate in a classroom discussion of language and feuding?
• Did student discussion help set the stage for 1.1?
• Did the students participate in the verbal duel with enthusiasm?

If you chose to have students look up definitions of the insult words, collect each student's insult and check to see if its definition is complete and accurate. Here is a grading suggestion:

• A definition that is complete and accurate	5 points
• A definition that is either complete or accurate	3 points
• A definition that is not attempted	0 points

HANDOUT 2

SHAKESPEAREAN INSULT SHEET

Directions: Combineth one word or phrase from each of the columns below and addeth "Thou" to the beginning. Make certain thou knowest the meaning of thy strong words, and thou shalt have the perfect insult to fling at the wretched fools of the opposing team. Let thyself go. Mix and match to find that perfect barb from the bard!

	Column A	Column B	Column C
1.	bawdy	bunch-backed	canker-blossom
2.	brazen	clay-brained	clotpole
3.	churlish	dog-hearted	crutch
4.	distempered	empty-hearted	cutpurse
5.	fitful	evil-eyed	dogfish
6.	gnarling	eye-offending	egg-shell
7.	greasy	fat-kidneyed	gull-catcher
8.	grizzled	heavy-headed	hedge-pig
9.	haughty	horn-mad	hempseed
10.	hideous	ill-breeding	jack-a-nape
11.	jaded	ill-composed	malkin
12.	knavish	ill-nurtured	malignancy
13.	lewd	iron-witted	malt-worm
14.	peevish	lean-witted	manikin
15.	pernicious	lily-livered	minimus
16.	prating	mad-bread	miscreant
17.	purpled	motley-minded	moldwarp
18.	queasy	muddy-mettled	nut-hook
19.	rank	onion-eyed	pantaloon
20.	reeky	pale-hearted	rabbit-sucker
21.	roynish	paper-faced	rampallion
22.	saucy	pinch-spotted	remnant
23.	sottish	raw-boned	rudesby
24.	unmuzzled	rug-headed	ruffian
25.	vacant	rump-fed	scantling
26.	waggish	shag-eared	scullion
27.	wanton	shrill-gorged	snipe
28.	wenching	sour-faced	waterfly
29.	whoreson	weak-hinged	whipster
30.	yeasty	white-livered	younker

INSULT HURLER: _____

INSULT:

Thou _____   _____   _____

DEFINITION:

You _____   _____   _____

LESSON 4 "Civil Brawls"

Acting 1.1

&

PLAY SECTIONS COVERED IN THIS LESSON

1.1.1–58 Sampson and Gregory, from the house of Capulet, encounter Abram and Servingman, from the Montagues.

LINES: Sampson, 32; Gregory, 22; Abram, 4; Servingman, 0

1.1.59–82 They fight. Tybalt, Benvolio, Lord and Lady Capulet, and Lord and Lady Montague join the fray.

LINES: Gregory, 2; Sampson, 3; Abram, 1; Benvolio, 4; Tybalt, 5; Citizens, 2; Capulet, 3; Lady Capulet, 2; Montague, 1; Lady Montague, 1

1.1.83–105 Prince Escalus breaks up the fight.

LINES: Prince, 23

&

WHAT'S ON FOR TODAY AND WHY

In this lesson, students will become actors and directors while reading, discussing, and dramatizing 1.1. With newspaper swords and scripts in hand, they will gain an active and dramatic approach to the text and its conflicts.

In addition, students will practice strategies that will help them learn to work through seemingly difficult language by:

- hearing the words as well as seeing them on the page
- using the words they know to understand words they don't
- holding problem words in suspension until they get the main idea of the passage
- feeling free to make guesses as to denotation
- learning to use resources like glossaries or dictionaries
- learning to rely on themselves to solve language problems
- focusing on how puns operate

Before this lesson, read "Three-Dimensional Shakespeare" by Michael Tolaydo (page 27), as our scene work today is based on his methods. Because this is our first venture into acting and because we will be setting up procedures that we'll use over and over again, we will not rush. Allow two days for this lesson.

WHAT TO DO

1. Puns (Day 1)

Think no further back than the morning show on the car radio to note examples of puns: "What do you do when your wheels wear out? *Retire*." "What did the boss say when he sold the carnival? It was a *fair* deal." From the cleverest repartee to the worst groaner, people use and respond to puns, but sometimes find them hard to define.

For the purpose of this lesson, say that a pun is a form of wordplay that occurs when two words pronounced and spelled somewhat the same contain different meanings. In this way the word *fair* above plays on two meanings, *fair* meaning carnival and *fair* meaning equitable, both contained in the same sound, "fair." It would not suit this unit to make students write and memorize the definition of pun, but it would help the comprehension of 1.1 if students were able to *make* and *recognize* puns. So begin by preparing students for the opening puns.

Write the *re-tire* pun on the board and ask a student to read it aloud. Ask students what sort of wordplay is at work in this bad joke. Come to a working definition and/or understanding of puns. Ask students to volunteer other examples. Discuss how puns work and why people enjoy them.

Write the following words and definitions on the board and explain that they will be used in puns in 1.1 of *Romeo and Juliet:*

carry coals: submit to humiliation
colliers: people who work with coal
in choler: angry
collar: hangman's noose

2. Punning in Verona (Day 1)

Pass out a script for 1.1.1–105, copied and confined, if possible, to one sheet of paper. Have the students put their chairs in a circle.

Divide the class in half and read the scene chorally, alternating between sides. Stop at line 82.

Side 1: Gregory, on my word we'll not carry coals.
Side 2: No, for then we should be colliers.
Side 1: I mean, an we be in choler, we'll draw.
And so on . . .

At the end of this reading, ask the students what their comprehension level is. (Tell them to use a scale of 1 to 10. Most of them will be low.)

Tell the students that it's their challenge to make sense of the words and sense of the entire scene. Going around the room, read the scene again, this time asking the students to read to full stops (periods, question marks, exclamation points, semicolons). Stop at line 82. After reading, ask the students to point out words they don't know. See if other students can explain the words. Let the students use footnotes or dictionaries if necessary.

Ask the students to work out the series of puns.

Going around the room, read the scene a third time, stopping at line

82. This time ask each student to read a complete sentence and then to paraphrase it into contemporary, easy-to-understand English. Don't rush, especially during the first 33 lines. The content is tricky.

After the third reading, ask questions such as: What's going on here? Who are these people? Are they related? What are they like? How do they feel about each other? What are the clues? (Be gentle with incorrect answers.)

Now ask students what their comprehension level is. (They should feel much more comfortable with the scene by this point.)

3. Acting 1.1.1–58 (Day 1)

Using Michael Tolaydo's casting techniques, assign parts. Have the rest of the class direct the characters through the scene. Start by asking them:

- Where exactly does this scene take place?
- Where and how should Gregory and Sampson make their entrance?
- Where have they been? Where are they going?
- What should they do while they discuss the feud and their attitudes?

Work through the scene a line or two at a time, always looking to the text for answers.

Continue:

- Where and how should Abram and Servingman make their entrance?
- How do Gregory and Sampson react when they see Abram and Servingman?
- How do the two sets of men react to each other during their verbal duel?

Stop at line 58. (This will be as far as you get in one period.)

4. Homework (Day 1)

Ask the students who were assigned roles during class to practice reading their parts.

Ask everyone to write a journal entry describing first impressions of *Romeo and Juliet* and first impressions of the language.

5. Acting 1.1.59–105 (Day 2)

Have the students sit in a circle and work with Prince Escalus's speech, 1.1.83–105.

Reading 1: Have the students read the speech aloud in unison.

Reading 2: Going around the circle, have the students read the speech a line at a time. After this reading, discuss and define together any words the students don't recognize.

Reading 3: Going around the circle, read the speech a third time. This time ask each student to read a complete sentence and then to paraphrase it into contemporary, easy-to-understand English.

Summarize the readings by asking the students to identify the key ideas of the speech.

Review the blocking for 1.1.1–58. Have the students who were assigned parts yesterday assume their roles. Ask the class to direct the characters through the rest of the scene. Ask them:

- Where and how should Benvolio make his entrance?
- How intense should the fight be?

Have the students choreograph a *brief* fight. Keep the steps simple, and tell the students to use the same routine each time they perform these lines. Use rolled-up newspapers or dowel rods as swords.

Continue:

- How should Benvolio break up the fight?
- What are the citizens doing before they join the fight?
- Do the Montagues and Capulets enter from the same place? And so on through line 105.

Once the blocking is complete, have the actors perform (with scripts in hand) 1.1.1–105. Have the rest of the class divide into two groups to support the two sides by hurling insults and booing and hissing when appropriate.

6. Analysis and Followup (Day 2)

Have the class return to their seats and discuss the effects of opening a play with a fight scene. (Students might recall movies like *Indiana Jones* that start with fights or raucous action.)

Have the students open their books to finish 1.1. Assign parts to new readers. Read the rest of the scene aloud. Encourage students to ask questions during the reading, but see if the other students can answer them.

7. Homework (Day 2)

Have students re-read 1.1.106–247 and write a brief outline of the events covered in these lines.

HOW DID IT GO?

No matter how weak or brilliant the performances, they were successful if the students actively participated in reading Shakespeare, in solving word problems, in envisioning the scene, and in making directing choices based on the lines Shakespeare wrote.

LESSON 5 "O Brawling Love"

Viewpoints on Love and Marriage

☙ _____

PLAY SECTIONS COVERED IN THIS LESSON

1.2 Capulet tells the County Paris that he can marry Juliet, but he must win her heart first, starting at a feast the Capulets are holding that night. Benvolio and Romeo intercept an invitation to the feast and decide to crash the party.

LINES: Capulet, 33; Paris, 4; Servingman, 20; Benvolio, 20; Romeo, 27

1.3 Lady Capulet tells Juliet and her nurse that Paris seeks Juliet for a wife.

LINES: Lady Capulet, 37; Nurse, 64; Juliet, 7; Servingman, 5

☙ _____

WHAT'S ON FOR TODAY AND WHY

Love is an experience filled with sighs, smiles, anger, regret, hope, passion, and fun, and it is sure to bring some interesting responses from your students. Ask them to explore their own thoughts on this topic and those of the characters in 1.2 and 1.3 through journal writing, group work, and class discussion. This lesson will allow the students to study characterization, to consider a key theme of the play and its application to their lives, and to develop independence in working with the text.

WHAT TO DO

1. Homework Review

Have the students trade the outlines of 1.1.106–247 they did for homework. Ask them to check each other's work. Let the students discuss what the key points on the outline should be, and ask the students to fill in any missing information on their partners' papers. Collect the papers.

Sample Outline:

1. Benvolio explains to Lord Montague how the fight got started.
2. Lady Montague asks where Romeo is, and Benvolio and Montague talk about Romeo's depression.
3. Benvolio talks to Romeo and discovers that Romeo loves Rosaline but Rosaline doesn't love him.
4. Benvolio encourages Romeo to cure his love for Rosaline by checking out other women.

2. Love and Marriage

Ask students: What are your thoughts and feelings about love and marriage? Let them write their answers in a journal or offer answers aloud.

Have students look for ideas about love and marriage in 1.2 and 1.3:

· Pass out Handout 3: The Love Connection.
· Divide students into groups of two.
· Tell the students to look up the lines that reveal each character's experience with, feelings about, or attitudes toward love and marriage. The students should write the lines down on the handout.
· Ask the students to write down what they feel each line reveals about its speaker's experiences, feelings, or attitudes.

(Note: The handout has one character, Paris, completed as an example. Have the students save Mercutio for homework.)

3. Reading 1.2 and 1.3

Have the students return to their seats to read 1.2 and 1.3. Assign parts and have the students read the scenes aloud, stopping to discuss any questions they have about the plot.

4. A Second Look at Love and Marriage

As a class, discuss the results of the group work on love and marriage. In the center of the board or on a transparency, place a copy of the empty chart. Ask the students to add to the class chart the lines and the students' discoveries for each character. Discuss the chart, making sure you elicit many views of love. Then ask:

· What is the effect of having such a variety of experiences, feelings, and attitudes about love and marriage in one play?
· What are some insights that you gained that made a strong impression on you?
· What are some complications that might arise because of these different viewpoints?
· In addition to the feud, what are some other problems that the young lovers will encounter?

Conclude the discussion by asking the students to answer one last question. (The students may write their responses in their journals and/or discuss them with the class.)

· Regarding the topic of love and marriage, with which character do you most identify and why?

5. Homework

Read 1.4 and add Mercutio to the chart.

HOW DID IT GO?

Ask yourself:

· How autonomous were the groups? Did they find the lines and comprehend them with relative ease?

• How accurate and insightful were student contributions during class discussion?

To evaluate the outlines, check for completeness and accuracy. Be flexible. Grading suggestion:

• A plot outline that is complete and accurate	5 points
• A plot outline that is either complete or accurate	3 points
• A plot outline that is not attempted	0 points

To evaluate the chart, just before discussion, collect *one* chart from each group. Evaluate it for completeness, accuracy, and aptness of conclusions. Assign the same grade to each member of the group.

HANDOUT 3

THE LOVE CONNECTION

Directions: Read the lines listed for each of the following characters. In the first column, write the lines as they appear in the play. Then draw some conclusions about each line or set of lines. What insights do they give into each character's experiences with, feelings toward, or attitudes about love and marriage? Jot down these insights in the third column.

CHARACTER	LINES	CONCLUSIONS
Romeo 1.1.195–199		
Benvolio 1.1.235–236 1.2.47–48		
Paris 1.2.12	"Younger than she are happy mothers made."	Paris is eager to marry. Age is not an issue.
Capulet 1.2.13 1.2.16–17		
Juliet 1.3.71 1.3.103–105		
Lady Capulet 1.3.75–79		
Nurse 1.3.101		
Mercutio 1.4.27		

6 "I Dreamt a Dream Tonight"

Mercutio's Queen Mab

ह▲ _____

PLAY SECTION COVERED IN THIS LESSON

1.4 On the way to the Capulets' feast, Romeo and his friends discuss dreams and hear Mercutio's treatise on this subject.

LINES: Romeo, 34; Benvolio, 13; Mercutio, 74

ह▲ _____

WHAT'S ON FOR TODAY AND WHY

We all dream. Dreams escape the subconscious at night to delight or torment our sleep. Dreams are important to *Romeo and Juliet*. Today, students will study Romeo's mention of dreams and Mercutio's speech on the fairy of dreams, Queen Mab, through journal writing, film, close study, and class discussion.

On several occasions throughout the unit, students will view scenes from Franco Zeffirelli's *Romeo and Juliet*, which is widely available. Before class, cue the film to 1.4, which begins with "What, shall this speech be spoke for our excuse?" and ends with "Strike, drum."

Make copies of the handouts at the end of this lesson. Also, locate a selection of Renaissance music to send home with the dancing masters, for example, *Dance of the Renaissance*, produced by Richard Searles and Gilbert Ysals for Sundown Records, 1985. Dance music by the Folger Consort—"Showers of Harmonie" on CD and "Dowland's Dances" on cassette—can be ordered by calling 1-202-675-0308. To prepare for the next lesson, save time at the end of class to talk about dancing masters.

WHAT TO DO

1. Homework Review

Check to see how well the students did with last night's homework. Since 1.4 is a tricky scene, ask the students what questions and reactions they have to the reading assignment. As much as possible, let the students resolve each other's questions without teacher intervention.

Ask the students what they discovered about Mercutio's thoughts and feelings on love when they added him to yesterday's chart.

2. Thinking About Dreams

Give students five minutes to write in their journals on this topic: Describe a dream of yours, either one that you've had while sleeping or a dream that you have for your life.

If time permits, ask some of the students to read their responses. If you like, tell the students about one of your dreams, too.

Ask the students: What are the advantages and disadvantages of dreams? (For example, they might say that dreams provide direction. They haunt. They inspire. They relieve the subconscious. They clarify our fears and desires. They may be unrealistic.)

3. Focusing on Mercutio's Explanation of Dreams

Remind the students that Queen Mab is a fairy who influences dreams. Also, ask the students to notice the moods of Romeo and Mercutio at the beginning of the scene.

Have each student complete with a partner Handout 4: I Dreamt a Dream Tonight. Discuss the students' answers to the questions and exhibit some or all of the drawings. Add some or all of the drawings to the bulletin board.

Show the excerpt of the Zeffirelli movie version of *Romeo and Juliet*. Draw the dream discussion to a close with a few final questions.

- This scene does not really further the plot. Why is it important to the play? (Students might say that it introduces Mercutio and shows his personality. It reveals Romeo's belief in dreams and in fate. It foreshadows tragedy.)
- What do we learn about Mercutio? About Romeo?
- What are the advantages and disadvantages of Romeo's dreaming?
- We know that Romeo's dream of Rosaline and his dream that evening make him unhappy. What do you suspect his next dream will be?

4. Homework

Assign 1.5 for reading.

5. Dancing Masters

Looking ahead to the next lesson, ask for student volunteers who have experience with dance, or enjoy dancing, to take home and study Handout 6: Pilgrims and Saints Dance. Also give them a tape or CD of Renaissance dance music. Let them have the handout and a few minutes to organize themselves. Tell them that they will be the dancing masters for *Romeo and Juliet*, that they will teach the class the Pilgrims and Saints Dance tomorrow. (Although the instructions look complicated to non-dancers, students who have had experience with dance will find the Pilgrims and Saints Dance easy to teach.)

HOW DID IT GO?

If students could verbalize the personality differences between Mercutio and Romeo, if they got a picture of Queen Mab in their heads, if they could follow Mercutio's thoughts as they worked through Handout 4, this lesson met its objective in helping students understand the importance of dreams in *Romeo and Juliet*.

To evaluate some of the ongoing methods, ask yourself:

- To what extent are students struggling with language problems and solving them on their own rather than turning to the teacher for answers?
- How accurate and insightful were student contributions during class discussion?
- How engaging was the film excerpt?

HANDOUT 4

"I DREAMT A DREAM TONIGHT"

ROMEO AND JULIET 1.4

1. We know that Romeo has at least two dreams, a dream of Rosaline and the dream he mentions in 1.4.

   a. What do we know about each dream?

   The dream of Rosaline:

   Romeo's dream that night:

   b. What do these dreams reveal about Romeo?

2. Mercutio has some interesting ideas about dreams, too.

   a. On a clean sheet of paper, sketch a simple picture of Queen Mab and her carriage according to Mercutio's description. The drawing does not need to be artistic, but it does need to be neat and clear.
   Label each part of your drawing with its corresponding line from the speech.

   b. According to Mercutio, what are the dreams that Queen Mab delivers for each of the following people?

   Lovers dream of:

   Courtiers (first mention) dream of:

   Lawyers dream of:

   Ladies dream of:

   Courtiers (second mention) dream of:

   A parson dreams of:

   A soldier dreams of:

   c. Is Queen Mab the queen of good dreams, nightmares, or both? Explain.

   d. Reread Mercutio's exchange with Romeo at the end of the scene. What does Mercutio think of dreams?

   e. Why do you suppose Mercutio told such a fantastic story to Romeo?

   f. What kind of person is Mercutio?

ॐ

HANDOUT 5

PILGRIMS AND SAINTS DANCE

First, form a circle. Use as many students as you like. Keep the number of dancers even, but you don't need equal numbers of boys and girls—if you were performing in Shakespeare's day, everyone dancing in this scene would be a guy anyway. If there is an odd number of students, make your teacher dance.

Give each step eight counts before moving on to the next. Repeat steps as needed to adapt to the music you select. (If need be, you can perform the dance steps without music.)

Stand in a circle with your partner by your side.

Honor your partner.
For eight counts, gentlemen bow to the ladies to their right, and ladies curtsy to the gentlemen to their left.

Honor your corner.
For eight counts, gentlemen bow to the ladies to their left, and ladies curtsy to the gentlemen to their right.

Doubles.
All the dancers in the circle take hands and, starting with the right foot, walk forward three steps and bring the left foot forward to meet the right foot on the fourth count. Then, starting with the left foot, they walk backward three steps and bring the right foot backward to meet the left foot on the eighth count.

Repeat.

Circle clockwise.
Still holding hands, the dancers circle clockwise for eight counts.

If the music is slow, the dancers can walk around the circle with a weaving step. Have each dancer take a step to the left with the left foot, step behind the left foot with the right foot, take a step to the left with the left foot, step in front of the left foot with the right foot, and so on for eight counts. Bring the right foot together with the left foot on the eighth count.

If the music is fast, the dancers can dance around the circle with a slipping step. Each dancer takes a step to the left with the left foot, brings the right foot toward the left foot with a hop, places the right foot where the left foot was, moves the left foot a step to the left, and so on for eight counts.

Circle counterclockwise.
Repeat the directions for circle clockwise (above) in the opposite direction for eight counts.

Right palms.
Partners face each other, raise their right hands, and place the hands together, palm to palm. Each pair of dancers walks around in its own circle for eight counts.

Left palms.
Partners face each other, raise their left hands, and place the hands together, palm to palm. Each pair of dancers walks around in its own circle for seven counts and returns to the large circle on the eighth count.

Gentlemen's double.
As in doubling above, men walk forward four counts into the circle then double back to their ladies for four more counts. They clap on the fourth count and on the eighth count.

Ladies' double.
Same as above, only ladies this time.

Alternating single.
Starting with the right foot, the men take one step into the circle and bring the left foot forward to meet the right foot on the second count. They clap on the second count.

While the men single back and clap on the fourth count, the women single forward and clap on the fourth count, too.

While the men single forward and clap on the sixth count, the women single back and clap on the sixth count.

The men single back and clap on the eighth count while the women hold their places and clap on the eighth count.

Honor your partner.

Honor your corner.

LESSON 7   "Give Room! And Foot It, Girls"

Elizabethan Dance

WHAT'S ON FOR TODAY AND WHY

Aiming for a fully choreographed performance of the ball scene, in this lesson students will practice an Elizabethan dance and receive instructions and motivation for making a mask. Have music and machine ready, and clear the floor for dancing. Also, prepare copies of Handout 6: "And Then We Masked."

WHAT TO DO

1. Dancing

Turn the class over to the dancing masters. Let them teach the students the basic steps to an Elizabethan circle dance. Practice the dance and put it to music. Tell the students that the dance will become a part of their performance of 1.5.

2. Making Masks

Give students Handout 6: "And Then We Masked." Take them through the instructions step by step, giving artistic suggestions and encouragement. If you prefer, have art supplies in the room and let students begin this project in class.

3. Homework

Ask each student to create a mask for tomorrow's lesson.

Ask everyone to reread 1.5. Assign the roles in 1.5 to some of the students, and ask them to be prepared to read their parts aloud in class tomorrow. Ask those who do not have an assigned role to make notes about where the actors should move in this scene. Remind them that the entire class will participate, some with speaking parts, some dancing and milling at the feast.

HOW DID IT GO?

Do not fret if the dancing was not up to professional standards. If students learned to do an authentic dance and practiced it enough to remember it in the upcoming performance, this lesson's objective was met. At this point, the first concern is to inspire and instruct students to learn the dance and make a mask so that everyone can participate in the ball scene in Lesson 8.

ર્જી

HANDOUT 6

"AND THEN WE MASKED"

No, it's not Halloween. You've just been invited to Capulet's feast tomorrow. A mask is part of the dress code, so you will need to make one tonight. Does it have to be artistic? No. Does it have to be complicated? No. Does it have to be pretty? Only if you want it to be. Have fun with this activity.

By the way—there are prizes at stake here. At the beginning of class tomorrow, we will decide on the following awards:

- most original design
- most colorful
- most unique materials
- most carefully done
- wildest
- funniest
- design that best reflects the personality of a character from *Romeo and Juliet*

What other kinds of awards to you think we should offer?

Materials: Use any materials you already have on hand at home, and feel free to take some construction paper with you from the class supply.
Suggestions:

cardboard	crayons	macaroni
felt	markers	magazine pictures
fabric scraps	sequins	ribbon
construction paper	glitter	paint
aluminum foil	stickers	fly tying supplies
tissue paper	feathers	hardware supplies

Directions for mask-making:

1. Select an outline for your mask or design an outline of your own.

   Basic outlines:

Design suggestions: animals, insects, flowers, geometric shapes, rock stars, moon, stars, planets, picture collages, etc., etc.

2. Draw your mask on cardboard and cover the front with felt, construction paper, or another material of your choice. If you don't have any cardboard, cut several copies of your mask out of construction paper and glue the layers together for added strength.

3. Decorate your mask.

4. Punch holes in the sides and attach strings.

LESSON 8 "And Then We Masked"

A Performance of 1.5

ঽ৯ _____

PLAY SECTION COVERED IN THIS LESSON

1.5 The ball scene. Romeo and Juliet meet.

LINES: First Servingman, 10; Second Servingman, 3; Third Servingman, 4; Capulet, 59; Capulet's Cousin, 3; Romeo, 27; Servingman, 1; Tybalt, 18; Juliet, 19; Nurse, 14; Benvolio, 1

ঽ৯ _____

WHAT'S ON FOR TODAY AND WHY

Sparkling music, spinning dancers, candlelight, young lovers meeting for the first time, an angry young man lurking in the shadows—*As the World Turns* has nothing on *Romeo and Juliet*. In this lesson, students will enter into the magic and tension of this wonderful scene by becoming guests at Capulet's party. As the students explore this scene through dance, performance, journal writing, and art work, they will have the opportunity to study the text as a script, to work together as a team, and to walk through the steps of the key characters in the scene.

Because there is much to do in this lesson, it will take two days.

WHAT TO DO

1. Revealing Masks (Day 1)

Have the students display their masks around the room before the start of class.

2. Planning a Performance of 1.5 (Day 1)

Following the basic procedure described by Michael Tolaydo on page 27 and used earlier for enacting 1.1, have the students read through and block 1.5.

- Provide the students with copies of the scene or let them use their books.
- Ask a student to take notes about the blocking decisions.
- Discuss any sections of the scene that are unclear.
- Use classroom furniture to suggest a set.
- Plan movements for every speech, and in between if necessary.
- Plan to use every class member (in masks, of course) in the dance scene.
- Plan how to incorporate music and dancing.

3. Dancing (Day 1)

Call up the dancing masters and go through the Elizabethan circle dance once for review.

4. Planning the Performance (Day 1)

Have the students who prepared readings last night assume their assigned roles.

Review the blocking: have the students who took notes on blocking decisions help walk the class through the scene.

5. Performance (Day 2)

Have the students perform the scene, incorporating text, blocking, dance, music, and masks. Optional: film the performance and play it for the students.

6. Reacting to the Performance (Day 2)

Have each student assume the persona of Romeo, Juliet, or Tybalt and write a journal or diary entry about her reactions to the evening.

Have some of the students read their entries aloud. Discuss the entries and the significance of the scene.

If students have studied sonnets, ask them to look carefully at 1.5 to find an embedded sonnet. Give them clues: a Shakespearean sonnet has 14 lines ... rhymes *ababcdcdefefgg* ... uses iambic pentameter (1.5.104–117). What is the effect of turning this exchange into a sonnet? What stage movement does the sonnet suggest?

7. Prizes (Day 2)

Award prizes for the masks, and add the masks to the *Romeo and Juliet* bulletin board.

HOW DID IT GO?

No matter how weak or brilliant the performances, if the students actively participated in the scene, they acquired, interpreted, and communicated Shakespeare's language. A grading suggestion is to give students who did all three activities (mask, dance, and scene) an A, to give students who did two of the activities a B or C depending on level of engagement, and students who did only one activity a D. If all went well, most students got As; if not, stop and work on getting all students involved.

LESSON **9** ## "Passion Lends Them Power"

Act 2 Prologue

ਏੈ _____

PLAY SECTION COVERED IN THIS LESSON

2.1.1–14 Act 2 prologue foretells how, despite their warring families, Romeo and Juliet fall in love.

LINES: Chorus, 14

ਏੈ _____

WHAT'S ON FOR TODAY AND WHY

It's time for an encore of choral reading. Working in groups, the students will prepare and present the Act 2 prologue to the class by dividing up the lines and reciting them or by setting the lines to a rhythm and reciting them. This lesson will help the students to improve fluency in oral reading, to develop interpretive reading skills, to gain some performance experience, and to study the content of the prologue.

Fresh from a successful performance in Lesson 8 and enlightened by choral reading of the prologue for Act 1, students should show improved confidence and ability in confronting language problems. Too, they should show broadening comprehension of plot and characters.

Teachers can choose from two options, or they can present both options and let the students choose which to do.

This lesson will take two days.

WHAT TO DO

1. Option 1: Ensemble Performance (Day 1)

Place the students in groups of seven. Tell the students that they should assign the lines of the prologue to the members of their group. The lines may be assigned in any manner; however, each student should have some part of the prologue to read aloud.

After the lines have been assigned, have the students decide how they will say their lines. For example, one voice could echo another voice on an appropriate word. Several voices could speak an important word, phrase, or line together.

Have the students decide on any movements or gestures that might enhance their presentation. For example, two members of the group might assume the identities of Romeo and Juliet, and these students might react to each other in pantomime based on the content of the lines.

2. Option 2: Rhythm Performance (Day 1)

Let the students get into groups of their own choosing.

Tell the groups that they should memorize the prologue by setting it to a rhythm—drill-team march, rap, chant, lullaby, rock. For example, if a group chooses the drill-team approach, the members might select a "sergeant" and follow that student's lead, repeating entire lines or parts of lines after the student. If a group chooses to rap, the members might repeat words and phrases, and they might select some lines to use as a refrain.

3. Rehearsal (Day 1)

Give the students the remainder of the class to rehearse their lines. Tell them that their performance will be graded on reading, interpretation, and group effort (or pass out sample evaluation forms).

Visit each group to encourage their efforts and act as a resource. Have the students decide how they will add movement and/or music to their presentation. For example, if a group sets the prologue to a drill-team march, the students might march in formation during their presentation. If a group uses the rock approach, the members might use some rhythm instruments.

4. Homework (Day 1)

Tell students to study their prologue lines. (Option 2 groups should memorize them. For Option 1 groups, memorization is not essential, but a thorough reading is.)

Also tell them to locate props or instruments they might use in their presentations.

5. Rehearsals (Day 2)

Let the groups practice their presentations once or twice.

6. Performance (Day 2)

Have the groups perform their prologues for each other.

7. Discussion (Day 2)

Ask for comments on interpretation.

Check for comprehension of the content: Are there lines whose meanings are still unclear?

Identify and discuss the contrasts that exist within the prologue. Suggestions:

old desire	young affection
deathbed	heir
Rosaline	Juliet
foe	lover
limited access for Romeo	even more limited for Juliet
extremities	extreme sweet

What do the contrasts add to the prologue? (Students might say that they add an awareness that Romeo's relationship with Juliet is stronger and more powerful than his love was for Rosaline, that they add a reminder of the complications provided by the feud, that they add a sense of Juliet's powerlessness.)

Discuss the possible purposes of this prologue. (Students might say that it reviews the story so far, that it prepares the reader for the upcoming romance.)

8. Homework (Day 2)

Have the students read 2.1.

HOW DID IT GO?

To evaluate the activities ask yourself:

- Did everyone participate in a group reading?
- Did the groups function effectively? (Were they able to approach the assignment with confidence? Did they make meaningful choices that enhanced the study of the prologue?)
- Did the students show increasing fluency and plot comprehension in the readings?

To evaluate the group performances, complete a grading guide like this one for each group while its members are working and performing. After the performance, give the completed grading guide to the group.

Act 2 Prologue Performance Evaluation

Group members:

_____ *Clarity of Reading*
Could the class hear and understand the words and the content of the prologue? (10 points)

_____ *Interpretation*
Did your presentation help to make the content of the prologue more meaningful for the class?
(10 points)

_____ *Group Effort*
Did your group make the most of its work sessions? Was your group organized and efficient during your presentation? (10 points)

_____ TOTAL

LESSON 10 "And I Must Conjure Him"

Praiseworthy Promptbooks

ࠔ
_____

PLAY SECTIONS COVERED IN THIS LESSON

2.1 Romeo leaves the Capulet feast. Benvolio and Mercutio search for him.

LINES: Romeo, 2; Benvolio, 9; Mercutio, 5

2.2 The balcony scene. Romeo and Juliet confess their love.

LINES: Romeo, 88; Juliet, 115; Nurse, 2

ࠔ
_____

WHAT'S ON FOR TODAY AND WHY

Promptbooks are copies of scripts that contain notes about performance—blocking, delivery of lines, setting, costumes, and so on. They are used by directors, actors, stage managers, and others involved in a production. In this lesson, students will create promptbook pages for 2.1 with the class, then do their individual promptbooks for 2.2, the balcony scene. In making promptbooks, students will envision the setting of the play, make choices about how lines might be delivered, suit movement to the words, and experiment with different but equally valid ways to stage a scene. All of these activities spring from the unit goal of getting students inside the play to interact with the language.

Prepare a transparency and copies of the stage directions. Prepare Handout 7 by copying 2.1, then pasting each page on a larger sheet of plain paper so that there is a large margin for notes. See the sample at the end of this lesson. Also prepare transparencies of the promptbook pages for 2.1.

This lesson will take two days.

WHAT TO DO

1. Introduction to the Promptbook (Day 1)

Show students examples of promptbooks. Local theaters might lend you promptbooks from a recent production. Facsimiles of Shakespearean promptbooks are sometimes available from university libraries, and they are wonderful visual aids and resources. A page from an 1868 *Romeo and Juliet* promptbook follows this lesson.

Talk about what a promptbook is, why it is needed. Notice how and where actors (or directors) put notes.

If possible, put some copies of promptbook pages on the bulletin board. (If you keep some of the promptbooks your students do, you will have good examples for next year.)

2. The Promptbook: Stage Directions (Day 1)

To prepare the students to work with a promptbook, draw an empty stage on the blackboard or on an overhead transparency. Give students a copy of this drawing, too. Explain basic stage directions.

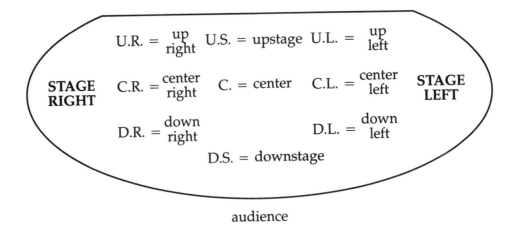

audience

3. The Promptbook: Set Design (Day 1)

Talk about the setting for 2.1. What would the set look like? Ask the students to direct you (or a student) in drawing the set on the blackboard or on an overhead transparency.

Some questions to prompt the design might include:

· What does the text indicate the scene needs—e.g., wall, trees, balcony for 2.2?
· Where should we place the wall? the trees? the balcony? Why? (The students will need to consider how their decisions may or may not facilitate the action.)
· What other props might be useful?

Ask each student to draw the set as it is drawn on the board.

4. The Promptbook: Notes in the Script (Day 1)

Give each student Handout 7: Promptbook Pages for 2.1. Place transparency copies of the promptbook pages on an overhead projector. Work on the overhead while students work on their handouts.

Using the large margins, make notes an actor would use. Mark entrances, exits, movements. Use the stage directions diagram to help. Example: Romeo enters u.l., moves u.r. Benvolio and Mercutio enter u.r., move center.

Keep a steady stream of questions about movement before the students: Where does Benvolio move? On what line? Why does he go there? What does the text say? Also, keep helping the students to become familiar with stage directions: Down is *toward* the audience.

After students have envisioned where each actor moves during the scene and have marked their scripts accordingly, ask them to find lines that need special delivery. Should Benvolio boom out his first line?

Should Mercutio whisper "I conjure thee by Rosaline's bright eyes . . . "? Make notes about delivery throughout the scene.

Complete the promptbook notes on 2.1.

Caution: This scene is not for the faint of heart. Mercutio's language is pretty racy, especially after line 20, so you will want to be prepared.

Option: If you don't have time to do promptbook pages for all of 2.1, just do the first 19 lines. There is plenty of material in those lines to give the students a clear understanding of how they should complete the pages of their promptbooks.

Put the transparencies aside and discuss (as appropriate for you and your teaching situation) lines 20–43.

5. Homework (Day 1)

Tell students to read 2.2 and to summarize the action by assuming the identity of one character and writing a postcard to another. Or, if they know about telegrams, write a telegram that picks up the key information of the scene.

Example:

Romeo and Juliet 2.2

ROMEO WAS IN MY GARDEN STOP THOUGHT I WAS ALONE STOP I SAID I LOVED HIM OUT LOUD STOP HE APPEARED AND SPOKE OF LOVE STOP NURSE ALMOST CAUGHT US STOP TWICE STOP HE LEFT AT DAWN STOP ORDER WEDDING CAKE STOP

6. Homework Review (Day 2)

Check student comprehension of last night's reading assignment. Have some of the students read their postcards or telegrams. Collect the papers.

Discuss any questions and/or reactions that the students have with regard to 2.2.

7. Promptbooks (Day 2)

Pass out copies of a drawing of an empty stage and promptbook pages for 2.2.

Tell the students that each one will complete a mini promptbook for 2.2. The promptbooks will be graded for:

• a neat, logical set design
• complete, thoughtful notations
• evidence of a clear understanding of the scene and its characters

Tell the students to design a set for 2.2. The design should reflect the needs expressed by the text, and it should facilitate the action of the scene. This drawing should be different from the one the class designed for 2.1.

Further, tell the students to complete promptbook pages for this scene, making notes about entrances, exits, movements, and line delivery. Allow the students to use annotated texts, a dictionary, and any other editions or glossaries that will help them research and understand the lines.

Let the students work on their promptbook pages for the rest of the class period.

8. Homework (Day 2)

Tell students to complete their promptbooks at home.

HOW DID IT GO?

Creating promptbooks requires strong focus power, especially if students are having to acquire the new language of stage directions. The goal of this lesson is not for students to perfect this language or to fill up a column with senseless notes. This lesson was a success only if students, while doing the promptbook, saw the characters moving around in their heads, used the lines to make choices, and came to a reasonable understanding of what the lines were saying.

As with previous homework assignments, assign points to the postcard or telegram based on completeness and accuracy. Reinforce with praise.

Will now deny to dance? She that makes dainty, she,
I'll swear, hath corns. Am I come near you now?—

Enter PETER, *showing in* MERCUTIO, ROMEO, *and* BENVOLIO,
masked, L.

You're welcome, gentlemen.—I've seen the day
That I have worn a vizor; and could tell
A whispering tale in a fair lady's ear,
Such as would please;—'tis gone, 'tis gone, 'tis gone!
—More light, ye knaves; and turn the tables up.
And quench the fire; the room is grown too hot.

Rom. Cousin Benvolio, do you mark that lady
Which doth enrich the hand of yonder gentleman?

Ben. I do.

Rom. Oh, she doth teach the torches to burn bright!
Her beauty hangs upon the cheek of night,
Like a rich jewel in an Ethiop's ear.
The measure done, I'll wait her to her place,
And, touching hers, make happy my rude hand.
Be still, be still, my fluttering heart!   [*They retire*

Tyb. This, by his voice, should be a Montague,
Come hither, covered with an antic face,
To fleer and scorn at our solemnity!   ——
Now, by the stock-and-honour of my race,
To strike him dead I hold it not a sin.

Cap. Why, how now, kinsman? wherefore storm you
   thus?

Tyb. Uncle, this is a Montague, our foe;
A villain, that is hither come in spite,
To scorn and flout at our solemnity.

Cap. Young Romeo, is't?

Tyb. That villain Romeo.

Cap. Content thee, gentle coz; let him alone
He bears him like a courtly gentleman,
And, to say the truth, Verona brags of him,
To be a virtuous and well governed youth;
I would not, for the wealth of all this town,
Here in my house, do him disparagement;
Therefore be patient, take no note of him.

Tyb. It fits, when such a villain is a guest:
I'll not endure him.

Cap. He shall be endured:

Page from *Romeo and Juliet* promptbook prepared, probably around 1868, by famous American actor and director Edwin Booth, showing directions for set arrangement and stage movement. Booth (the brother of John Wilkes Booth) cut many lines from the play but none on this page.

SAMPLE: HANDOUT 7

PROMPTBOOK PAGE FOR 2.1

Teachers, this is an example of what the first promptbook page for 2.1 might look like *after* we add notes. Each production is different, of course, so each time you teach this unit you and your class will make different notes. What you need to give students for Handout 7 is a copy of 2.1 that looks just like this only with *no notes.*

Romeo enters up right, moves center, stops, exits center right.

enter up right, move center

searches c.l., then d.l.

sighs— making fun

line up arrow in bow, aim at B.

B. falls

M. moves center, makes shape of woman, B. admires.

Enter Romeo alone.

ROMEO
Can I go forward when my <u>heart</u> is here?   *excited*
Turn back, dull earth, and <u>find thy center</u> out.   *He withdraws.*
    pause   *say faster*

Enter Benvolio with Mercutio.

BENVOLIO
Romeo, my cousin Romeo, Romeo!

MERCUTIO
He is wise
And, on my life, hath stol'n him home to bed.

BENVOLIO
He ran this way and leapt this orchard wall.
Call, good Mercutio.

MERCUTIO   *singsong voice*
                    Nay, I'll conjure too.
Romeo! Humors! Madman! Passion! Lover!
Appear thou in the likeness of a sigh.
Speak but one rhyme and I am satisfied.
Cry but "Ay me," pronounce but "love" and
    "dove."
Speak to my gossip Venus one fair word,   *quiet*
One nickname for her purblind son and heir,
Young Abraham Cupid, he that shot so trim
When King Cophetua loved the beggar maid.—
He heareth not, he stirreth not, he moveth not.
The ape is dead, and I must conjure him.—
I conjure thee by Rosaline's bright eyes,   *M. pretends to be serious*
By her high forehead, and her scarlet lip,
By her fine foot, straight leg, and quivering
    thigh,

And the demesnes that there adjacent lie,
That in thy likeness thou appear to us.

BENVOLIO
An if he hear thee, thou wilt anger him.

MERCUTIO
This cannot anger him. 'Twould anger him
To raise a spirit in his mistress' circle
Of some strange nature, letting it there stand
Till she had laid it and conjured it down.

LESSON **11** ## "What Satisfaction Canst Thou Have Tonight?"

The Balcony Scene in Film

WHAT'S ON FOR
TODAY AND WHY

From the very start of this unit, we have asked students to be actors and directors. Today they are going to join the brotherhood of professional Shakespeareans. After praise and discussion of their promptbook work with 2.2, they are going to view two movie versions of the same scene. Thus they will see with their own eyes that there is more than one way to read Shakespeare's lines, that the best acting choices are based on the lines themselves, and that the lines were written for actors.

Before this lesson, in fact before this unit, teachers should locate at least two productions of *Romeo and Juliet*:

- The 1936 MGM production directed by George Cukor and starring Leslie Howard and Norma Shearer is available through Facets Multimedia (1-800-331-6197).
- The 1954 Verona Productions version directed by Renato Castellani and starring Laurence Harvey and Susan Shentall is available through The Writing Company (1-800-421-4246).
- The 1969 Franco Zeffirelli version starring Leonard Whiting and Olivia Hussey is available in most video stores.
- The 1978 British Broadcasting Company version directed by Alvin Rakoff and starring Patrick Ryecart and Rebecca Saire is available through Ambrose Video (1-800-526-4663).
- The 1988 Thames TV production starring Christopher Neame and Ann Hasson is available through The Writing Company (1-800-421-4246).
- The 1996 Baz Luhrmann *Romeo + Juliet*, set in a hip, modern-day Verona Beach, California, features television newscasts, customized cars, and guns rather than swords, but maintains Shakespeare's language. It stars Leonardo DiCaprio as Romeo, Claire Danes as Juliet, Paul Sorvino as Capulet, Brian Dennehy as Montague, and John Leguizamo as Tybalt.

Have the films cued up to 2.2. (Romeo: "He jests at scars that never felt a wound.")

WHAT TO DO

1. Promptbook Display

Discuss the completed promptbooks, asking the students to show their work and talk about some of the choices they made for the scene.

2. Comparative Video

Show two different movie versions of 2.2 from *Romeo and Juliet*. As students watch, ask them to keep their promptbooks open to compare their choices with those of the directors. Tell students to watch for cuts, characterization, tone, pace.

Have students write in their journals about similarities and differences among the movie versions and their own versions.

Discuss the similarities and differences the students noted, and discuss student preferences.

3. More Promptbook Display

Collect promptbooks. Invite students to display them in the room if they like.

HOW DID IT GO?

If students produced promptbooks that showed careful thought about the set, movement, and line delivery, they were listening to the language of the play in a very attentive manner. You have led them well. To evaluate their work, assign a set number of points to the items you listed in Lesson 10:

- a neat, logical set design
- complete, thoughtful notations
- evidence of a clear understanding of the scene and its characters

If students, in viewing the film scenes, voiced approval or argument about scene choices, you know they are seeing themselves in the role of director or actor—a very different role from that of a student laboring through an incomprehensible text.

LESSON 12 "The Gray-Eyed Morn"

Language Tricks

❧ _____

PLAY SECTIONS COVERED IN THIS LESSON

2.3.1–22 Friar Lawrence admires the dawn as he sets out to gather herbs.

LINES: Friar Lawrence, 22

2.3.23–93 Romeo tells Friar Lawrence he loves Juliet Capulet and asks the friar to marry them that day.

LINES: Friar Lawrence, 54; Romeo, 25

❧ _____

WHAT'S ON FOR TODAY AND WHY

Moving from the big picture to the individual word, students will do a close study of "the gray-eyed morn" passage. To recognize and analyze some of the language tricks Shakespeare uses, students will explore the passage with the teacher's guidance, then set off in groups to discover these tricks in the rest of Act 2. The emphasis of this lesson is on studying how the language works rather than on memorizing the names of the tricks.

Prepare a transparency and copies of Handout 8: Shakespeare's Language Tricks.

WHAT TO DO

1. The Gray-Eyed Morn: Close Reading

Ask the students to read Friar Lawrence's speech in unison. (You might want to pass out copies of this speech so the students can write on them.)

Discuss the language tricks that Shakespeare uses in this speech. Focus on the line "The gray-eyed morn smiles on the frowning night." Point out that in this line, Shakespeare attributes to morn and night human actions. Ask the students to show you which actions (smiles, frowns). Tell them (or remind them) that this trick is called *personification*. Have the term written on the board or on a transparency along with the example line.

Focus on the phrase "check'ring the eastern clouds with streaks of light." Ask: What picture do you get in your mind when you hear this phrase? Do you see a sky with areas of dark and light? Why might Shakespeare have used the word *check'ring*? What does that word contribute to the pattern of dark and light you see? Does it invite a comparison with a checkerboard? Point out that this comparison is called a *metaphor.* Again, have the term written on the board or on a transparency along with the example phrase.

Focus on the line "And fleckled darkness like a drunkard reels." Remind the students that if the comparison uses *like* or *as,* it is called a *simile.* Ask if this line is a metaphor or a simile. (Someone will point out that it is also a personification.) Ask: What is being compared to what? Again, have this term written on the board or on a transparency.

Focus on the phrase "From forth day's path and Titan's fiery wheels." Together, find out who Titan is. Explain that references to ancient Greek and Roman mythology are called *classical allusions.* Again, have this term and example listed on the board or on a transparency.

2. Gray-Eyed Morn: Reversals

Again look closely at 2.3.1–22. Focus on the word *upfill* (line 7). Ask the students to identify what is unusual about this phrase. (They will say that "upfill" is reversed, that we usually say "fill up.")

Focus on "The earth that's nature's mother is her tomb; / What is her burying grave, that is her womb" (lines 9–10). Ask the students to identify what is unusual about these ideas. (The thoughts are reversed. What gives birth serves as a grave; what serves as a grave gives birth.) Point out that these lines contain reversed thoughts.

Focus on "And from her womb children of divers kind / We sucking on her natural bosom find" (lines 11–12). Ask the students to identify what is unusual about the wording of the sentence (other than the fact that it sounds like a foreign language). The wording is an example of reversed sentence construction. Ask the students to unscramble the sentence. For example, students might say that this is the "normal" word order: And we find children of divers kind from her womb sucking on her natural bosom.

All of these examples are listed on Handout 8.

3. Generating Language Tricks

Pass out Handout 8: Shakespeare's Language Tricks. Review all the tricks, and ask students to generate examples of their own for each. Have them read some of their examples aloud.

4. A Last Look at Morn

Divide the students into groups of two or three. Give them 10 minutes to study the rest of the speech for more examples of these devices. Have the students present their discoveries.

Draw some conclusions about this speech:

• What does Friar Lawrence explain about the nature of these herbs?
• How does this nature lesson apply to life in general?
• How does this nature lesson apply to the relationship between Romeo and Juliet?
• How does the use of these language tricks enhance this speech for you?

5. Close Reading 2.3.23–93

Let the students return to their groups and study the rest of the scene. Collect a list of 2.3 language tricks from each group at the end of class.

6. Homework

Ask students to read 2.4–6 and write a summary of these scenes.

Summary suggestion: Tell the students to write their summaries in a letter format as if writing to a friend. The students should pretend to be aware of the entire situation between Romeo and Juliet, and they should share the latest developments in the relationship (2.4–6) along with their concerns for or approval of the young lovers.

Tell the students that you'll award a bonus point to any student who includes an original example of a language trick in the letter.

HANDOUT 8

SHAKESPEARE'S LANGUAGE TRICKS

The list below contains some of the language tricks that Shakespeare used when writing *Romeo and Juliet,* and it provides an example of each trick from Friar Lawrence's opening speech, 2.3.1–22.

personification   "The gray-eyed morn *smiles* on the *frowning* night"

metaphor   "*check'ring* the eastern clouds with streaks of light"

simile   "And fleckled darkness *like* a drunkard reels"

classical allusions   "From forth day's path and Titan's fiery wheels"

reversed word   "upfill"

reversed thought   "The earth that's nature's mother is her tomb; / What is her burying grave, that is her womb"

reversed sentence   "And from her womb children of divers kind / We sucking on her natural bosom
  construction   find"

Experiment with Shakespeare's language tricks. Write an original example of each of the devices listed below.

1. personification

2. metaphor

3. simile

4. classical allusion

5. reversed word

6. reversed thought

7. reversed sentence construction

LESSON 13 "If You Should Deal Double"

More Language Tricks

❧ _____

PLAY SECTIONS COVERED IN THIS LESSON

2.4.1–37 Mercutio tells Benvolio that Tybalt has sent a challenge to Romeo.

LINES: Mercutio, 29; Benvolio, 8

2.4.38–103 Benvolio, Mercutio, and Romeo trade witticisms.

LINES: Benvolio, 3; Mercutio, 42; Romeo, 21

2.4.164–219 Romeo asks Juliet's nurse to tell Juliet to meet him at Friar Lawrence's cell today so they can be married.

LINES: Nurse, 35; Romeo, 20; Peter, 1

2.5.1–55 Juliet is eager for her nurse to come home and tell about her meeting with Romeo, but the nurse takes her time in reporting.

LINES: Juliet, 36; Nurse, 19

2.5.56–83 After much evasion, the nurse tells Juliet she is to marry Romeo today.

LINES: Juliet, 10; Nurse, 18

2.6 Juliet joins Friar Lawrence and Romeo for her wedding ceremony.

LINES: Friar Lawrence, 18; Romeo, 12; Juliet, 7

❧ _____

WHAT'S ON FOR TODAY AND WHY

Because the recognition, identification, and analysis of language tricks takes a great deal of focus and practice, students will spend another day with these activities.

WHAT TO DO

1. Homework Review

Collect the letter summaries of 2.4–6 from the students. If you like, hear a few of the student-generated language tricks.

2. More Practice with Language Tricks

Review yesterday's discussion of language tricks. Make a transparency that compiles the lists collected at the end of yesterday's class. Discuss the successfully identified and labeled examples. Work through the incorrectly labeled examples, problem tricks, and problem lines.

Divide the class into seven groups for a language-study activity. Assign each group one of the following passages:

2.4.1–37
2.4.38–103
2.4.164–219
2.5.1–55
2.5.56–83
2.6

Ask each group to study its passage and to complete the following activities:

- Prepare a summary of your group's lines.
- Identify three examples of language tricks used in your group's lines. Discuss how these specific tricks enhance the passage for your group.
- Identify what your group thinks is the most important line, and be prepared to explain why it is important.

Allow twenty minutes for group work. Then let each group present its discoveries in brief oral reports.

Ask the students what else they noticed about the language of their passages. If they can identify examples of other types of word tricks (e.g., hyperbole, puns, contracted words, and more), discuss them. Also, if they noticed rhyme or rhythm patterns, talk about them.

3. Homework

Ask the students to read 3.1 and write a summary of the scene.

Summary suggestion: Tell the students to write their summaries in a "lazy sonnet" form. Using only one word per line for 14 lines, each student should try to capture the essence of 3.1.

Example:

Mercutio
by
Tybalt—
slain.
Tybalt
by
Romeo—
slain.
Romeo
by
banishment—
slain.
Hate
fate.

HOW DID IT GO?

To evaluate the 2.3 language tricks identified by the groups in Lesson 12, ask yourself:

- Were the groups able to identify and label most of the remaining examples correctly?

· Did any of the tricks or any of the lines seem to cause problems for most of the groups?

Read through the summary letters for 2.4–6 and complete a quick grading guide for each one: Was the summary complete? Accurate? Did the student include personal reactions to the events? Award a bonus if the student included an original example of a language trick. Staple some of the letters to the bulletin board.

To evaluate the group reports, use this grading guide:

· Summary: Did the summary help to orient the class to your lines in a clear, complete manner? (5 points)
· Language tricks: Did your group correctly identify and label three examples of language tricks found in your set of lines? Did your group discuss how these language tricks enhanced your passage for you? (15 points)
· Important line: Did your group remember to identify which line you thought was most important, and did you explain why you selected this line? (5 points)

LESSON 14 "Hold, Friends!"

Tableaux Vivants for 3.1

❧ _____

PLAY SECTIONS COVERED IN THIS LESSON

3.1.1–35 Benvolio and Mercutio say they should get off the street and avoid the Capulets, but they don't.

LINES: Benvolio, 9; Mercutio, 26

3.1.36–86 Benvolio and Mercutio encounter Tybalt and the Capulets. Romeo tries to be friendly, but Tybalt challenges him. Mercutio draws on Tybalt. Romeo tries to break them up, but they fight.

LINES: Benvolio, 5; Mercutio, 24; Tybalt, 12; Romeo, 10

3.1.87–120 Romeo steps between Tybalt and Mercutio as they fight. Tybalt wounds Mercutio by running his sword under Romeo's arm.

LINES: Romeo, 14; Petruchio, 1; Mercutio, 18; Benvolio, 1

3.1.121–143 Benvolio reports Mercutio's death. Romeo vows revenge, slays Tybalt, and then flees.

LINES: Benvolio, 9; Romeo, 12; Tybalt, 2

3.1.144–207 Citizens of Verona summon the prince, who banishes Romeo.

LINES: Citizen, 4; Benvolio, 30; Prince, 16; Lady Capulet, 11; Montague, 3

❧ _____

WHAT'S ON FOR TODAY AND WHY

Tableaux vivants (living pictures) are used in the worlds of art and theater to recreate famous works of art using backdrops, props, costumes, and live models. The technique may also be used to recreate scenes from Shakespeare or from any type of literature. These scenes are easy to develop because only a few key lines from the original work are needed. Like frozen statues, the actors arrange themselves in an appropriate opening tableau; then one at a time each actor comes to life, speaks a line, and changes position. In this lesson, students will create tableaux vivants to pinpoint key lines, actions, and feelings in 3.1 that help to make the scene a turning point in the play. Our objective is to involve every student, offer a simple and less threatening approach to acting, and provide an excellent starting point for the discussion of 3.1.

To allow time for careful reading and researching of 3.1, we will give the students two days for this lesson.

WHAT TO DO

1. Homework Review (Day 1)

Start the class by having some of the students read their "lazy sonnets" summarizing 3.1.

2. Forethought: Anger (Day 1)

Have the students think, and talk, about the power of anger. Ask them to write journal entries about a time when they were so angry that they acted without thinking. Also ask the students to write about the consequences of this impetuous action.

Allow some volunteers to read their entries, and discuss some of the insights students expressed. After student volunteers read their entries, settle on one incident from those read. On the board make a chain-reaction diagram, real or predicted.

Example:

You told a friend you liked Sally's boyfriend.
The friend told Sally.
Sally snubbed you in the hall.
You put down Sally to mutual friends.
Sally wrote you a note saying, "Why are you spreading these lies?"
And more . . .

Discuss how quickly anger can spread and damage relationships. As the students prepare to work with 3.1, tell them to watch the way that anger controls the characters in the scene.

3. Tableaux Vivants (Day 1)

Divide 3.1 into five sections—see Play Sections Covered in This Lesson, above. Divide the students into five groups, one group for each set of lines. The size of each group will be determined by the number of actors needed for the scene. If there are more students in a group than there are parts, put the extra students in charge of directing the tableaux, and have them present the opening and closing remarks. Make sure everyone has something to say aloud.

Briefly explain tableaux vivants and pass out Handout 9: Shakespearean Snapshots and a copy of the grading guide. Let the groups work on their presentations. Each student should complete a copy of the handout. The student can then take this handout home and review the tableau before class tomorrow.

Tell each group member to assume a role and the task of searching the scene for one of his character's most significant lines. The line could clearly reveal character, a feeling, an important moment in the plot, or a prediction of coming events. The group should make sure that the lines will work well together, and some of the actors may need to speak more than one time during the tableau.

Teachers circulating from group to group should keep in mind:

· The group members should identify each student's role and line on the handouts.
· The students should decide in what order each actor will speak.

- The group members should record the speaking order on the handouts.
- The students should begin to block the scene by first arranging themselves in an appropriate opening tableau and then freezing.
- The students should practice saying their lines in order, and they should decide what actions would best accompany their lines.
- The group members should describe each student's action on the handout.
- The group should rehearse its tableau. One at a time each character should come to life, say her line, change positions, and freeze.
- The closing tableau should reflect the outcome of the lines spoken.
- Each group should prepare a brief opening and closing to accompany its presentation.
- The opening should identify the scene and each student's role.
- The closing should briefly explain why the group selected the lines that it did.
- The group members should include the opening and closing on their handouts.

4. Homework (Day 1)

Tell students to memorize the lines assigned to them by the group and the order in which the lines in their group will be presented.

5. Tableaux Vivants (Day 2)

Let the groups rehearse their tableaux a few minutes. Then have them perform their tableaux in the order in which the lines appear in 3.1.

Stop after each tableau and discuss the performances with the class: What do these lines reveal about the characters? Conflict? Anger? What other lines might have been equally appropriate? Why? What is the significance of this scene relative to the scene before? To the play as a whole? Why is this scene identified as a turning point in the play?

6. Homework (Day 2)

Ask students to make a chain-reaction diagram of the major events that led to disaster in *Romeo and Juliet*.

HOW DID IT GO?

Check student comprehension by reading the summary "lazy sonnets." Assign points for each sonnet that captures the key events of 3.1. Staple some of the sonnets on the bulletin board.

To evaluate the tableaux vivants activity, ask yourself:

- Did the students pinpoint key lines from each passage?
- Were the tableaux helpful, interesting, fluid, organized?
- Did the presentations facilitate the discussion of 3.1?

If you like, use the following grading guide to evaluate each group while its members are presenting the tableau. After the presentation, give the completed grading guide to the group.

Shakespearean Snapshots 3.1 Grading Guide

Group members:

_____ Clarity and helpfulness of content of opening and closing (5 points)

_____ Appropriateness of lines chosen for each character (10 points)

_____ Organization, clarity, and effectiveness of the tableau (15 points)

⁊

HANDOUT 9

SHAKESPEAREAN SNAPSHOTS 3.1

Each group member should fill out this sheet.

Group Members:

1.   4.

2.   5.

3.   6.

ACTOR	CHARACTER	SPEAKING ORDER	LINE	ACTION

Write an opening that will identify your scene and each group member's role:

Write a closing that will briefly explain why you selected the lines that you did:

⁊

LESSON 15   "And Bring in Cloudy Night"

A Word Study of 3.2

ə̃

PLAY SECTIONS COVERED IN THIS LESSON

3.2 Juliet's nurse brings her the news that Romeo has slain Tybalt.

LINES: Juliet, 125; Nurse, 32

ə̃

WHAT'S ON FOR TODAY AND WHY

Certain words take on lives of their own in Shakespeare's plays. The word *night*, for example, is used repeatedly in *Romeo and Juliet*, and this repetition calls to mind a variety of meanings, associations, and pictures that add imagery to the play. Read "Triple-Threat Shakespeare" (page 3) for an excellent discussion of *night* by Jeanne Roberts.

In this lesson, students will study the word *night* in 3.2 by brainstorming, writing, reading, and analyzing activities. As a result of this lesson, the students will see how the repetition of a single word is one of Shakespeare's language tricks, and they will develop sensitivity to the power of a word in their own writing.

WHAT TO DO

1. Night: Brainstorming

Prepare the students to work with the word *night* in 3.2 by having them draw upon their own understanding of the word.

Place the students in groups of four or five and ask them to brainstorm a web of definitions, synonyms, ideas, and images that they associate with the word *night*. An example might be:

Make a collective web on the board or on the overhead projector. Ask each group to add some of their best findings, and have the students take notes.

2. Writing About Night

Ask each student to select four to six words from the web (examples: stars, dreams, darkness, nightmares, peace, chaos), then use these words in a paragraph or a poem that produces a picture of night in the reader's mind. Example:

<blockquote>
Night

Stars glitter,
    dusting dreams with imagination
Darkness creeps,
    suffering sleep with nightmares
How quickly peace yields to chaos
</blockquote>

After they have completed the writing assignment, ask the students:

- Why did you choose the words you did?
- Did you learn through your writing?
- If yes, what?

Students may see that they bring personal memories to the word *night.* Talk about how some words produce images, pictures in the mind. (*Apple* does, *the* does not.)

Have some or all of the students read their pieces to the class. Put some of their pieces on the bulletin board.

3. Repetition of *Night* in 3.2.1–33

Explain to the students that Shakespeare would take a word like *night* and use it throughout a play. Each time the audience hears the word *night,* certain pictures or images pop in their heads, so we say that repetition of the word creates *imagery.*

Pass out copies of Juliet's opening speech, 3.2.1–33, and ask the students to read the speech to themselves, lightly circling any words that are unfamiliar.

Discuss any trouble spots, working together to define the unfamiliar words and to clarify confusing lines.

Ask the students to listen carefully while you slowly read 3.2.1–33 aloud to them.

Have the students individually scan 3.2 for the phrases containing the word *night.*

As a class, have the students analyze their discoveries. Ask one student to take notes on the board or on an overhead transparency as the students identify the lines that contain *night.* For example:

"and bring in cloudy *night* immediately" (line 4)
"love-performing *night*" (line 5)
"Come, gentle *night*" (line 21)

Ask the students to analyze this imagery:

- What are some of the different denotations or associations given to the word *night*? (For example, students might say that Juliet associates night with privacy, intimacy, and Romeo.)
- What does the night imagery add to the scene? (Students will think it adds sexual tension, romance, a sense of anticipation.)

4. *Night* in the Rest of 3.2

Assign parts and read the rest of the scene aloud.

Discuss any questions the students raise with regard to plot.

Ask students:

- Did you find more *night*s? (Don't overlook *knight* in 3.2.156.)
- How conscious of the imagery would you be if you had read the scene before our work in class today?
- Would it have mattered if you didn't pick up on the imagery?
- Why or why not?
- At what point does the scene begin to use the word *night* again?
- Romeo and Juliet have been eagerly anticipating night. How do you think the recent events will change the meaning of *night* for them?

5. Writing Option

Consider having the students revise their pieces on *night*.

6. Homework

Ask the students to read 3.3–5 and summarize the scenes.

HOW DID IT GO? Did students see images of night in their heads? Did they feel the texture, notice the color, see it move? Did they talk about images, write about images, count images, notice what images do to a passage? If so, you have shown students how bits of sound or smudges of ink call forth from our memory shimmering sights. Not a bad day.

16 "Romeo Is Banished, and All the World to Nothing"

Cutting the Script

ટ**

PLAY SECTIONS COVERED IN THIS LESSON

3.3 Friar Lawrence tells Romeo that he has been banished by Prince Escalus. They, along with Juliet's nurse, agree that Romeo can see Juliet this night, but he must leave before the watch the next morning.

LINES: Friar Lawrence, 92; Romeo, 73; Nurse, 21

3.4 Capulet tells Lady Capulet that Juliet will marry Paris next Thursday.

LINES: Capulet, 31; Paris, 5; Lady Capulet, 2

3.5 As in a classical aubade, Romeo and Juliet regret the coming of the dawn. Romeo leaves. Lady Capulet tells Juliet she will marry Paris on Thursday. Juliet begs her father to release her from the marriage, but he angrily refuses. Juliet sends her nurse to consult with Friar Lawrence.

LINES: Juliet, 105; Romeo, 24; Nurse, 24; Lady Capulet, 38; Capulet, 64

ટ**

WHAT'S ON FOR TODAY AND WHY

Cutting an original script is a fact of life for directors. Time constraints, budgetary concerns, and other considerations mean that words, lines, and even scenes must be eliminated. This cutting, however, must be done with care so the work itself is not destroyed. An excellent exercise for the students is to assume the role of the director, reading scenes and making decisions about what may be eliminated without ruining the sense of the play. Have the students take a director's eye to 3.3–5. They will become closely and independently involved with the scenes; they will consider the essential elements of the play that must be communicated to an audience; and they will develop an appreciation for the work of Shakespeare and for the directors of his plays.

Time this two-day lesson so that the bell does not ring in the middle of the film presentation. To lead students to see and hear the characters as they plan an imaginary performance, be thorough in questions during the group reports.

Before the lesson, preview the excerpt and cue up the film. Make copies of 3.3 and 3.5 so students can mark on the script freely.

WHAT TO DO

1. Homework Review

Collect the summaries of 3.3–5 and work together to resolve any questions that the students have about the reading assignment.

2. Cutting the Script

Talk to the students about cutting and about why a director cuts a play. Ask the students to assume that they are directors preparing to film *Romeo and Juliet* and that they need to decide what they will do with 3.3–5. Ask them if one of the scenes could be cut without ruining the sense of the play. (They will say 3.4.) Ask them if they have to include every line of the other two scenes. Divide them into groups and have them do some cutting. Assign half the groups 3.3 and the other half 3.5. Pass out copies of 3.3 and 3.5 to the appropriate groups. Tell them to cut at least one-third of the lines and to make cuts without destroying the scene. Tell them to write in pencil directly on the duplicated copies.

3. Script Cutting: Reports (Day 1)

Hear each group read its newly cut scene. Discuss the results. Ask the groups to defend their choices.

If you like, place a transparency of each scene on the overhead, and ask the groups to explain where they made their cuts.

4. Script Cutting: Reports (Day 2)

If some groups did not have a chance to report on their script cuts yesterday, let them do so today.

5. Script Cutting: Zeffirelli

Show students what Franco Zeffirelli did with 3.3–5. (The beginning of the scene is cut. It starts with a knocking on the door. 3.5 has some nudity, which you might need to know in case you don't get a chance to preview. The film excerpt of these scenes has a viewing time of 16 minutes.)

Compare and contrast the students' versions with Zeffirelli's version. Discuss points of interest and/or controversy.

HOW DID IT GO?

If, in the course of arguing about why one phrase is essential to the scene and another is not, students were reading the scene and comprehending the action in it, this lesson met its objective. If students gave permanent places in their minds to some of the words and characters they encountered, they have exceeded the mark.

Ask yourself:

· Were the students actively engaged in the group work?
· Did the students cut their scenes in effective and appropriate ways?
· Did the students eagerly discuss their scene cuts and Zeffirelli's?

If so, their close reading and literary analysis skills are up to speed.

LESSON 17 "Take Thou This Vial"

Subtext, Stress, and Inflection

"**S**he kissed me after school." The preceding statement is worded clearly, and most people would agree on its basic meaning; however, depending upon how the speaker conceives and presents the line, those five words can mean anything from "She usually boxes my ears" to "Ordinarily she kisses me *before* school." The thought we suppose a character is thinking while saying the lines is the *subtext,* and subtext controls the way an actor reads a line.

An understanding of subtext is especially important in 4.1–2 of *Romeo and Juliet,* since these scenes are full of interior thoughts and intentions: What is Friar Lawrence thinking as he tells Juliet to take the vial? What is Juliet thinking when she agrees to marry Paris or when she begs her father's forgiveness? In this lesson the students will role-play one series of lines with a variety of subtexts, consider possible subtexts for the characters in 4.1–2, and do some 4.1–2 readings for each other that reflect an understanding of subtext. These activities will help the students develop an awareness of the presence and importance of subtext in a play.

For further work on subtext, read Lessons 8 and 9 of the *Midsummer Night's Dream* unit. We will begin by borrowing a few exercises from that unit, then continue with more exercises designed by Paul Cartier.

WHAT TO DO

1. Subtext: An Introduction

Introduce the students to the idea of subtext by leading them through the "I'm glad you're here" exercise found in Lesson 8 of the *Midsummer* unit.

Lead students to an understanding of subtext: thoughts we imagine characters to have as they speak certain lines.

2. Subtext: I'm Late

Do a second subtext exercise. Divide the class into pairs, and tell the students that each pair will be given the same set of lines that everyone else has, but the characters and the scenario will be different. Caution them not to tell anyone about their characters or scenario.

The lines:

CHARACTER 1 You're late.
CHARACTER 2 I know. I couldn't help it.
CHARACTER 1 I understand.
CHARACTER 2 I thought you would.
CHARACTER 1 I have something to give you.

CHARACTER 2 Really?
CHARACTER 1 Yes, this.

Some suggested characters and scenarios:

- Two friends—The late friend has just arrived at what will be a surprise party for him or her.
- Pizza delivery man and customer—The pizza delivery is late.
- Bride and groom—One has arrived late for the wedding.
- Spies—They are meeting secretly to exchange information.
- Lovers—They are meeting at a romantic restaurant.
- Teacher and student—The student is handing in a late paper.

Give each pair a card or paper with the lines and their scenario written on it. Tell them to develop the dialogue so that when they present it, the scene is completely different from everyone else's, even though they're using exactly the same words. *Tell them to make sure their reading reflects their assigned scenario.*

Model this activity for the students before they begin to work. With another teacher or a student, prepare and present the same lines that you've just given to the students. (For example, your scenario might be a shop that just closed, and your characters are a grumbling shopkeeper and a customer who is late to pick up a package. Prepare your scene before class.) Ask the students to identify your characters and scenario.

After you perform, consider each character one at a time and ask students what that character was thinking while delivering the lines. (This seems obvious, but get them to say the subtext aloud.) Then ask them what they did to convey the subtext. To help them identify the tools that actors use, list these terms on the board.

Subtext Tools:

- Stress—emphasis placed on a word when pronounced
- Inflection—the way the voice goes up or down when a word is pronounced
- Pause—break in reading for emphasis
- Nonverbal communication—gestures, posture, the presence or absence of eye contact

Suggest ways to mark the script for each of these—underlines, arrows, for example.

Let the students develop and practice their scenes for 10 minutes. Encourage them to experiment with all four tools in preparing their presentations and to make notations about delivery on their papers.

Have each group present its scene, and have the audience identify the characters and the scenario after each presentation. List the characters and scenario on the board.

Review with the students the fact that even though their lines were identical, the readings revealed different characters and scenarios because each reading was shaped by a different subtext.

3. Homework: Shakespearean Subtext: 4.1–2

Ask the students to read 4.1–2 and to write a two-paragraph journal entry, one for each scene:

- For 4.1, select Paris, the Friar, or Juliet, and write a paragraph describing what you think your character's subtext is during this meeting.
- For 4.2, select Juliet or her father, and write a paragraph describing what you think your character's subtext is during this meeting.

HOW DID IT GO?

- Were the "I'm Late" readings varied?
- Did they reflect an understanding of subtext and how it affects delivery?
- Did students show in their work an increasing awareness of subtext and how to demonstrate it with stress, inflection, pause, and nonverbal means?

If so, you have doubled the messages students receive from Shakespeare's lines. If not, keep trying. Lesson 18 is also devoted to subtext.

LESSON 18 "And All Things Shall Be Well"

Shakespearean Subtext

ɜ♣ _____

PLAY SECTIONS COVERED IN THIS LESSON

4.1 Juliet encounters Paris. Friar Lawrence explains to Juliet a plan in which she takes a potion that makes her appear dead.

LINES: Friar Lawrence, 56; Paris, 23; Juliet, 50

4.2 Juliet begs her father's forgiveness and agrees to marry Paris.

LINES: Capulet, 27; Servingman, 5; Nurse, 2; Juliet, 12; Lady Capulet, 3

ɜ♣ _____

WHAT'S ON FOR TODAY AND WHY

Continuing the work of Lesson 17, students will read 4.1 for subtext, then participate in a coached reading that will show them how to connect subtext to line delivery.

So students can mark on their scripts, teachers should prepare duplicated copies of 4.1.1–32.

WHAT TO DO

1. Imagining Subtext for 4.1–2

Divide the class into five groups. Make sure each student is placed in a group where he may use one of the two journal entries written for last night's homework.

Group 1—4.1 Juliet
Group 2—4.1 Friar Lawrence
Group 3—4.1 Paris
Group 4—4.2 Juliet
Group 5—4.2 Capulet

Tell the students that each member of the group should read his or her paragraph aloud, and the group should compile a list of the thoughts that might be the character's subtext during that scene. Inappropriate comments should be eliminated; important comments should be highlighted.

Hear and discuss the groups' findings. Take the characters one at a time. List the ideas that might be the character's subtext on the board. Be sure to ask the students to justify their ideas with evidence from the text. (An example for Juliet in 4.1: "I can't believe Paris wants me to tell him I love him. He makes me sick, but if I don't answer him, he might suspect something." Our justification for this subtext would be that Juliet's abhorrence of Paris is supported by her willingness to die rather than marry him.)

Compare each character's subtext with the surface meaning of his lines. (Students may say that Paris's subtext runs parallel to his words because they are honest and heartfelt. Juliet's subtext is hidden because she must conceal her true feelings. The irony of her words may be evident to the audience but not to Paris.)

2. Connecting the Subtext to Line Delivery

Ask students to read a short passage and decide how the lines might be delivered. Tell them to work independently. Have one-third of them focus on lines 4.1.1–8, one-third focus on lines 4.1.23–29, and one-third focus on lines 4.2.18–31. Tell them to read the passage to themselves several times, keeping in mind the subtext and how it influences delivery. Ask them to make notations on their papers to indicate how the lines should be delivered. (Display the list of the subtext tools, Lesson 17, as they work.)

3. Coached Reading

Have the class use these notations to help you coach several students in a reading of each passage. Ask for two volunteers to do a coached reading of 4.1.1–8, and have them stand in the front of the room. Lead the class in coaching the actors:

- In this passage Friar Lawrence is trying to hide his subtext. Ask the students how much of the Friar's subtext should slip through into the reading. Ask them to consider *why* it should slip through and *how*.
- Have the students read the passage one line at a time, stopping and letting the class make suggestions for stress, inflection, pauses, and nonverbals. Have the readers reread each line, incorporating the suggestions.
- Work through all eight lines, having the students do one final reading where they deliver the entire passage without stopping.

Do coached readings for the other two passages. (In these passages Juliet is the one who is trying to hide her subtext.)

4. Concluding Discussion

To review how subtext works in a scene, ask students:

- How do you feel about Paris and Capulet in these scenes? What do they want?
- How do you feel about Juliet and Friar Lawrence in these scenes?
- What does an awareness of subtext add to the scene? (Students may say it adds irony, audience concern for Juliet and Friar Lawrence. They may say subtext adds characterization for Juliet, that in expressing Juliet's subtext an actress can convey Juliet's sense of desperation, her isolation from family, her determination, her courage. Students may also say that subtext adds to the suspense—will Juliet's plans be discovered?)

HOW DID IT GO?　Monitor participation in the group work by checking to see which students completed the journal assignment. Count this journal exercise as a homework grade, awarding points for a completed entry.

Did the students identify a plausible subtext for each character in 4.1–2? Did the class effectively coach volunteer readers in their portrayals of the characters in 4.1–2?

You have spent two lessons trying to show students an invisible but potent dimension attached to every line in the play. If, after working through the subtext exercises, they understand it, their experience with *Romeo and Juliet* will be much richer. If not, let it go for the moment.

LESSON 19 "Cold Fear"

Imagery in 4.3

❧ _____

PLAY SECTION COVERED IN THIS LESSON

4.3 Juliet bids her nurse and mother good night and resolves to drink the potion.

LINES: Juliet, 57; Lady Capulet, 3.

❧ _____

WHAT'S ON FOR TODAY AND WHY

Act 4 belongs to Juliet. The activities and emotions in all five scenes revolve around her, and at no place is this focus more evident than in 4.3. It is in this scene that Juliet resolves to drink the potion that will take her close to death, and she draws the audience to her as she speaks her desperate fears aloud. There is no need to explore a subtext. Juliet's soliloquy is her subtext. Here she tells the truth as she knows it and reveals her painful internal conflicts. To underscore those conflicts, students will play the part of warring consciences in a role-play technique designed by Folger teacher Donna Denizé of St. Albans School, Washington, D.C.

Journal writing, focused listening, scene setting, discussion, and role-play will help the students to understand and visualize the fearful imagery and atmosphere present in Juliet's mind in 4.3. To give students the clearest picture possible of the tomb Juliet imagines, they will build it out of props, an activity designed by Folger Institute participant Suzanne Peters from Tucson, Arizona.

So students can mark on their scripts, teachers should duplicate 4.3. Also, notice that the building the tomb activity calls for props and an audio recording of *Romeo and Juliet*.

WHAT TO DO

1. Prewriting: Fear

Prepare the students to be sensitive to Juliet's fears. Have them write and, if they choose, talk about moments in their lives when they were really frightened.

Discuss how fear affects people mentally and physically.

2. Searching Out the Images

Tell the students that Juliet will be facing a terrifying moment in 4.3. Pass out copies of the scene and ask the students to read 4.3 to themselves and to circle any words that are unfamiliar. After the reading, discuss and define together these words.

Read 4.3 aloud. The reading may be done chorally or by one person, but ask the students to listen closely and to remember the images that are especially vivid for them. You might tell them, "As you hear these words, pictures will appear in your head. Be aware of them so that you can list the most memorable ones." As soon as the reading is finished, ask the students to list those images on a sheet of paper.

Ask the students to talk about the images they noted and to make a list of the images on the board. Consult every student in this compilation, for it will be revealing to see which images were noted most, which were seen in the most vivid detail, or what other patterns evolved. Ask: What effect do these images have on you?

3. Building the Tomb

Create a concrete picture of Juliet's mental picture of the tomb. Begin by asking the following questions:

- If we were going to build the tomb as Juliet sees it in 4.3, what props do we need/want?
- How should we arrange the props? (Have some props handy—fake dagger, vial, shroud, even bones.) Use some classroom furniture and some students to suggest biers and bodies.

Let the students arrange the props as suggested by the text.

Play a recording of the scene, or have a student read 4.3 a third time. Ask them to listen carefully and to look at the setting they created in the classroom.

Discuss the mood felt in this reading. Ask: Were the props helpful? Why? To what extent did the words create the mood?

4. Role-Play: Warring Consciences

Tell students that this soliloquy, like many of Shakespeare's soliloquies, focuses on the character's internal conflict. Ask the students to state Juliet's internal conflict. (Students might say it is her love for Romeo vs. her fears.) Ask students to identify Juliet's specific fears. Which is the worst?

Ask for three volunteers—one to play Juliet and two to play her "consciences." Have Juliet sit, vial in hand, in a chair in the middle of the tomb setting, and have the consciences stand on either side of her. Tell the two consciences to argue with Juliet and each other. One argues for taking the potion. One argues against it.

Discuss the role-play by asking the following questions:

- How have Juliet's fears affected her?
- How well do you think she is coping?
- What do you think of Juliet in this scene? Why?
- Would you be willing to take the risks that Juliet does? Why or why not?

5. Concluding Discussion

Conclude by discussing why this scene is important to the play as a whole. (Students might say, for example, that it contributes intensity, it sets the tone for the tragic ending, or it lets the audience inside Juliet's mind.)

6. Homework

Assign 4.4–5 for reading. Ask students to write a plot outline of the events in those scenes.

HOW DID IT GO?

If the students actively participated in the writing, reading, discussing, "mind set" designing, and role-playing for 4.3, they entered Juliet's mind and saw the images and fears there. No small feat, considering that Juliet is a fictional character. Too, if students were inside Juliet's mind, they got there through words. As readers and scholars, they have been a success. And they learned something about the power of language.

LESSON 20 "Go Waken Juliet"

Looking for Multiple Causes

ða _____

PLAY SECTIONS COVERED IN THIS LESSON

4.4 Capulet, acting like a "cot-quean" (man who plays housewife), oversees preparations for the wedding feast.

LINES: Lady Capulet, 3; Nurse, 4; Capulet, 22; First Servingman, 1; Second Servingman, 2

4.5.1–96 The Nurse and Capulet try to awaken Juliet but find her "dead." Capulet, Lady Capulet, the Nurse, Friar Lawrence, and the County Paris lament her "death."

LINES: Nurse, 29; Lady Capulet, 13; Capulet, 28; Friar Lawrence, 20; Paris, 6

4.5.97–151 Peter argues with the musicians about what music to play and how to play it.

LINES: Friar Lawrence, 5; First Musician, 13; Nurse, 2; Peter, 28; Second Musician, 6; Third Musician, 1

ða _____

WHAT'S ON FOR TODAY AND WHY

There is great distress in 4.5 when Juliet's "death" is discovered. Surrounding this lamentation is the lightness of 4.4 (the cot-quean scene) and the comic touches at the end of 4.5 (Peter's argument with the musicians). In this lesson, students will review *Romeo and Juliet* to consider many possible causes for the tragic moment in 4.5. They will also consider how the surrounding passages provide comic relief. Their tools are textual study, discussion, and poetry-writing. The results are increased understanding of motivation, characterization, and balance.

WHAT TO DO

1. Homework Review

Review and discuss the plot of 4.4–5. Ask the students if they have any questions about or reactions to the reading. Working together, resolve any unanswered questions. Check to make sure each student has completed a plot outline for 4.4–5.

As a class, come up with a model plot outline for 4.4–5. Let the students suggest the key events that should be in this outline, and write these events on an overhead transparency.

2. Comic Relief

Have the students focus on 4.4 and 4.5.97–151. Ask:

- Where are comic touches used in these two scenes? (The opening of the outline should reflect the "cot-quean" scene of 4.4, and the closing of the outline should reflect the encounter between Peter and the musicians at the end of 4.5.)
- Where is the tragedy located? (The students should notice that the tragedy is at the heart of the two scenes and that the comic touches surround the tragedy.)
- Why do you suspect there is this balance of comedy and tragedy? (The students should pick up on the value of the contrast and the comic relief.)
- What would be the effect if a director omitted these two scenes as Zeffirelli did in his production?

3. Who's Responsible for Juliet's "Death"?

We hear much weeping and wailing by the Nurse, Lady Capulet, Capulet, and Paris. If they only knew that their actions and reactions helped to push Juliet to make her drastic decision. . . . Have the students consider the multiple causes of Juliet's "death."

Ask the students who they think is responsible for Juliet's "death." Don't discuss their answers, just make a list of the characters the students name. (The students will probably list almost every character in the play, including Romeo and Juliet.)

Draw a circle on the board. Write "Juliet's 'Death'" in the center. Draw spokes out from the circle, one spoke for each character who might have contributed to Juliet's death. Write the character's name on the spoke. Leave one spoke blank; it will be completed later. Ask the students to copy this diagram on their own paper:

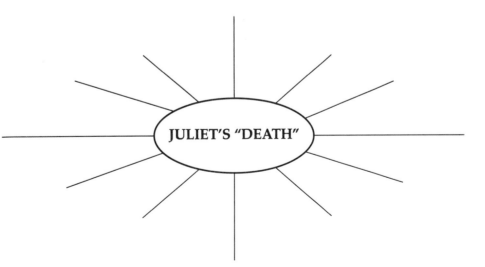

Tell each student to research the character that he or she believes is the most responsible for Juliet's predicament. The student should search throughout the play for words and actions of the character that might have made Juliet feel that she had to take such a drastic course of action. (Make sure that every character is chosen by at least one student.) Tell the student to add these words and actions to the end of the spoke with the character's name. Allow 15 to 20 minutes for research.

Discuss the discoveries made for each character, placing important information on a transparency of the web. Have the students add the notes to their copies of the web.

Ask the students if they've changed their minds about who's to blame. Ask them to explain their responses. (Chances are the students will say that Juliet's isolation is a product of all the actions and reactions of the people in Juliet's life, including her own.)

4. Homework

Ask students to read 5.2 and 5.3.

Optional writing assignment: Ask each student to write a poem.

- Select a character from the web who intrigues you. You may work with the same character you studied earlier, or you may work with a different one. Focus your work on how this character relates to Juliet. Example: The Nurse
- List five or more strong verbs or verbals that you think of when you think of your character: betraying, protecting, caring, talking, complaining
- Select one of those verbs or verbals and identify a moment in the play when the character really performs that action. Example: betraying— the Nurse tells Juliet to marry Paris.
- Turn the event into a poem that says something powerful and/or insightful about the character from the isolated incident.
- The poem should be at least six lines long, and it should contain at least one quotation from the character that works well with the incident.

Write a practice poem with the students on an overhead transparency so that the process is clear.

Example:

The Betrayal

The Nurse watches her weeping charge.

Shall Juliet be
married
widowed through banishment
married . . .
All within a week?
Ah, life is too simple.
Loss and Gain
Loss and Gain

Like Susan and my husband
(God rest all Christian souls!)

Calmly, practically, coolly, she says the words that
slice the young girl's heart in two:

"Romeo is banished. . . . I think it best you married with
the County"

HOW DID IT GO?   Reinforce student effort by checking the plot outlines. Award points for
this homework assignment based on completeness.

To evaluate the lesson, ask yourself:

- Were the students able to recognize the presence and the contributions
  of comedy and tragedy?
- Did the students find examples of words and actions that show how
  the different characters contributed to Juliet's predicament?
- Did they show logic in tracing the plot line to find how their character
  contributed to the tragedy?

LESSON **21** "Fortune's Fool"

The Fate Debate

PLAY SECTIONS COVERED IN THIS LESSON

5.1 Balthasar brings Romeo the news that Juliet is dead. Romeo, vowing "Juliet, I will lie with thee tonight," plans to return to her tomb in Verona and take poison.

LINES: Romeo, 73; Balthasar, 11; Apothecary, 7

5.2 Explaining how he was barred entry from Mantua because guards suspected him of being from a house with the plague, Friar John returns to Friar Lawrence with the letter to Romeo undelivered.

LINES: Friar John, 13; Friar Lawrence, 17

5.3 Romeo visits Juliet in the tomb, drinks his poison. Juliet awakens, finds Romeo dead, stabs herself with his knife. Friar Lawrence, the prince, the Capulets, and Montague lament the deaths, and the warring families promise to end their feud.

LINES: Paris, 32; Page, 9; Romeo, 82; Balthasar, 21; Friar Lawrence, 75; Juliet, 13; First Watch, 20; Second Watch, 2; Third Watch, 3; Prince, 39; Capulet, 10; Lady Capulet, 5; Montague, 10

WHAT'S ON FOR TODAY AND WHY

A well-intentioned but inaccurate message, an undelivered letter, an unusual dream, poor timing—these acts of fate and/or accidents conspire against Romeo and Juliet, leaving little room for doubt that, among other problems, the young lovers are "star-crossed." Discussion, a film clip, and journal writing will show students how unlucky events hasten Romeo and Juliet down their tragic path.

In this lesson we will lead the students in a discussion of the role of fate in *Romeo and Juliet*. Our purpose is to give students an opportunity to use their mastery of text to answer questions about ideas. For 5.1 and 5.2, students will read the script for support to their answers. For 5.3, they will listen and view the script as they watch a filmed performance.

Teachers should have the film of their choice cued up to 5.3, and they should have their "Juliet's 'Death' " transparency from Lesson 20 handy.

WHAT TO DO

1. Homework Review

If students did the optional writing assignment, collect their poems. In their homework reading assignment, they confronted the powerful ending of the play. Give them an opportunity to talk it out. Ask for questions, reactions.

2. Considering Fate

Prepare the students to think about the idea of fate in *Romeo and Juliet*. Place the following quotations about fate on the board:

> "The best of men cannot defend their fate: The good die early and the bad die late."
>
> —Daniel Defoe, 18th century

> "Our hour is marked and no one can claim a moment of life beyond what fate has predestined."
>
> —Napoleon, 19th century

> "What fates impose, that men must needs abide;
> It boots not to resist both wind and tide."
>
> —Shakespeare, *Henry VI, Part 3*

Discuss the quotations. Ask the students how they would define fate. (They will probably arrive at the idea that fate is an impersonal force that directs one's life.)

Ask students if they know people who believe that their lives are ruled by fate. What are the advantages of believing that fate rules life? (Students might say that fate can always be blamed when events don't go well.) What are the disadvantages in believing that fate rules life? (Students might say that a belief in fate creates a sense of helplessness.)

Ask the students: How is fate a part of *Romeo and Juliet?* (Students will probably be quick to say that the tragedy was caused partly by bad luck, accident, fate.) Suggest to students that they add another "character" to yesterday's diagram—Fate. (Now you know why we left one spoke blank.) Write "Fate" on the empty spoke from yesterday's transparency. Pose the question: Does fate cause the tragedy of Romeo and Juliet? Invite students to look at the play for evidence to answer this question yes or no.

3. Fate in Acts 1–4

Ask the students where and how fate has shown itself to play a part in Romeo and Juliet's relationship prior to the last act. Insist that students find examples from the playscript to support their answers. For example:

- From the beginning: "star-crossed lovers"
- Before they meet: ". . . for my mind misgives / Some consequence yet hanging in the stars . . ."
- Right after they meet: "Prodigious birth of love it is to me / That I must love a loathèd enemy."

Have the students add the examples to their webs while you add the examples to the transparency.

4. Fate in 5.1–2

Ask students: What is Romeo's mood at the beginning of 5.1? Support your answers with evidence from the text. (Students might look at 5.1.1–12, at the interpretation of his dream, and say that Romeo is joyful.)

Ask students to skim 5.1–2 and identify the examples of fate that are present. (They might mention Balthasar's inaccurate message, Friar Lawrence's miscarried letter, or Romeo's comment—"Then I defy you, stars!") Have the students add these examples to their webs while you add the examples to the transparency.

Ask: What is Romeo's mood after he hears of Juliet's "death" from Balthasar? Support your answers with evidence from the text. (Students might say Romeo is defiant—"Then I defy you, stars!"—or reckless— "Come, cordial and not poison, go with me / To Juliet's grave; for there must I use thee.")

Ask: How does fate affect Romeo when he believes Juliet is dead? (Students might say that he decides to take control in his own hands by drinking poison. His belief system makes him feel as though he has nothing more to lose and nothing more to gain since fate seems to destroy what he values. Or they might point out that Romeo will get to the tomb before the friar and commit suicide.)

Ask: To what degree is fate responsible for the tragic turn of events? (Answers may be mixed. Some students will recognize the presence of fate as a factor in the tragedy, but they probably won't say that fate is solely responsible. Others may disagree. Indeed, at this point you may have a coalition of "There's no such thing as fate" advocates. No matter. You are not trying to get students to accept one particular theory; you are teaching them to use the text to support their own theories.)

5. Looking for Fate in 5.3: Film Presentation

Show a film excerpt of 5.3, the tomb scene. Ask the students to identify some new examples of fate. (For example, Romeo arrives before the friar, Juliet awakens after Romeo dies.)

Have the students write a journal entry in which they consider how the presence of fate does or does not affect the power of the ending.

Ask some or all of the students to read or discuss their journal entries. (When discussing fate, some students may say that the accidents of fate seem too coincidental. Others may say that the accidents make Romeo and Juliet seem even more helpless; therefore, the reader feels more pity for the couple and a sense of his own helplessness.) Praise them for using examples and/or lines from the play.

6. Homework

Ask the students to reread 5.3.

HOW DID IT GO?   If you elected to use the optional writing assignment, grade each student's character poem, making sure that the student included a key incident that reveals something important about the character, added at least one quotation from the character, and wrote a minimum of six lines.

To evaluate this lesson, ask:

- In discussing the presence of fate in *Romeo and Juliet,* did students demonstrate a knowledge of the text? A knowledge of characters? A knowledge of plot?
- Did they know the play well enough to come up with good examples and/or lines to support their ideas about the role of fate?
- Are they reading with more confidence? Are they more willing to tackle the language problems on their own? Do they help each other solve language problems? Do they show that the characters are up and walking around in their minds?

"How Oft When Men Are at the Point of Death"

A Close Study of Romeo's Last Speech

PLAY SECTION COVERED IN THIS LESSON

5.3.88–120 Romeo confronts Juliet and death, then drinks the poison.

LINES: Romeo, 33

WHAT'S ON FOR TODAY AND WHY

The sense of joy and expectation felt by the lovers in the early acts is gone. Romeo believes his beloved Juliet is dead, and he prepares to commit suicide in the hope that they will be together in eternity. Students will look closely at his last words. Choral reading, close study, discussions, and writing will provide some insights into these words and into the play as a whole.

Prepare a transparency and copies of Handout 10: Final Words.

WHAT TO DO

1. Close Reading with Ears Open

Have the students sit in a circle and read Romeo's final passage, 5.3.88–120.

- Reading 1: Read the passage aloud in unison. After the reading, discuss and define together any words the students don't recognize.

- Reading 2: Going around the circle, have the students read the speech, changing readers at every mark of punctuation.

  First Student: "How oft when men are at the point of death / Have they been merry, . . ."

  Second Student: "which their keepers call / A light'ning before death."

  Third Student: "O," and so on . . .

  After the reading, discuss any questions the students have about content.

- Reading 3: In this read-through, have the students read to end stops (semicolons, question marks, exclamation points, and periods, not commas). This time, ask them to try to read as if the words were all spoken by one voice, without lengthy pauses between readers and with some expression. After the reading, ask the students what comments they have about the passage. What did they notice? What ideas or images made an impression upon them?

• Reading 4: Have the students read the passage aloud in unison.

2. Close Reading with Pencil in Hand

Have the students work in pairs to complete the chart in Handout 10: Final Words. Give them 20 minutes. Discuss the discoveries as a class. Let the students fill in any information they missed on their charts while you compile the information on an overhead transparency of the chart.

Have the students complete a writing assignment that draws some conclusions about the chart. Tell them: Select one component of your close study chart—Comparisons, Personifications, Word Categories, Repetitions, Sentence Types, or Personal References. Draw some conclusions about your component. The following questions may help:

• How does your component reflect Romeo's mental state?
• How does it relate to the larger themes of the play?
• How does it contribute to the effect of Romeo's final words?

Ask students to write a paragraph that summarizes their findings. When possible, support your statements with additional evidence from the text.

3. Homework

Ask the students to complete and revise their paragraphs for class tomorrow.

HOW DID IT GO?

As to classroom procedure:

• Did hearing the passage read aloud foster comprehension?
• Did students complete their charts accurately and thoughtfully?

To evaluate the paragraph:

• Were the conclusions the student reached accurate and appropriate?
• Did the students support their conclusions with evidence from the text?

HANDOUT 10

FINAL WORDS 5.3.88–120

Carefully read and study Romeo's final words. Look for the language tricks listed in the left side of the chart. Put your discoveries in the corresponding column on the right side of the chart.

LOOK FOR . . .	DISCOVERIES
COMPARISONS—List any metaphors and similes that you can find in the passage.	
PERSONIFICATIONS—List any examples of personification you can find.	
WORD CATEGORIES—Look for two or more words that relate to a category, such as plants, time, the heavens.	
REPETITIONS—Identify sounds or words that are repeated or that echo each other.	
SENTENCE TYPES—Find the number of times commands, questions, statements, and exclamations appear.	
PERSONAL REFERENCES—Find what Romeo says about himself.	

LESSON 23 "O, the People in the Street Cry 'Romeo' "

Acting Companies

WHAT's ON FOR TODAY AND WHY

As a culminating activity, have the students form small acting companies to prepare and perform scenes from *Romeo and Juliet*. (See Lesson 21 of *A Midsummer Night's Dream* for more information about shaping this activity.) In banding together for a final performance, the students will "own" a part of the play, work in teams, draw together language and performance skills they have developed throughout the unit, and enjoy an exciting final event.

Including instructions, rehearsals, and performance, this lesson takes four days.

WHAT TO DO

1. Organizing the Companies (Day 1)

Tell students that for a final *Romeo and Juliet* project they will perform a scene and develop a promptbook for that scene.

Pass out Handout 11: Promptbook Instructions and Handout 12: Scenes for Final Performance. Explain the activities that the students will be completing in their acting companies. Field all questions and concerns.

Don't let the students consider scenes that were blocked and performed earlier in class. With student input, select the scenes that are the most popular and/or performable, and make certain that enough scenes are selected so every student will be able to have a part.

Set up the acting companies by letting the students volunteer for parts in their favorite scenes. (It is a good idea to identify the more demanding roles before the students make their requests.) Send students to meet in their acting companies.

To help each company begin to develop a sense of unity and identity, post the cast lines and have each group of students give its company a name.

Give each company a copy of the promptbook and performance evaluation forms.

2. Companies: Starting Promptbooks (Day 1)

Direct attention back to Handout 11: Promptbook Instructions. Allow the students to work on activities as outlined in the handout for the rest of the period.

3. Companies: Planning and Rehearsal (Days 2 and 3)

Allow the students five minutes at the beginning of class to study their lines. They might look over their lines quietly or sit in a circle with their company members and read through the script.

Let the students work on the promptbook activities. To help the students make the most of their time, set goals for them at the beginning of each class (e.g., "By the end of the period, you should have completed activities 1 and 2"). They should assign themselves homework if they are getting behind in their work or if they want more time in class for rehearsing.

Have the students use the last 10–15 minutes of class to work on blocking and delivery. (After the first two days of this lesson, the promptbook activities will be nearing completion, and the students will be able to spend more time on rehearsal.)

4. Companies: Performance (Day 4)

Have a master or mistress of ceremonies introduce each company and its scene.

Options: Consider awarding prizes that celebrate significant achievements or moments of great fun. Avoid competitive awards.

Videotape the performances and let the students see their efforts.

HOW DID IT GO?

Check each company's paraphrase (Promptbook Procedure 1.c. in Handout 11) as early in the rehearsal process as possible. Award points based on completeness and accuracy and return the paraphrase immediately so students can correct misunderstood passages before performance.

Complete an evaluation for each company's promptbook. Focus on qualities such as completeness, accuracy, and effort.

Complete an evaluation for each company's performance. Focus on qualities such as memorization, delivery, characterization, blocking, and costumes and props.

ẽᴑ

HANDOUT 11

PROMPTBOOK INSTRUCTIONS

GOALS: To gain a clear understanding of the scene that you will be performing
To visualize your set and its appropriate props and traffic patterns
To interpret your company's lines and how they will be read
To consider an effective way to costume your actors
To understand your characters

PROCEDURE:

1. Your acting company should carefully read through and study your scene.
   a. Circle any unfamiliar words and define them using a dictionary, C. T. Onions's *A Shakespeare Glossary*, or the notes in your copy of the play.
   b. Complete the company handout.
   c. On an extra copy of the script, paraphrase the lines. (Turn this script in separately and as early in the rehearsal process as possible.)

2. Decide how you want to stage the scene and then draw the stage set. For a finishing touch, write a key line from your scene under the set design.

3. Complete the promptbook pages.
   a. Cut out an extra copy of the scene you have chosen and paste it onto plain paper. Place the lines to the far right. You will use the left side of the paper for notes and sketches.
   b. You may make cuts in your scene by crossing out lines, but Shakespeare's words must appear in their original sequence without changes in their meaning. In the margin, briefly justify the reasons for your cuts. Work in pencil.
   c. Make production notes for the way you want the scene to be played. These notes should include the following information: pauses, tone of voice, gestures and facial expressions, notes or diagrams of action and movement.

4. Decide how you will costume your players.
   a. Provide a drawing or description of your company's costumes.
   b. Provide a justification for selecting them. (If you do the scene in modern dress or in another time period, explain your reasons.)

5. Each student in your company will complete a character report for the character that he is portraying.

6. Please assemble your promptbook in the following order and turn it in on_____: cover, set design, prompt pages, costume drawing/description and justification, character reports (one per actor).

ẽᴑ

డ

HANDOUT 12

SCENES FOR FINAL PERFORMANCE

1.2.47–108   Benvolio and Romeo intercept an invitation to the Capulet feast.
Lines: Benvolio, 20; Romeo, 30; Servingman, 12

1.3.1–113   Juliet, her nurse, and her mother talk about her childhood and a possible marriage to Paris.
Lines: Lady Capulet, 37; Nurse, 64; Juliet, 7; Servingman, 5

2.4.1–103   Mercutio and Benvolio tease Romeo about his new love.
Lines: Mercutio, 71; Benvolio, 11; Romeo, 21

2.4.104–219   Mercutio, Benvolio, and Romeo joke around with Juliet's nurse and Peter. Romeo tells the nurse about the wedding arrangements.
Lines: Romeo, 32; Mercutio, 21; Nurse, 55; Peter, 7; Benvolio, 1

2.5   Juliet and her nurse discuss the merits of Romeo.
Lines: Juliet, 46; Nurse, 37

3.3.1–87   Friar Lawrence, Romeo, and the nurse talk about Romeo's banishment.
Lines: Friar Lawrence, 31; Romeo, 54; Nurse, 2

3.4   Capulet and Paris agree on a wedding date.
Lines: Capulet, 31; Paris, 5; Lady Capulet, 2

3.5.1–68   Romeo and Juliet curse the dawn because Romeo must leave.
Lines: Juliet, 40; Romeo, 24; Nurse, 3; Lady Capulet, 1

3.5.69–130   Lady Capulet tells Juliet she must marry Paris.
Lines: Lady Capulet, 31; Juliet, 31

3.5.131–215   Juliet tells her father she refuses to marry.
Lines: Capulet, 64; Lady Capulet, 6; Juliet, 11; Nurse, 4

4.1.1–50   Friar Lawrence, Juliet, and the County Paris meet outside Friar Lawrence's cell.
Lines: Friar Lawrence, 12; Paris, 23; Juliet, 15

4.2   Juliet begs her father's pardon.
Lines: Capulet, 27; Servingman, 5; Nurse, 2; Juliet, 12; Lady Capulet, 3

5.3.195–321   The prince, the Capulets, Montague, and Friar Lawrence try to understand what caused the deaths of Romeo and Juliet.
Lines: Prince, 39; Capulet, 10; Lady Capulet, 5; First Watch, 6; Montague, 10; Friar Lawrence, 46; Balthasar, 6; Page, 5

డ

HANDOUT 13

PROMPTBOOK—COMPANY REPORT

After you have read your scene aloud, answer the following questions:

1. What happens in your scene? Outline the basic events.

a.

b.

c.

d.

2. What do you think are the key purposes of your scene?

a.

b.

c.

(Keep these purposes in mind as you make decisions about blocking and characterization.)

3. What are your reactions to this scene?

ಏ

HANDOUT 14

PROMPTBOOK—CHARACTER REPORT

No matter how big or small the part, every actor needs to know the answers to the following questions:

1. What does your character want in this scene?

2. What is your character's motivation for doing what he or she does?

3. What obstacles stand in his or her way?

4. What happens when your character confronts these obstacles?

5. Are there any distinctive elements in your character's way of speaking? (Is his or her language elaborate, plain, musical, or what?)

6. What is your character thinking during the scene? (How does he or she react to the other characters and events?)

ಏ

෧

PROMPTBOOK EVALUATION

ACTING COMPANY:

COMPANY MEMBERS:

_____ 1. Completeness (60 points total)
     a. Company Report (10 points)
     b. Set Design (10 points)
     c. Prompt Pages (20 points)
     d. Costume Drawing/Description and Justification (10 points)
     e. Character Reports (10 points)

_____ 2. Accuracy (20 points)

_____ 3. Effort (10 points)

_____ 4. Neatness/Appearance (10 points)

_____ TOTAL

COMMENTS:

෧

PERFORMANCE EVALUATION

ACTING COMPANY NAME:

SCENE PERFORMED:

CHARACTER	PLAYED BY	COMMENTS

POINTS POSSIBLE	POINTS AWARDED	TO WHAT EXTENT DOES THE PERFORMANCE SHOW:
15		Careful Reading and Rehearsal
15		Understanding of Characters
15		Understanding of Plot
20		Understanding of Language
15		Ability to Use Language to Portray Character
10		Well Planned Movements
10		Well Planned Use of Props and Costumes
(BONUS)		Something Extra
100 TOTAL (+ BONUS)		

COMMENTS:

Macbeth

·

CHRISTOPHER D. RENINO
EDITOR

Dear Colleagues,
    You enter *Macbeth* to a question:

> When shall we three meet again?
> In thunder, lightning, or in rain?

Then blood runs under cloak of night; a ghost shakes gory locks at a usurping king. And several murders, apparitions, and a suicide later, you exit darkness, invitation to a coronation in hand. At the very least, you feel entertained. With any luck you will feel flat out elevated.

Try telling that to most teenagers. The classroom spokesperson for the vast majority groans, "Shakespeare? This is going to be impossible. Forget it, I can't read books written in Old English." The can-do kid responds from the front of the room, "Oh, come on, just try. It'll make sense once you translate it." Optimism and determination aside, these two are twins: they see Shakespeare's plays as printed words in a dead language, a bookworm's aerobics.

Why are some captivated while others are turned off? After all, the play's words never change. Macbeth always says, "I have done the deed." Macduff always says, "Turn, hell hound, turn!" Too often we communicate that the plays are sacred texts, and we distribute them with the well-intentioned but misguided assumption that our students should eagerly study them with the same reverent devotion that monks dedicate to their holy books. God knows teenagers are not monks. Look at how they spend their days. They like wooing and sword-swinging and bragging and swearing and vengeance. *Macbeth* is loaded with those things. So how do you get a kid to see that?

By teaching the play as living spoken language, best experienced on stage by every comer. I mean that literally. I have designed this unit with the belief that putting the words of *Macbeth* into the mouths of students and giving them the chance to become actors, directors, and artistic consultants of their own staged scenes leads them to enjoyment and understanding of the play. There will be times when the dictionary is the best tool in the shed and when there will be no substitute for asking students to write about what they have learned; but those activities will be the supplements, not the core, of this unit.

Most of the lessons in this unit build on what students learned in previous lessons. Likewise, the culminating activities call for application of the skills taught in the daily lessons. For this reason, I recommend that you teach all the lessons. However, those who don't have time to teach the whole play or who want to dip into a few scenes might use the following two-week sequence of lessons:

WEEK ONE
Lesson 2: "All Hail, Macbeth!"
Lesson 3: "There to Meet with Macbeth"
Lesson 6: "Look Like th' Innocent Flower . . ."
Lesson 7: "If It Were Done When 'Tis Done"

WEEK TWO
Lesson 9: "I Dreamt Last Night of the Three Weird Sisters"
Lesson 13: "Fly, Good Fleance, Fly!"
Lesson 14: "Thou Art the Best o' the Cutthroats"
Lesson 15: "Hold, Enough"

Those teaching a two-week unit to students who are capable of reading and understanding the play on their own might use the following sequence of lessons:

WEEK ONE
Students read the first two acts on their own and follow these in-class lessons:
   Lesson 2: "All Hail, Macbeth!"
   Lesson 3: "There to Meet with Macbeth"
   Lesson 5: "Blood Will Have Blood"
   Lesson 6: "Look Like th' Innocent Flower . . ."

WEEK TWO
Students read the last three acts on their own and follow these in-class lessons:
   Lesson 10: "There's Daggers in Men's Smiles"
   Lesson 12: "Ride You This Afternoon?"
   Lesson 18: "Hell Is Murky"
   Lesson 20: "Out, Out Brief Candle"

I wish you best of luck with this unit; I hope it helps you to exorcise those demons that insist a Shakespeare unit with teenagers is an unavoidable annual penance. If you do succeed, you will likely be as grateful as I am to the participants and instructors of the Teaching Shakespeare Institute of the Folger Shakespeare Library whose work inspired this unit. And I hope your success will help you to understand why I wish to give special recognition to Kathleen Breen, Louisville, Kentucky; Lynn Frick, Madison, Wisconsin; Mary Beth Maitoza, North Providence, Rhode Island; and Michael LoMonico, Stony Brook, New York, whose work on this unit demonstrates that they know as much about teaching *Macbeth* to secondary students as anyone you'll ever meet.

Chris Renino
Scarsdale Senior High School
Scarsdale, New York

UNIT CALENDAR FOR
Macbeth

❧ 1	❧ 2	❧ 3	❧ 4	❧ 5
LESSON 1 Introductory Exercises	LESSON 2 Taking the Plunge Text: 1.3.1–112	LESSON 3 Staging a Scene Text: 1.1–2	LESSON 4 Denotation, Connotation, Stress, and Inflection in 1.3–4 Text: 1.3–4	LESSON 5 Tracing a Word from the Play
❧ 6	❧ 7	❧ 8	❧ 9	❧ 10
LESSON 6 Text and Subtext, 1.5–6 Text: 1.5–6	LESSON 7 Soliloquies for Everyone Text: 7.1–96	LESSON 8 Modeling the Word Journal	LESSON 9 The Promptbook Text: 2.1–2	LESSON 9 The Promptbook *(cont.)* Text: 2.1–2
❧ 11	❧ 12	❧ 13	❧ 14	❧ 15
LESSON 10 Character Committees	LESSON 11 Act 2 Word Journals	LESSON 12 The Promptbook Revisited Text: 3.1	LESSON 13 Editing a Text and Performing a Murder Text: 3.2–3	LESSON 14 Comparative Film Text: 3.4
❧ 16	❧ 17	❧ 18	❧ 19	❧ 20
LESSON 15 Choral Reading, Staged Reading Text: 3.5–4.1	LESSON 16 Reports from Act 3 Word Journals	LESSON 17 Looking at Macduff Text: 4.2–3	LESSON 18 Lady Macbeth's Decline Text: 5.1	LESSON 19 Concluding the Reading of the Play Text: 5.2–8
❧ 21	❧ 22	❧ 23	❧ 24	❧ 25
LESSON 19 Concluding the Reading of the Play *(cont.)* Text: 5.2–8	LESSON 19 Concluding the Reading of the Play *(cont.)* Text: 5.2–8	LESSON 20 The Concluding Word Web	LESSON 21 Culminating Performances	LESSON 21 Culminating Performances *(cont.)*
❧ 26	❧ 27	❧ 28	❧ 29	
LESSON 21 Culminating Performances *(cont.)*	LESSON 21 Culminating Performances *(cont.)*	LESSON 21 Culminating Performances *(cont.)*	LESSON 21 Culminating Performances *(cont.)*	

LESSON **1** "Hail, Brave Friend"

Introductory Exercises

WHAT'S ON FOR TODAY AND WHY

In this unit, we want students to engage with *Macbeth* as completely and personally as possible. Lying between the students and this goal is Shakespeare's language—rich, complex, archaic, timely, poetic, confusing, and clear. In this lesson, students will confront that language on the idea level and on the word level. First, students will improvise and perform short skits based on scenarios that anticipate the characters, events, and conflicts they will encounter in the early acts of *Macbeth*. Then they will speak lines in an exercise that gives them a chance to hear and feel the bloody language of the play cross their teeth. Finally, they will connect to *Macbeth* by writing personal experiences based on a *Macbeth* theme.

If students are not already using a journal—or log, or notebook, or portfolio—we need to take a few minutes to establish one, since we will use a *Macbeth* journal (i.e., spiral notebook) for writing assignments, notes, summaries, or drawings almost every day.

You may gulp when you see that right from the beginning we ask teachers to stand out of the way and let students do Shakespeare. Certainly this approach results in some oddly pronounced words and stammered lines, but we are willing to tolerate beginners' mistakes in order to activate students' engagement with the play.

WHAT TO DO

1. Improvisation

Divide the class into small groups, and give each group a card with one of the following situations written on it:

- Situation 1: While walking home together, two close friends are told by a reliable source that each will get the thing he or she covets more than anything else: a date with that special someone; the one and only car of its kind; the last ticket to the best seat for the greatest performance of a favorite band or team. Big problem: there are two friends but only one date or car or ticket, and each of the friends wants it.

- Situation 2: An ambitious man sees an illegal way to become head of his company or country, but his cautiousness and loyalty make him indecisive about pursuing his goal. His motto: "Maybe tomorrow." He shares his ambition with his equally ambitious wife, who is refined and elegant on the outside but a "killer" within. Her motto is "Just do it."

- Situation 3: Several longtime friends get together for a meal. After the ice cream they take a siesta only to be suddenly awakened by the cries of one of the guests, who discovers that his money is missing.

Give each group five minutes to brainstorm a list of scenarios that might result if this situation were to take place.

Each group should now take 15 minutes to create a short skit based on one of these scenarios. Have each group present its skit for the whole class.

Class size will probably require that a given scenario be performed by more than one group. Once the skits have been presented, lead a short discussion of the different choices made by groups working with the same scenario. In what ways were the moods of the skits different? Then explain that these scenarios anticipate the play that students will begin reading in class the next day.

2. Tossing Lines

Push back the desks. Place eight chairs in a small circle at the front of the room, and ask for eight volunteers to take those seats. Give each one a card that has one of the following lines from Act 1 of *Macbeth* written on it:

> Fair is foul, and foul is fair . . . (1.1.12)

> So foul and fair a day I have not seen. (1.3.39)

> If chance will have me king, why, chance may crown me
> Without my stir.   (1.3.157–159)

> Stars, hide your fires;
> Let not light see my black and deep desires. (1.4.57–58)

> Yet do I fear thy nature;
> It is too full o' th' milk of human kindness . . . (1.5.16–17)

> Come, you spirits
> That tend on mortal thoughts, unsex me here . . . (1.5.47–48)

> Look like th' innocent flower,
> But be the serpent under 't. (1.5.76–78)

> If it were done when 'tis done, then 'twere well
> It were done quickly.   (1.7.1–2)

Allow each student a moment to become familiar with his quotation. Then ask him to shout it out as the rest of the class listens. After each volunteer has been heard, give one of them a tennis ball or bean bag; he is to shout out his line, then toss the ball to another person in the circle. (Extra credit for throwing strikes. Spit balls are banned.) The recipient calls out his line and passes the ball to another reader in the circle, and so on. After several rounds, put the ball away and ask the class to join in and recite each line in chorus.

TOMORROW AND TOMORROW AND TOMORROW

Journal entry: Has there ever been a time in your life when someone told you that something improbable would happen and it did? Did the fact that the event was "predicted" cause you to behave differently than you would have otherwise and make it more likely for the event to occur? Or did the event simply seem to occur without any assistance from you?

Recall what happened and include your feelings when you heard the event predicted and when it occurred.

HOW DID IT GO?

If students enjoyed the skits and were able to recall the lines from Act 1 with some accuracy, the day was a success because students are already making their own discoveries about the plot and language of *Macbeth*.

LESSON **2** "All Hail, Macbeth!"

Taking the Plunge

PLAY SECTION COVERED IN THIS LESSON

1.3.1–112 Macbeth and Banquo meet three witches who prophesy great things for them.

LINES: First Witch, 35; Second Witch, 12; Third Witch, 14; Macbeth, 15; Banquo, 27; Ross, 16; Angus, 4

WHAT'S ON FOR TODAY AND WHY

Students' first exposure to the play will involve reading aloud and acting the parts of characters, things they will do throughout this unit. Although this lesson will work with any scene in Shakespeare, we will use 1.3.1–112 because it introduces several important characters and an important part of the plot. It will serve as a preview to *Macbeth*, and students will greet it as an old friend when we come to it again.

WHAT TO DO

1. Actors' Circle

Arrange the room so students are seated in a circle. Pass out a script of 1.3.1–112. (See page 28 of Michael Tolaydo's "Three-Dimensional Shakespeare" for instructions on script preparation.)

Tell students they will read, in turn, one line of text. (Many times the line will end in the middle of a thought.) Tell students to listen for and underline any words, phrases, or ideas they don't understand. After the reading, ask students to point out words they don't know. Ask if others can explain the meaning of the words. Brief explanations of Elizabethan constructions will be helpful here—see Lesson 4 of *A Midsummer Night's Dream*.

Go around the room again (in the opposite direction so students will be reading different lines), only this time have each student read until she encounters a long pause (colon, semicolon) or full stop (period, question mark, exclamation point). Ask after the reading: "What's going on here? Who are these people? What clues do you get about them and about the action?"

Try another round, this time letting each student read until the passage indicates a change in the character who delivers the lines, whereupon the next student in the circle begins reading. As students read, they should try to use their voices to convey the mood or emotion suggested by the words. Ask questions that are more specific: "What do the witches look like and what is the 'charm' they refer to in line 38? What predictions do the witches make for Macbeth and Banquo, and how do these men receive them? What news do Ross and Angus bring Macbeth and Banquo?"

Assign two students to each part (Witches 1, 2, and 3, Macbeth, Banquo, Ross, Angus). Get one "cast" on its feet and up in front of the class. Ask these students to read the script aloud. Then ask the second cast to do the same. As each cast reads, try some variations:

- Cast 1: Macbeth and Banquo are confident men who eagerly follow Witches 1, 2, and 3 around the room, hungry for news. The witches avoid their pursuit, finally vanishing.
- Cast 2: Turn out the lights and have Macbeth and Banquo enter looking fearful. They jump in fright when the witches appear. The witches' pursuit of *them* causes them to retreat coweringly.

If time permits, do the scene a third time with student suggestions.

2. Conclusions

Ask which variation worked best and why. Then explain that tomorrow's lesson will deal with the play from the beginning and provide background information that will lead to a better understanding of the significance of this scene's events.

TOMORROW AND TOMORROW AND TOMORROW

Divide students into groups of four or five. Tell them that tomorrow they will do a project for which each group will need the following materials: a duplicated copy of *Macbeth* 1.2, a shoe box, crayons or markers, a dozen or so buttons, coins, Legos, or other similar objects of various colors and shapes. Give the groups five minutes to meet and divide up the tasks of who will bring what.

HOW DID IT GO?

There will still be heads shaking and exclamations of puzzlement at the end of the lesson, but if students showed by questions and comments that they have a beginning understanding of the characters and conflicts in *Macbeth*, you have led them into the play.

LESSON **3** "There to Meet with Macbeth"

Staging a Scene

ဒ&_____

PLAY SECTIONS COVERED IN THIS LESSON

1.1 The witches confer.

LINES: First Witch, 6; Second Witch, 6; Third Witch, 5

1.2 Duncan hears reports of Macbeth's valor and the thane of Cawdor's disloyalty. He orders Cawdor's execution and gives his title to Macbeth.

LINES: Duncan, 16; Malcolm, 6; Captain, 35; Lennox, 3; Ross, 18

ဒ&

WHAT'S ON FOR TODAY AND WHY

Students will work in groups as teams of "directors" to make decisions about entrances, exits, positioning, and movement of characters in 1.2. While focusing on these decisions, they will read, read, read the script.

Throughout the unit, we will stop and show excerpts from film versions of *Macbeth.* There are many available:

- The 1948 Republic Pictures and Mercury Films production directed by Orson Welles and starring Orson Welles and Jeanette Nolan is available through The Writing Company (1-800-421-4246).
- The 1954 Hallmark Hall of Fame production has the same cast as above, but unlike that one which was filmed on location, this was a studio production. It is available through The Writing Company (1-800-421-4246).
- The 1960 Hallmark Hall of Fame production directed by George Schaefer and starring Maurice Evans and Judith Anderson is available through Insight Media (1-800-233-9910).
- The 1971 Playboy Productions movie directed by Roman Polanski and starring Jon Finch and Francesca Annis is available through Facets Multimedia (1-800-331-6197).
- The 1979 Royal Shakespeare Company and Thames TV production produced by Trevor Nunn, directed by Philip Casson, and starring Ian McKellen and Judi Dench is available through Films for the Humanities (1-800-257-5126).
- The 1981 Bard Series production starring Jeremy Brett and Piper Laurie is available through The Writing Company (1-800-421-4246).
- The 1982 BBC: The Shakespeare Plays production directed by Jack

Gold and starring Nicol Williamson and Jane Lapotaire is available through Ambrose Video (1-800-526-4663).

- The 1982 Lincoln Center production directed by Sarah Caldwell and starring Philip Anglim and Maureen Anderman is available through Films for the Humanities (1-800-257-5126).
- The 1988 Thames TV production stars Michael Jayson as Macbeth and Barbara Leigh as Lady Macbeth. It is available through The Writing Company (1-800-421-4246).
- The 1998 English Shakespeare Company's production, directed by Michael Bogdanov, was originally shown in installments on Britain's Channel Four. Set in a post-apocalyptic world, the film features Sean Pertwee as Macbeth and Greta Scacchi as Lady Macbeth.

Before this unit, choose at least two productions and have them on hand. For today's lesson, cue up one of the productions to 1.2. If you like, also locate an audio recording and cue it up to 1.1.

WHAT TO DO

1. Listening to 1.1 and 1.2

Play a recording of 1.1 and 1.2, and ask students to read along in their books as they listen to it, or cast the parts and ask students to read aloud. Talk about the characters, the setting, and the plot. Where does this take place and what is the weather like? How does Macbeth behave in battle? How does Duncan view this behavior? How does the battle end? What pronouncement does Duncan make at the end of the scene? Add your own questions as you see fit, but keep the discussion crisp. The goal here is to familiarize students with the scenes.

2. Shoe Box Staging

Convene the groups you established yesterday. Tell each group to take its "stage" (the shoe box) and "characters" (the buttons, coins, etc.), identify a setting, and draw it inside the box. Then have each group reread 1.2 and move their "characters" around inside the box as they see fit, based on the scene's dialogue. Students should note their movements on their scripts. Circulate as students do this activity. Let students make their own decisions about the scene, but urge them always to use the script as their authority. If they get stuck, prod them with questions such as the following:

- When and how do the various characters move as the Captain delivers his lines?
- Who stands closest to Duncan? Why?
- Does any character move as he speaks? How and where?
- Do any characters touch? When? How?
- In what direction does the Captain exit (after line 48), and from where do Ross and Angus enter (after line 48)?
- What is their mood?
- How does the scene end, and how do the characters exit: Together? Separately? Who leads? Why?

Have groups get together and demonstrate their staging choices to one another.

3. Checking with Professional Directors

Show a film version of this scene to give students a chance to compare their choices with those of the film director. Discuss the differences. For this scene, the Roman Polanski production is the best because the camera shows many full-body shots so students can see where actors move—it even shows Cawdor hanging. The Royal Shakespeare Company and BBC productions emphasize staging but show more closeups. In the Welles version, 1.2 is omitted.

TOMORROW AND TOMORROW AND TOMORROW

Journal entry: Choose two of the characters you have met to this point and draw or cut from a magazine a picture of them. Under each picture, list three words that capture the character's personality.

HOW DID IT GO?

You will be able to judge the success of this lesson as you watch and listen while the groups stage their scenes and discuss their choices with one another. If students took charge of the scene, visualized a set, moved characters around in it, and used Shakespeare's lines as the authority for all of this, they are **doing** *Macbeth*. If when you showed them the film they thought they did the scene better than Polanski (or Gold or Nunn), you know that they sank their teeth into this scene.

LESSON 4 "Is Execution Done on Cawdor?"

Denotation, Connotation, Stress, and Inflection in 1.3 and 1.4

ཨེ๑

PLAY SECTIONS COVERED IN THIS LESSON

1.3 Soon after the three witches prophesy that Macbeth will be the thane of Cawdor, Ross and Angus arrive with the news of Macbeth's new title. Macbeth then contemplates the witches' other prophecies: that Banquo will be the father of kings, and that Macbeth will be king.

LINES: First Witch, 35; Second Witch, 12; Third Witch, 14; Macbeth, 54; Banquo, 42; Ross, 16; Angus, 13

1.4 Duncan announces that his son Malcolm will be the heir to the throne and says that he will spend the night at Inverness, Macbeth's castle.

LINES: Duncan, 37; Malcolm, 10; Macbeth, 16; Banquo, 2

ཨེ๑

WHAT'S ON FOR TODAY AND WHY

Students will work with denotation, connotation, stress, inflection, and nonverbal communication. As well as helping students read more carefully for nuances in the words of the play, these exercises will help them in subsequent lessons, particularly Lesson 6, which deals with subtext.

For additional work with denotation and connotation, stress and inflection, and nonverbal communication inspired by Paul Cartier, Folger teacher from Providence, Rhode Island, see Lesson 8 of *A Midsummer Night's Dream* and Lesson 17 of *Romeo and Juliet*.

WHAT TO DO

1. Reading 1.3 and 1.4

Assign parts and get students in front of the class to read 1.3 (which should be familiar) and 1.4. Ask questions: How does Banquo feel about the witches' predictions? How does Macbeth feel? Who is the topic of conversation at the start of scene 4? How might Duncan's words to Macbeth, as Macbeth enters, seem ironic? How does Macbeth feel now that Malcolm has been named Prince of Cumberland? Do we have any clues about how he will behave in the future?

2. Denotation and Connotation

Write the following words on the board—*thin, woman, man*—and have students create a list of synonyms for each. Ask these questions: What are the differences in meaning between the words in a given list? (For example: *thin, skinny,* and *svelte.*) Which are the more powerful words in each list and why? Now define denotation (the literal meaning of a word) and connotation (a secondary meaning suggested by a word in addition to its literal meaning). Discuss how a word's power is determined in part by the associations one brings to the word. Now write the following sentence on the board:

So foul and fair a day I have not seen.

Ask students for a list of synonyms for the words *foul* and *fair.* Rewrite a sentence a number of times using these synonyms. For example:

- So cloudy and clear a day I have not seen.
- So nasty and beautiful a day I have not seen.
- So rotten and just a day I have not seen.
- So ugly and adequate a day I have not seen.

Discuss how the denotations and connotations of these replacement synonyms affect our understanding of the sentence. This might be a good time to talk about the paradoxical nature of the sentence and how it might be confusing. Question: Who can recall other contradictions in this scene? Examples:

- The witches seem to be women, but they have beards (lines 47–49).
- "Lesser than Macbeth and greater" (line 68)
- "Not so happy, yet much happier" (line 69)

Tell students that paradoxes will continue to appear throughout the play and that they should keep this in mind as they read.

3. Stressing Stress

Write the following sentence on the board:

He was a gentleman on whom I built an absolute trust.

Define *stress:* the relative force with which a sound or syllable is spoken. Have six students read the sentence, each stressing a different one of the following words: *he, was, gentleman, I, absolute,* and *trust.* Discuss how the meaning of the sentence changes with each reading. For example, when *I* is stressed, the meaning is "*I* trusted him and he betrayed *me.*" When *absolute* is stressed, the sentence suggests a trust without qualification and, therefore, indicates the speaker's surprise or disappointment at being betrayed.

4. Inflection

Write the following sentence on the board:

Is execution done on Cawdor?

Define *inflection:* a change in pitch or tone of the voice. Have two students read the sentence. The first student's voice should rise as he reads the sentence (implying a question); the second student's voice should go down as he reads (implying a statement). Discuss the difference in meaning between the two readings. The first might suggest that

Duncan is uncertain that his order has been carried out; perhaps he is even fearful of being disobeyed. The second convinces the speaker and the listener alike that Duncan presumes that the execution has been done; he seems strong and confident.

Ask for one more reading of this line, coaching the speaker to pause for two seconds before saying "on Cawdor?" Ask students to describe how the meaning of the sentence is affected by the pause.

5. Adding Nonverbal Communication

Call a student to a seat in the front of the room and dub him Malcolm. Name a second student Duncan and tell him to walk slowly toward the seated Malcolm, cross his arms, and stare at him without saying a word. Explain that this is *nonverbal communication* and ask what meaning was implied without words. Have the students repeat this scenario, with Duncan finally saying his line: "Is execution done on Cawdor?" How does the meaning change?

TOMORROW AND TOMORROW AND TOMORROW

Journal entry: Write three sentences often said to you by someone close to you: a parent, a brother or sister, a friend. Indicate the typical inflection and meaning for each; then vary the inflection and tell how this changes the meaning.

HOW DID IT GO?

Student understanding should be evident from class discussion and journal entries. Ask yourself:

- Did students practice speaking and reading skills that will help them to interpret the script?
- To what extent are they able to distinguish between denotation and connotation?
- Can they vary the message conveyed in a line by varying stress and inflection?

If they picked up on any of these skills, their thoughts while reading *Macbeth* will expand to include not only the surface message of the words but also the implied messages associated with them.

LESSON 5 "Blood Will Have Blood"

Tracing a Word from the Play

WHAT'S ON FOR TODAY AND WHY

Among the most important, frequently appearing words in *Macbeth* are *blood* (41 times), *hand* (33 times), *night* (35 times), and *sleep* (32 times). (These counts are from WordCruncher, a computer program mentioned below; the counts include the words' various forms—e.g., *blood* and *bloody, night* and *tonight.*) Each student will adopt one of these words and record its use in an assigned act. Concentrating on how the denotations and connotations of the words are related to the people who say them, students will come to conclusions about characters and ideas in *Macbeth* based on key words and their contexts.

There are, of course, many other important, frequently used words in addition to these four. This assignment might be expanded, for an advanced class, to include these words, and such a group might trace their use throughout the entire play rather than in a single act. For a list of words and the frequency of their appearance in the play as counted from a concordance, see Skip Nicholson's Key Word Frequency List: *Macbeth* at the end of this lesson. (You will notice that Nicholson's count and the WordCruncher count do not match. This is because the WordCruncher computer program counts all forms of the word.)

For our work today, we will need to prepare Handout 1: Tracing a Word in *Macbeth* plus a transparency of the sample word journal contained in the handout. It is desirable but not mandatory to have in the classroom a Shakespeare concordance (e.g., *The Harvard Concordance to Shakespeare*). Teachers with computers in the classroom would benefit from one of the Shakespeare software programs like WordCruncher or Shakespeare on Disk that allow users to search a word throughout a play or part of a play.

WHAT TO DO

1. Tracing a Word in *Macbeth*

Distribute Handout 1 to students and ask them to read it. Discuss and clarify the information.

2. Modeling the Word Trace

To demonstrate the assignment, assume the part of a student and do a word trace for *blood* in Act 1. Put on the overhead a transparency of the sample word journal in Handout 1, and use a cover sheet to reveal the information little by little. As you "work" the assignment, solicit student help. It is the conclusion part of this assignment, rather than the recording or paraphrasing portion, that students find most challenging.

You can assist them by suggesting that they consider questions like the following as they make their conclusions:

- Does one character use the word most frequently? If so, who?
- Does the word's meaning change as different characters use it?
- What is happening in the play at the time the word is spoken? Is there any connection between these events and others that precede them?
- What emotions does the speaker feel as he uses the word? Why does he feel as he does?

3. Organizing Future Word Traces

Tell students that each of them will trace the use of one of these words—*blood, hands, night,* or *sleep*—in either Act 2 or Act 3. Assign a word and act to each student. Tell them to start on their assignment as soon as we get to their act. Give them an approximate date for their report.

TOMORROW AND TOMORROW AND TOMORROW

Assign 1.5 and 1.6 for reading. If time permits, start this assignment in class.

HOW DID IT GO?

To evaluate this lesson, ask yourself:

- Did students focus on a single word and its messages?
- Did they see how the messages accrue as different speakers use the word?
- Did they see how the messages varied with the changing context?
- Were they able to relate the word to character and situation?

If so, they are using a word as a way into *Macbeth,* and they have a basis for drawing conclusions about characters.

ও

HANDOUT 1

TRACING A WORD IN *MACBETH*

During our study of *Macbeth*, you will each be responsible for keeping a "word journal" in which you identify how the meaning of a specific word is shaped by the situation in which it is used and the character who uses it.

Starting at the beginning of the act you were assigned, find the word every time it appears. A concordance or computer program is a great help here, but if these are not available, reading the act and scanning for the word is fine. Each time you find the word, make an entry in your word journal.

Guidelines for Each Entry

1. Write out the passage that contains your word and give act, scene, and line numbers—for example, 2.3.3–5. Record enough of the passage to make its meaning clear; avoid cutting it off in mid-thought. Identify the speaker.

2. Clarify the meaning of the passage by putting it into your own words. This is called paraphrasing. Then briefly explain what is happening in the play at the time the words in this passage are spoken.

3. Draw conclusions about how the word is used. For example, compare the passage to one you recorded earlier by explaining how the meaning of your word is affected by the character who uses it and the situation in which it is used.

4. At the end of your act, use the journal to draw more conclusions: What character uses the word most often? How does the denotation and connotation of the word change from character to character? Is there an unusual use of the word? How does this word affect the act you studied?

Sample Word Journal

This is what an entry might look like for the word *blood* in Act 1.

1. a. Quotation and speaker	Duncan: What bloody man is that? He can report, / As seemeth by his plight, of the revolt / The newest state. (1.2.1–3)	
b. Paraphrase and clarification	Who is that bloody man? It looks like he has been fighting against the revolt and can give us the latest news of the battle. King Duncan is on or near the battlefield and wants to know how the fight is going.	
c. Conclusions	First quote; no comparison yet. Duncan trusts a bloody soldier whose blood gives him the authority to report on the battle.	
2. a. Quotation and speaker	Captain: For brave Macbeth (well he deserves that name), / Disdaining Fortune, with his brandished steel, / Which smoked with bloody execution, / Like valor's minion, carved out his passage / Till he faced the slave . . . (1.2.18–22)	

  b. Paraphrase and clarification — In spite of our troops' bad luck, brave Macbeth carved his way with his executioner's sword through the ranks of rebel soldiers until he faced the traitor who led the revolt. The captain reports to King Duncan that Macbeth fought fiercely to spill the blood of the traitors who rebelled against Duncan and Scotland.

  c. Conclusions — In the first passage, the loyal Scottish captain is bloody because of the rebels' uprising. Because of his bravery, fierceness, and loyalty, Macbeth makes the rebels bloody.

3. a. Quotation and speaker — Lady M.: Make thick my blood. / Stop up th' access and passage to remorse . . . (1.5.50–51)

  b. Paraphrase and clarification — Make my blood thick so I can be cold-hearted and feel no sorrow or guilt about planning this murder. Lady Macbeth wants to convince Macbeth to kill Duncan. In order to do so, she hopes to become more mannish and heartless.

  c. Conclusions — Early in the play, soldiers get bloody as they try to overthrow Scotland. Then Scottish soldiers get bloody overthrowing the rebels. Lady Macbeth wants to overthrow King Duncan, so she is going to have to get bloody too. But before she can make Duncan's blood flow, she is going to have to change her blood—slow it down, make it cold. She talks as if she can change her personality by changing her blood.

General Conclusions for Act 1:

1. In Act 1 it is a good thing to be bloody, especially for *men* to be bloody—the king trusts the bloody soldier, and people admire Macbeth because he has a bloody sword and has killed lots of soldiers. Lady Macbeth thinks it might be good for her and her husband to be bloody—she wants to slow down her blood and be like a man and make Duncan's blood flow.

2. Even before we meet him, Macbeth is bloody—he comes onstage with a bloody sword.

KEY WORD FREQUENCY LIST:

MACBETH

Rank	Frequency	Word	Rank	Frequency	Word
1	52	come	38	15	dead
2	51	good	39	15	friend(s)
3	44	time	40	15	heaven
4	42	Macbeth	41	14	air
5	40	king(s)	42	14	bloody
6	39	say	43	14	God
7	35	fear	44	14	name
8	34	lord	45	13	dare
9	33	hand(s)	46	13	Duncan
10	31	great	47	13	father
11	31	see	48	13	noble
12	29	man	49	13	pray
13	29	sir	50	13	sword
14	26	sleep	51	13	think
15	25	thane	52	13	wife
16	24	thought(s)	53	12	fly
17	23	blood	54	12	keep
18	23	look	55	12	leave
19	22	Banquo	56	12	new
20	22	eye(s)	57	12	Scotland
21	22	heart	58	11	bed
22	22	night	59	11	knock
23	21	Cawdor	60	11	peace
24	20	death	61	11	stand
25	20	live(s)	62	11	welcome
26	20	nature	63	11	wood
27	19	love	64	10	Birnam
28	18	day	65	10	face
29	18	hear	66	10	fight
30	18	life	67	10	grace
31	17	show	68	10	honor
32	17	worthy	69	10	hour
33	16	hail	70	10	place
34	16	Macduff	71	10	tonight
35	16	men	72	10	woman
36	16	poor	73	10	words
37	16	strange			

LESSON 6 "Look Like th' Innocent Flower, but Be the Serpent Under 't"

Text and Subtext in 1.5 and 1.6

❧ _____

PLAY SECTIONS COVERED IN THIS LESSON

1.5 Lady Macbeth reads a letter from her husband telling about his promotion and saying that King Duncan will be visiting in their castle tonight. She greets him with plans of regicide.

LINES: Lady Macbeth, 77; Messenger, 5; Macbeth, 4

1.6 Lady Macbeth welcomes Duncan to Inverness.

LINES: Duncan, 19; Banquo, 9; Lady Macbeth, 11

❧ _____

WHAT'S ON FOR TODAY AND WHY

Today's lesson is about *subtext*, which can be defined as the thoughts we imagine a character has as he speaks the words in the text. The work we did with denotation, connotation, stress, and inflection in Lesson 4 is a basis for work on subtext. Students will create their own characters, scenarios, and subtext from a given dialogue, work with a pair of lines from 5.7, then apply what they have learned to 1.5.61–86. Our goal is to help students ascribe interior thoughts to characters by carefully reading their lines. For further work on subtext, read Lesson 8 of *A Midsummer Night's Dream* and Lesson 17 of *Romeo and Juliet*.

WHAT TO DO

1. Reviewing the Techniques to Convey Subtext

Spend a few moments reviewing denotation, connotation, stress, inflection, pauses, and nonverbal communication (Lesson 4).

2. Defining and Practicing Subtext

Write this sentence on the board: "You've made me very happy, dear." Ask the class to say it aloud in unison. Then ask various students to say the sentence with one of the following thoughts in mind:

- "You just promoted me to a better job."
- "You just told me I won the lottery."
- "You just wrecked my new car."
- "It's not Janie I care about; you are my hero."

Lead a discussion:

· Were all the messages the same?
· What was the same each time? What changed?
· How did that work? Why?

Students will quickly see that although the words (or text) are the same in each repetition, those words are spoken differently as the underlying thought changes. Tell the class that the term for those underlying thoughts is *subtext* and give them this definition: Subtext is the thought we imagine a character has as he speaks the words in the text.

3. More Subtext Exercises

Do another exercise. Ask five student volunteers to make up and write down on a piece of paper a subtext for this line: "Oh, no you won't."

Call on each to deliver the line with the subtext in mind. (It might be helpful to suggest a character who says this line: father, lover, spy.) Let the class guess what the subtext might be.

Repeat this exercise, using subtexts suggested by students, for the following lines:

· "Is that a new hairdo?"
· "So you want to borrow my car?"

4. Reading Subtext from Stress and Inflection

Work backward from stress and inflection. Put this sentence on the board: "He never had a single chance."

Call on different students to read the sentence aloud, stressing a different word each time. ("*He* never had a single chance," "He *never* had a single chance," and so forth.) After each reading, ask the class what subtext is implied.

5. Shakespearean Subtext

Work with Shakespearean subtexts. Start with a very short exchange from 5.7, written on the board or distributed in a handout:

YOUNG SIWARD What is thy name?
MACBETH Thou'lt be afraid to hear it.

Changing student actors, run the scene many times with students on their feet, using a variety of subtexts:

YOUNG SIWARD This is boring. I wish I were back in Kansas with Dorothy.
MACBETH I'm going to scare the wits out of this little nerd.

YOUNG SIWARD I'm scared spitless of this monster.
MACBETH I'm going to rip this guy apart.

YOUNG SIWARD I hate this killer.
MACBETH What's the use of fighting any longer?

6. Subtext in 1.5

Assign parts, reread 1.5 aloud, and clarify plot questions. Then give students a copy of 1.5.61–86. Tell each student to choose five sentences and write a subtext for each. Discuss responses.

7. Subtext in 1.6

Ask students to read 1.6 silently. Elicit subtext suggestions. Cast and read aloud in light of the suggestions.

TOMORROW AND TOMORROW AND TOMORROW

Journal entry: Have you ever faced a situation in which you wanted something from someone but realized it would be best to pursue it indirectly rather than asking for it outright? If not, can you imagine such a situation? Describe your indirect approach for getting what you wanted, or write a brief dialogue between two characters in which one person attempts this with another.

Assign 1.7 for reading.

HOW DID IT GO?

Do students understand subtext? Can they see that the reading of the text changes as subtext changes? Can they imagine a subtext for the text? If so, they are moving into the territory of scholars, actors, and directors, working with variant textual readings.

LESSON

LESSON 7 "If It Were Done When 'Tis Done"

Soliloquies for Everyone

ॐ _____

PLAY SECTIONS COVERED IN THIS LESSON

1.7.1–28 The "If it were done . . ." soliloquy.

LINES: Macbeth, 28

1.7.29–96 Lady Macbeth convinces Macbeth they should murder Duncan.

LINES: Lady Macbeth, 46; Macbeth, 22

ॐ _____

WHAT'S ON FOR TODAY AND WHY

Students are often leery of soliloquies because of their length, the density of their language, and the seeming stagnation of the action that occurs when the stage contains only one character and dialogue isn't being exchanged. This lesson treats the soliloquy in 1.7 as an internal dialogue that reveals Macbeth's conflicting feelings. Our goal is to get students into Macbeth's mind, listening to battling voices there. Toward this end, we will ask students to view a professional actor doing the soliloquy, then have them look at the lines and pick out various voices and read them as an argument.

To prepare for this lesson, we will cue a film to 1.7.1. Ian McKellen's performance in the Royal Shakespeare Company version of the play would be an excellent choice.

WHAT TO DO

1. Viewing the Soliloquy

Play a film version of the soliloquy, 1.7.1–28. Students should watch and listen *with books closed;* otherwise they tend to get tangled up in difficult words or phrases and miss out on the flow of words and clues to mood and meaning suggested by the actor's performance. (Teachers who are unable to show a film should read the soliloquy aloud or play an audio recording.)

2. Verbalizing the Inner Arguments of the Soliloquy

Distribute copies of the soliloquy. Push the desks back and have students form a circle. Assign a student to begin reading aloud from the beginning of the soliloquy until he encounters a period, semicolon, question mark, or exclamation point, at which time the student next to him will pick up the reading and so on. For example:

FIRST STUDENT If it were done when 'tis done, then 'twere well
  It were done quickly.
SECOND STUDENT If th' assassination
  Could trammel up the consequence and catch
  With his surcease success, that but this blow
  Might be the be-all and the end-all here,
  But here, upon this bank and shoal of time,
  We'd jump the life to come.
THIRD STUDENT But in these cases
  We still have judgment here, that we but teach
  Bloody instructions, which, being taught, return
  To plague th' inventor.

Have two students enter the circle and face one another. The first reads aloud from the beginning of the soliloquy until he encounters a period or semicolon, at which time the second student picks up the reading and so on. Then ask for clarification of what's being said: "When does Macbeth think he should commit the murder? What reasons does he give against murdering Duncan? Which reasons are strongest?"

Now repeat the reading in this way, but use the entire class, broken into two choruses. Before they begin, tell students to increase their volume as they read, so that by the time the reading has been finished it sounds as if the two groups are yelling angrily at one another.

Ask students: What conflicting feelings does Macbeth have as he contemplates the murder of Duncan? Divide students into groups of six and give them their mission: to break the soliloquy up so that it reads like an argument conducted by the many voices of Macbeth's personality, debating the wisdom of going through with the murder. They are to indicate on the script each new reason for or against committing the murder by enclosing those lines in a box. Once finished, tell groups to assign one of the boxes of lines to each member.

Form a circle again. Ask the members of a volunteer group to arrange themselves in a tight circle within the larger circle. Tell them that they will read the soliloquy again with each member of the group reading his boxed lines. Urge them to build volume and energy as they read. The various voices of the six students should sound like six internal voices in Macbeth discussing the planned murder.

3. Discussing the Soliloquy

Ask students to explain their breakdown of the soliloquy by identifying specific reasons Macbeth gives for pursuing or questioning his plan of murder. Examples include the following:

- "But in these cases . . ." (line 7)
- "He's here in double trust . . ." (line 12)
- "Besides, this Duncan . . ." (line 16)

Follow up with a discussion of Macbeth's state of mind, the depth of his resolve, etc.

4. The Seduction Scene

Read 1.7.29–96 several times. First ask the females to read Lady Macbeth and the males to read Macbeth. Stop and have students clarify words they don't understand. Talk about what is happening in the scene.

For the second reading, cast Macbeth and Lady Macbeth. Ask the rest of the class to act as student directors. Establish acting objectives for both characters. Ask: At the beginning of the conversation, what does Macbeth want? What obstacles lie in his way? What does Lady Macbeth want? What obstacles lie in her way? Have the actors read with these thoughts in mind. Have the directors listen for these objectives, plus *all the arguments Lady Macbeth uses to get her way*. List these after the reading.

Divide the students into pairs. Get them on their feet to read the scene one last time. Tell them to keep in mind all the objectives and arguments and to read with all the stops out. As they read, circulate, encourage, applaud.

TOMORROW AND TOMORROW AND TOMORROW

Ask students to reread Handout 1: Tracing a Word in *Macbeth*, and to pay special attention to the sample word journal.

HOW DID IT GO?

Listen in on group work and review the class discussion to check the extent to which students understand this lesson. Did students accept their mission and get inside the minds of Macbeth and Lady Macbeth? Did they battle the fears and desires there? If so, they have traveled a long way since they stood on the edge of *Macbeth* with frightening texts in their hands.

LESSON **8** "Make Thick My Blood"

Modeling the Word Journal

WHAT'S ON FOR TODAY AND WHY

Today's lesson uses the word journal assignment (see Lesson 5) to wrap up Act 1 and introduce Act 2. Focusing on a specific word from the play—and other words that are associated with it because of denotation, connotation, or imagery—will lead students to a deeper understanding of character, theme, and atmosphere in the play.

WHAT TO DO

1. The Word Web

Break students into four groups. (It will save time if groups are determined by the word they will trace in the word journal assignment: *blood, hands, night, sleep.*) Print and circle, on the blackboard, the word *blood.* Give each group several minutes to compose a list of 15 or 20 words it associates with the word *blood.*

Invite a student to come to the board, write one of those words on the board, connect it with a line to the word *blood,* and explain the basis of the connection. For example:

- Blood and family: Duncan and Malcolm are blood relatives.
- Blood and cut: Many people are cut and bleed: the captain, Macdonwald, and more.
- Blood and heart: Lady Macbeth is cold-blooded and heartless.

As students add their words, one by one, to the board, a web or spoked wheel will form. There are no "right" answers here. Their product *might* look like this:

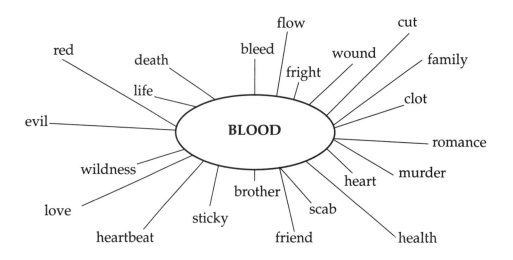

Once the spokes are formed, ask students to randomly choose a character from the play. Then randomly select three words from the board, and explain how that character, those words, and *blood* might be connected. For example:

- Macbeth: friend—brother—heart—blood: Because Macbeth is a blood relative and friend of Duncan, his heart tells him it is wrong to murder him.
- Lady Mac: wildness—blood—bleed—flow: Lady Macbeth's wildness and boldness give her the force necessary to make blood spill and flow.

2. Making the Synonym List

Following this discussion and exercise, students will write their own word (*blood, hand, night,* or *sleep*) in large capital letters on a piece of paper, circle the word, then compile a list of 15 or 20 words that are synonymous or associated with their word. Again, there are no right answers here. *Tell students to save this work, as it will be used during Lesson 11.*

TOMORROW AND TOMORROW AND TOMORROW

Journal entry: Capture a person or a setting in a poem or a paragraph that includes several of the words that your group collected. Your piece of writing could also use a line or phrase from the play that contains one of your words.

Assign 2.1 and 2.2 for reading.

HOW DID IT GO?

You will know that this lesson was successful if students were able to use the word *blood* to show a good understanding of character, theme, and atmosphere in the play. This shows that they can understand what is going on in *Macbeth*, and that they can form theories that are based on words in the text.

At this point in the unit, the end of Act 1, students should have a reasonable comprehension of the plot, characters, and language of *Macbeth*. If you think they are lagging behind in comprehension, stop and give them the Act 1 test (Handout 2, which follows this lesson) so they can have another opportunity to tackle the language and learn what's going on in the play.

&

HANDOUT 2

ACT 1 EXAM

Choose ten of the twelve following quotations from *Macbeth* and (a) identify the speaker, (b) identify to whom she or he is speaking, and (c) explain what is happening in the play when the words are spoken.

1.   He's here in double trust:
First, as I am his kinsman and his subject,
Strong both against the deed; then, as his host,
Who should against his murderer shut the door,
Not bear the knife myself.

2. Stay, you imperfect speakers. Tell me more.
By Sinel's death I know I am Thane of Glamis.
But how of Cawdor? The Thane of Cawdor lives . . .

3. Bring forth men-children only.
For thy undaunted mettle should compose
Nothing but males.

4.   Sons, kinsmen, thanes,
And you whose places are the nearest, know
We will establish our estate upon
Our eldest, Malcolm, whom we name hereafter
The Prince of Cumberland.

5.   To beguile the time,
Look like the time. Bear welcome in your eye,
Your hand, your tongue. Look like th' innocent flower,
But be the serpent under 't.

6. The Prince of Cumberland! That is a step
   On which I must fall down or else o'erleap,
   For in my way it lies. Stars, hide your fires;
   Let not light see my black and deep desires.

7. Fair is foul, and foul is fair,
   Hover through the fog and filthy air.

8.   Come, you spirits
   That tend on mortal thoughts, unsex me here,
   And fill me from the crown to the toe top-full
   Of direst cruelty.

9. No more that Thane of Cawdor shall deceive
   Our bosom interest. Go, pronounce his present death,
   And with his former title greet Macbeth.

10.   Give me your hand.
    Conduct me to mine host. We love him highly
    And shall continue our graces towards him.
    By your leave, hostess.

11. We will proceed no further in this business.
    He hath honored me of late, and I have bought
    Golden opinions from all sorts of people,
    Which would be worn now in their newest gloss,
    Not cast aside so soon.

12. Glamis thou art, and Cawdor, and shalt be
    What thou art promised. Yet do I fear thy nature;
    It is too full o' th' milk of human kindness
    To catch the nearest way.

LESSON 9 "I Dreamt Last Night of the Three Weird Sisters"

The Promptbook

ċ&_____

PLAY SECTIONS COVERED IN THIS LESSON

2.1 Macbeth and Banquo discuss the witches' prophecies. Banquo vows to keep his conscience clear. Macbeth "sees" a dagger before him and goes to kill King Duncan.

LINES: Banquo, 26; Fleance, 2; Macbeth, 49

2.2.1-73 Excited and bold after drugging the guards and laying out their daggers, Lady Macbeth waits as her husband kills the king. Macbeth returns. He is horrified by what he has done and brings with him the bloody daggers, which Lady Macbeth places by the guards to incriminate them.

LINES: Lady Macbeth, 41; Macbeth, 32

2.2.74-95 Lady Macbeth and Macbeth hear knocking at the castle gate. They hastily retire to their chamber to appear as if they had been asleep during the murder.

LINES: Macbeth, 11; Lady Macbeth, 11

ċ&_____

WHAT'S ON FOR TODAY AND WHY

In Lesson 3, students arranged the entrances, exits, and positioning of characters in 1.2, noting these directions on their scripts of the scene. Today's lesson builds on that work. Once again, students will become "directors," but now they will consider all the aspects of performance: setting, props, movement, and vocal interpretation. They will make records of their decisions on script copies of 2.2. This record is called the director's promptbook. For example, read Sue Biondo-Hench's work on promptbooks in Lessons 10, 11, and 23 of *Romeo and Juliet*.

Before this lesson, we will need to prepare promptbook pages for 2.2—see instructions in Handout 11, Lesson 23, in *Romeo and Juliet*. Also, we will need to make copies of the *Romeo and Juliet* handout plus copies of Handout 3: Promptbook Questions, following this lesson.

This lesson will take two days.

WHAT TO DO

1. Tossing Lines

Begin class with an introduction to some key lines from Act 2 by using the exercise in Lesson 1. The procedure, once again: Push back the desks, place five chairs in a small circle at the front of the room, and ask for five volunteers to take those seats. Give each a card containing one of the following lines from Act 2 of *Macbeth:*

> Is this a dagger which I see before me,
> The handle toward my hand? (2.1.44–45)

> I have done the deed. (2.2.19)

> Methought I heard a voice cry "Sleep no more!
> Macbeth does murder sleep" . . . (2.2.47–48)

> A little water clears us of this deed. (2.2.86)

> There's daggers in men's smiles. The near in blood,
> The nearer bloody. (2.3.165–166)

Allow students a moment to become familiar with their quotations. Then ask each to shout out the line as the rest of the class listens. After each volunteer has been heard, give one of them a tennis ball or bean bag: she is to shout out her line, then toss the ball to another person in the circle. The recipient calls out his line and passes the ball to another reader in the circle, and so on. After several rounds, ask the class to join in and recite each line in chorus.

2. Summarizing 2.1

Ask students to summarize 2.1 from their reading last night. Do this quickly and move on.

3. Promptbooks (Day 1)

Distribute the promptbook pages for 2.2 to each student. Also distribute Handout 11: Promptbook Instructions taken from Lesson 23 of *Romeo and Juliet* and Handout 3: Promptbook Questions at the back of this lesson.

Explain that as a director prepares a script for stage, he or she constructs a promptbook, making notes about choices for the set, props, movement, the tone or volume or pace in which lines of dialogue are to be delivered. Tell students to make a promptbook for 2.2.1–73 by making notes on the promptbook pages according to the instructions in Handout 11. Remind them that there are no "right" answers; however, all choices should be supported by the dialogue and knowledge about character, setting, and other matters. Tell them to keep in mind the promptbook questions on Handout 3.

4. Acting from the Promptbook

Call on student volunteers to act 2.2.1–73 using the stage directions they noted on their promptbooks. This will likely take more than one attempt. Students who are not reading can be called upon to serve as directors who offer suggestions about how to stage the scene.

5. Promptbooks (Day 2)

Divide students into pairs. Ask them to do promptbooks for the rest of 2.2. Circulate to see that they are following instructions.

Call for volunteer pairs to act the scene according to their promptbook notes.

Collect the promptbooks.

TOMORROW AND TOMORROW AND TOMORROW

Assign 2.3 and 2.4 for reading.

Remind students who are doing word journals for Act 2 to work on them.

HOW DID IT GO?

You can judge the success of this lesson by reading the students' promptbooks with these questions in mind:

- Can students visualize the set? The characters? The movements?
- Do students read the lines with reasonable accuracy?
- Do students make choices based on what the lines say?

To evaluate progress in the unit so far, ask yourself:

- What are students doing with Shakespeare's language?
- Are they paraphrasing it, reading it for subtext, using it as a basis for conclusions about movement and characterization?

If so, they are becoming their own Shakespeare experts. If not, stop and work on getting students actively engaged with the text—repeat selected exercises, and/or choose a scene the unit does little with (e.g., 2.1) and go through the Michael Tolaydo techniques with it. (See "Three-Dimensional Shakespeare," page 27.)

ം

HANDOUT 3

PROMPTBOOK QUESTIONS

As you work on your promptbook, keep the following questions in mind:

1. Where does the action take place?

2. Who is speaking to whom?

3. What happens in this passage?

4. Where should the characters be positioned on stage? From where and to where are entrances and exits made? Why?

5. What props are required by the passage?

6. Especially important are questions about the characters:

   • What motivates these characters to say what they say?

   • Do the characters' objectives change in this passage? If so, when and why? Or do only tactics change? What obstacles stand in each character's way? What happens when objectives meet obstacles?

· Where would you place vocal pauses?

· In what tone of voice is the line spoken? Why?

· How would the characters move here? What facial expressions might accompany the delivery of this line?

LESSON 10 "There's Daggers in Men's Smiles"

Character Committees

ਦੋ ‾‾‾‾‾‾‾‾‾‾‾‾‾‾‾‾

PLAY SECTIONS COVERED IN THIS LESSON

Acts 1 and 2

ਦੋ ‾‾‾‾‾‾‾‾‾‾‾‾‾‾‾‾

WHAT'S ON FOR TODAY AND WHY

Students will work in groups reviewing the first two acts to collect textual evidence that will lead them to a better understanding of a specific character. This lesson builds on and expands the work done in Lesson 17 in *A Midsummer Night's Dream*.

WHAT TO DO

1. Homework Review

Review the previous night's reading assignment and answer any questions about it. As much as possible, let students supply answers before you intervene.

2. Character Committees

Divide the class into ten committees and assign a character to each committee: Duncan, Macbeth, Banquo, Macduff, Fleance, Lady Macbeth, the Three Witches, the Porter, Malcolm and Donalbain, Lennox and Ross. Tell students assigned to the witches and the last two committees that they have been given more than one character because those characters have relatively few spoken lines. Remind them to deal with each character as a separate personality—to distinguish among each of the three witches, between the two brothers, and between the two soldiers.

Ask each committee to choose a scribe to record findings.

Tell each committee to collect from the first two acts lines said by or about its character that reveal something about her appearance or personality. Because students will report their findings to the class, exact citation is important. Require a standard format that includes the character's name, the line or lines, reference, and insight about the character. Encourage brief responses on paper, longer ones in discussion. For example:

> MACBETH If chance will have me king, why, chance may crown me / Without my stir. (1.3.157–159)

This passage shows Macbeth to be ambitious. Does his caution reveal loyalty or a fear of acting?

Students will perceive the ambiguity that a line like this reveals about Macbeth's character. This exercise should encourage them to discuss that ambiguity, rather than simplify their analysis into a single-word summary.

Collect papers from each committee at the end of class. After class, duplicate them and give each student a copy for each character. Keep the extras in a character file for future use.

TOMORROW AND TOMORROW AND TOMORROW

Remind students who are tracing a word from Act 2 that they must bring their finished word journals to the next class and be prepared to present their findings.

HOW DID IT GO?

The committee papers will show the depth of student understanding of their characters. To evaluate character committee reports, ask:

- How many personality-revealing lines did the student find?
- On a scale of 1 to 10, how accurate were the citations?
- On a scale of 1 to 10, how insightful were the comments about the character? (If students wrote "What a guy!" for every line, they were not looking to the language for character clues.)

LESSON 11 "How Goes the Night, Boy?"

Act 2 Word Journals

WHAT'S ON FOR TODAY AND WHY

Students will work in word journal groups to discuss the evolution of the word they are tracing, then share their findings with the entire class.

The purpose of this extensive work on a single word is to show students that every word contributes to the communicative power of the play, and that they themselves bring some of this power to the word via their own associations. We have no idea what Shakespeare "meant" when he used these words. What we do know is that the frequent appearance of certain words influences what we get from the text.

WHAT TO DO

1. Word Journal Reports: Act 2

Each student should have a copy of the word association list he created in Lesson 8. Ask students to find that list.

Divide students into groups according to words they were assigned: *blood, hand, night,* and *sleep.* Half of the students in each group will have completed word journals for Act 2. The other half (those assigned Act 3) will not. Students who kept word journals for Act 2 will lead their group in a discussion of their findings, giving special emphasis to the "conclusion" section (part c) of the assignment, which focuses on how the word's meaning is affected by the character who uses it and by the events occurring in the play at the time of its use.

Teachers should make the rounds of the groups, listening in on their discussions and fueling them with leading questions, if necessary. Examples: Is night a solace or a menace to this character? What happens when this character really sees blood? This exercise should take about 15 minutes.

2. Making Webs from the Reports

Tell each student to choose a character from the play, select three words from his word association list, and write a sentence explaining the connection between that character, those words, and the word journal word. Here's an example for those tracing *sleep:*

BANQUO: rest—peace—nightmare—sleep. Banquo is very tired and would like to rest, but he's afraid that going to sleep will lead him to dream about the witches' predictions.

MACBETH: darkness—silence—death—sleep. By murdering Duncan, Macbeth makes the temporary darkness and silence of Duncan's sleep eternal darkness and silence.

Divide the blackboard into four sections. Call on a member of the *sleep* group to write "SLEEP" in one quadrant, circle it, connect his three words to one another and to "SLEEP" with lines, and read his sentence aloud to the class. Do the same with *hand, night,* and *blood.* Repeat the process several times, asking leading questions and clarifying ambiguities when necessary. The criss-crossing connecting lines will quickly make a mess of the board, but will also reveal the interrelation of these words.

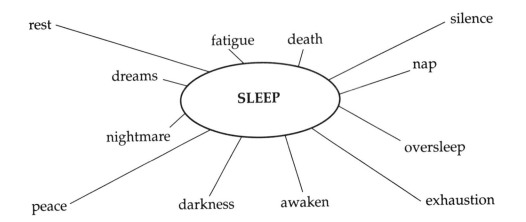

TOMORROW AND TOMORROW AND TOMORROW

Remind students who are keeping word journals for Act 3 that they are to start with 3.1 tonight.

Ask for student volunteers to prepare summaries and readings of four sections of Macbeth's soliloquy, 3.1.52–77:

- Section 1: lines 52 through the middle of 59
- Section 2: the middle of line 59 through line 65
- Section 3: lines 66 through 70
- Section 4: lines 71 through 77

Students who accept this assignment should first paraphrase the lines, then write what they think Macbeth's thoughts and feelings are as he says the words. Finally, they should plan and practice a reading of the lines that reflects all of the above.

HOW DID IT GO?

Listening in on the group discussions and monitoring the class presentations should help you to check student work.

To evaluate the word journals for Act 2, assign from one to ten points in each of the following categories:

- Completeness: Did the student find all the references to the assigned word? Did he complete the chart?
- Accuracy: Did he quote the line correctly and identify the speaker?
- Paraphrase: Did the student show clear understanding of the lines?

Then assign from one to fifteen points for the aptness of the conclusions students drew.

LESSON **12** "Ride You This Afternoon?"

The Promptbook Revisited

&

PLAY SECTIONS COVERED IN THIS LESSON

3.1.1–51 Macbeth requests Banquo's presence at a supper that evening. He learns that Banquo and Fleance will go riding that afternoon.

LINES: Banquo, 21; Macbeth, 26; Lady Macbeth, 3; Servant, 1

3.1.52–77 Macbeth soliloquizes about killing Banquo.

LINES: Macbeth, 26

3.1.77–162 Macbeth arranges for Banquo and Fleance to be killed on their afternoon ride.

LINES: Macbeth, 69; First Murderer, 10; Second Murderer, 9

&

WHAT'S ON FOR TODAY AND WHY

Lesson 9 introduced students to the promptbook and taught them that the preparations for staging a scene include recording insights about such issues as subtext, movement, and vocal interpretation suggested by the scene. This lesson, which focuses on 3.1, will give students a second opportunity to practice constructing and using a promptbook.

We will need to prepare copies of Handout 4: Taking Care of Banquo.

WHAT TO DO

1. Staging 3.1.1–51

Distribute Handout 4: Taking Care of Banquo, an edited excerpt from 3.1, to each student.

Ask the class to read the scene and explain what these characters are saying about one another.

Call on two volunteers to take the parts of Banquo and Macbeth and call them to the front of the room. Tell them to read Banquo's lines that open the excerpt and Macbeth's lines that close it.

> BANQUO   Thou hast it now—King, Cawdor, Glamis, all
> As the Weird Women promised, and I fear
> Thou played'st most foully for 't.
>
> MACBETH   To be thus is nothing,
> But to be safely thus. Our fears in Banquo
> Stick deep, and in his royalty of nature
> Reigns that which would be feared.

Now ask the volunteers to read the entire excerpted dialogue aloud. Then recall the work done on subtext and inflection in earlier lessons, and discuss with the class what's happening here. Talk about the characters' feelings and motives. Ask students for suggestions about how these feelings and motives might lead the actors to play this scene. Who looks at whom when speaking? How? When? What tone of voice is used? Where do the characters stand in relation to one another?

Tell students to create a promptbook for this scene by recording some of these observations on their handouts.

Call on three new volunteers (adding Lady Macbeth to the scene). Tell them to read 3.1.1–55 aloud, using some of the class's suggestions about how to play the scene. Discuss the results.

2. Fruitless Crown: Macbeth's Soliloquy

Call to the front of the room those who agreed, at the end of Lesson 11, to prepare summaries and readings of Macbeth's soliloquy (3.1.52–77) and ask them to summarize, in turn, Macbeth's thoughts and feelings in the soliloquy. They should answer any questions the class has about the soliloquy, then follow up by giving a clear and dramatic reading of it, each reading the section for which she is responsible. Those sections, once again:

- lines 52 through the middle of 59
- the middle of line 59 through line 65
- lines 66 through line 70
- lines 71 through 77

3. Vile Blows and Buffets

Call on three new volunteers to take the parts of Macbeth, First Murderer, and Second Murderer. Finish reading the scene aloud.

Discuss Macbeth's intentions, as well as the response of the murderers to his plans.

TOMORROW AND TOMORROW AND TOMORROW

Ask four volunteers to read 3.3 for homework. Assign them the roles of Banquo and the three Murderers and tell them they will act the scene during the next lesson. Tell each of the murderers to bring a suitable disguise to that lesson.

Ask the other students to read 3.3 with the eye of a director.

Remind students who are keeping word journals for Act 3 to stay strong in the task.

HOW DID IT GO?

Students' understanding will be evident from their directorial suggestions, their reading of the excerpt and scene, and the ability of those who prepared the reading of the soliloquy to clarify and perform the soliloquy for the class. While making their acting and directing choices, students have read the text with careful eyes.

HANDOUT 4

TAKING CARE OF BANQUO

This is an edited excerpt from *Macbeth* 3.1.

BANQUO   Thou hast it now—King, Cawdor, Glamis, all
As the Weïrd Women promised, and I fear
Thou played'st most foully for 't.

Sennet sounded. Enter Macbeth.

MACBETH   Here's our chief guest.
Tonight we hold a solemn supper, sir,
And I'll request your presence.

BANQUO   Let your Highness
Command upon me, to the which my duties
Are with a most indissoluble tie
Forever knit.

MACBETH   Ride you this afternoon?

BANQUO   Ay, my good lord.

MACBETH   Is 't far you ride?

BANQUO   As far, my lord, as will fill up the time
'twixt this and supper.

MACBETH   Fail not our feast.

BANQUO   My lord, I will not.

MACBETH   Goes Fleance with you?

BANQUO   Ay, my good lord.

MACBETH   Farewell.

Banquo exits.

MACBETH   To be thus is nothing,
But to be safely thus. Our fears in Banquo
Stick deep, and in his royalty of nature
Reigns that which would be feared.

LESSON **13** "Fly, Good Fleance, Fly!"

Editing a Text and Performing a Murder

❧ _____

PLAY SECTIONS COVERED IN THIS LESSON

3.2 Macbeth and Lady Macbeth discuss the doubts and torments that have come with their new positions. Macbeth tells his wife to be attentive to Banquo at supper.

LINES: Lady Macbeth, 18; Servant, 2; Macbeth, 43

3.3 Banquo and Fleance are murdered.

LINES: First Murderer, 11; Third Murderer, 9; Second Murderer, 9; Banquo, 3

❧ _____

WHAT'S ON FOR TODAY AND WHY

As they view or listen to performances of the play, students are quick to notice lines that have been edited or rearranged. Their first reaction is often surprise, their second shock, and if they have really invested time in their reading and study of the play, they may even feel outrage that "their" play has been violated. Giving students a chance to edit a scene helps them to understand how and even why directors sometimes edit Shakespeare's script. This lesson will start by asking students to edit 3.2 and move on to a full performance—replete with blood and guts—of 3.3.

So students can work freely on the script and change their minds if they like, we will prepare copies of 3.2 and urge them to work with pencil.

WHAT TO DO

1. Editing 3.2

Distribute copies of 3.2, assign parts, and give the scene a reading. (This is a somewhat difficult scene. Choose readers carefully, and don't be discouraged if you have to read the scene more than once.)

Ask questions: How do the Macbeths feel now that they rule the kingdom? Why do they feel that way? How do they intend to make themselves feel better? Who seems to be in control in this scene? How do you know?

Tell students that directors sometimes edit or rearrange a play's lines to clarify the play, shorten it, or quicken its pace. Explain that they will now edit 3.2. Divide the class in half and assign the left side of the room lines 1–29 and the right side lines 30–63. Working in groups of three or four, they are to cut their half of the scene to about ten or fifteen lines by crossing out those lines they think are "dispensable." They may abbreviate sentences, but they must also remain true to the plot and characterizations. Tell them to work in pencil.

Call a group that edited the first half of the scene to the front of the room and ask the students to reproduce their edits on a transparency for an overhead projector. Alternatively, they may read their scene aloud. Either way, they must justify their cuts. Needless to say, other groups treating this portion of 3.2 will have different products. Have them share their versions and explain their choices. Repeat the process with those groups editing the second half of the scene, then wrap up with discussion about where all of this leaves Macbeth and Lady Macbeth.

Collect the editing sheets.

2. The Murder Scene: A Performance

Call yesterday's volunteers to the front of the room and invite them to conduct a spirited murder (3.3). Let them act the scene two times, once as they planned it and once with suggestions from the class.

TOMORROW AND TOMORROW AND TOMORROW

Tell students to watch at least ten minutes of a television show tonight and pay attention to how it is shot. They are to notice how the camera moves and record in their journals one camera technique the director used. If they know terms like *zoom*, *fade*, *close-up*, or *body shot*, fine; if not, tell them to explain in their own words what the camera did. They should also describe the scene in which the camera technique was used, and explain how the technique added to the drama or mood of the scene.

Remind students who are keeping word journals for Act 3 to keep working.

HOW DID IT GO?

Use the editing sheets, along with the presentations each group made, to evaluate learning. The ability to cut a scene indicates that the students know what's going on in the scene and that they are making choices with regard to text. Thus they are learning to read the scene in a very sophisticated way.

If you wish to reinforce their editing efforts, (1) give each edited script a grade based on how appropriate the cuts are and (2) add comments and questions.

As for 3.3, judge the murder by the spirit with which it's conducted and by the knowledge it shows of text and staging.

LESSON 14 "Thou Art the Best o' th' Cutthroats"

Comparative Film

ᐱ‚_____

PLAY SECTION COVERED IN THIS LESSON

3.4 The banquet scene. Macbeth sees Banquo's bloody ghost while entertaining the court.

LINES: Macbeth, 111; Lords, 3; Lady Macbeth, 43; Murderer, 6; Lennox, 6; Ross, 7

ᐱ‚_____

WHAT'S ON FOR TODAY AND WHY

To this point, students will have had many opportunities to stage and perform scenes. In this lesson students will have a chance to view the work of professional actors and directors and to respond to it. Using all the previous work of this unit as a background, students will (1) focus on problems of character and staging of 3.4, (2) see several solutions to these problems, and (3) evaluate the solutions according to what the lines in the script suggest.

In the various film performances of *Macbeth,* each banquet scene is very different from the next. The Royal Shakespeare Company production of 3.4 takes 11 minutes; there is no visible ghost. The BBC production takes 11 minutes; there is no visible ghost. The Orson Welles production takes 10 minutes; there is a visible ghost. The Roman Polanski production takes 7 minutes; there is a visible ghost. For this lesson, we will choose two or three productions and cue them up to 3.4.

Also, we will need to prepare handouts of the issues to be considered (see section 1 under "What to Do") or write the issues on the board.

WHAT TO DO

1. Planning the Staging of the Banquet Scene

Start by summarizing 3.4.

Next, distribute to students (or have them copy from the blackboard) a list of some of the issues that a theater company must address in staging this scene. This list is only a tool to focus students' viewing of the scene. They will no doubt raise issues or questions of their own after viewing performances of the scene. Issues:

- How should the lords at the feast react to Macbeth's side conversation with the murderer? What will the audience conclude from these reactions?
- How should Banquo's ghost be portrayed? Who sees it? How will these portrayals affect the mood of the performance and the emotions or sympathies of the audience?

- How should Lady Macbeth react to Macbeth's fit? What will the audience conclude from these reactions?
- How do the lords at the feast react to Macbeth's fit? What do you conclude from these reactions?
- How can we use camera angles, cuts, close-ups, or other techniques to influence the audience?

Assign each student two issues from the list. Tell them that as they watch each film version of 3.4 they are to pay close attention to how the director deals with those two issues. (Make sure that all the issues are assigned.)

Additionally, for each production that you view, tell students to list a word that captures Macbeth's mood or frame of mind at the end of the scene. Do the same for Lady Macbeth.

Show the first version of the scene and answer any questions students have about who's who, what happened, or general logistics. Then canvass the room for observations about how the performance dealt with the issues listed above. Probe, question, and clarify.

Show a second performance of 3.4 and ask students to talk about the similarities or differences that exist in the way the two versions treat the issues they are watching for.

If time permits, show a third version and ask how this version differed from the two previous ones.

Follow up with a general discussion of the scene, being sure to give students a chance to discuss issues that are not part of the list you gave them. Ask them to evaluate the various directors' decisions based on what the lines in Shakespeare's script suggest.

TOMORROW AND TOMORROW AND TOMORROW

Write the following passage on the board. Ask students to copy it, and then ask for a clarification of its meaning.

> MACBETH   I am in blood
> Stepped in so far that, should I wade no more,
> Returning were as tedious as go o'er.

Journal entry: Recall a time in your life when you were involved in a tough situation, had to make a decision about whether to turn back or push on, and found both options equally difficult. What did you do? Why?

Encourage students working on word journals for Act 3 to be vigilant in their assignment.

HOW DID IT GO?

The discussion that follows each version of 3.4 will tell you if students are reading and viewing the scene with care:

- Did students demonstrate a fairly complex knowledge of characters, their relationships, their politics, their inner struggles?
- Did students use lines from the script to justify their comments about the issues they were assigned?
- Did students pick up on subtle nuances, shifts, and inflections in the productions?
- Did students, in their comments, connect camera techniques to the director's purposes in staging the scene?

LESSON **15**   **"Fire Burn, and Cauldron Bubble"**

Choral Reading, Staged Reading

𝒆𝒂 _____

PLAY SECTIONS COVERED IN THIS LESSON

3.5 The witches meet on the heath.

LINES: First Witch, 2; Hecate, 34

3.6 Lennox hears a report that Macduff is in England raising an army to put Malcolm on the throne.

LINES: Lennox, 35; Another Lord, 21

4.1.1–38 The witches cook up a charmed pot of hell-broth.

LINES: First Witch, 13; Second Witch, 15; Third Witch, 20

4.1.39–177 Macbeth consults with the three witches.

LINES: Hecate, 5; Second Witch, 13; Macbeth, 81; First Witch, 28; Third Witch, 9; First Apparition, 2; Second Apparition, 4; Third Apparition, 5; Lennox, 6

𝒆𝒂 _____

WHAT'S ON FOR TODAY AND WHY

In this lesson, students will practice some of the skills they will use in the performance activity that is the culmination of this unit: in a choral reading of 4.1.1–38, they will experiment with sound effects; in 4.1.39–176, they will focus on character objectives.

WHAT TO DO

1. Summaries: 3.5 and 3.6

Begin class with a quick summary of 3.5 and 3.6. (Check the notes in the Folger edition about 3.5. Many Shakespearean scholars agree that this scene, as well as part of 4.1, was not part of the original *Macbeth*, that it was not written by Shakespeare, but was added later, perhaps by Thomas Middleton.)

In 3.6, emphasize that the lords use irony to reveal their suspicions of Macbeth, and that Macduff is in England attempting to rally support to overthrow Macbeth.

2. Choral Reading: 4.1.1–38

Distribute Handout 5: A Choral Reading of Macbeth and the Witches, an edited version of 4.1. Arrange students in a large circle and count them off randomly—1, 2, 3, 1, 2, 3, etc. Then choose three students whose voices are distinct in pitch—one high and light, one deep, one medium. Cast them as the three witches. Practice with group 1 the sounds of wind (see Handout), with group 2, the sounds of hooting owls, and with group 3 the sounds of howling dogs. Then practice all three for a while. (You'll know when enough is enough.) Encourage volume and variety.

Read through the scene once with the witches and no sound effects. Then read it through again with sound effects. Before doing so, however, remind students producing the sound effects that they must pay attention to their cues and that the witches must be heard. There will be a lot happening here; feel free to stop students and start over if they don't listen to one another. (On the other hand, this exercise can't be done without a little mayhem.)

During a second or third complete reading, students might experiment with lighting (adjusting the shades or turning the lights out) and movement (e.g., the three witches might move to the center and form their own circle at the words "Round about the cauldron go . . ."). Wind, owls, and dogs might also move around.

Stop to discuss the experience. Ask students what feelings they had as they read the scene. How did the background sounds affect them? Then ask: What do you think is going on in this scene? Discuss.

If you like, read the scene aloud a final time with half the class reading the lines, while the other half adds the sounds of wind, owls, and dogs at random. Discuss the effects. Experiment with combinations (i.e., one-third of the group reads Witch 1, one-third reads Witch 2, and one-third reads Witch 3).

3. Staged Reading: 4.1.39–177

Assign the following parts and continue on with a reading of the remainder of the scene: Witches (1, 2, and 3), Hecate, Macbeth, Apparitions (1, 2, and 3), Lennox. It might be fun and interesting to assign several students to the part of each apparition, and have them read the part in chorus from the back of the room.

Because this is a pivotal scene, give it your full attention. Talk about objectives: What does Macbeth want? What is in his way? How does he try to surmount the obstacles? Do his objectives change in the course of the scene? What about the witches—what do they want? What do they do to get it?

TOMORROW AND TOMORROW AND TOMORROW

Remind those who are keeping word journals on Act 3 that they are to bring their completed word journals to the next lesson. Tell those who completed word journals for Act 2 to bring them to the next class as well. In addition, all students should bring to the next lesson the word association lists they created in Lesson 8.

HOW DID IT GO?

To evaluate this lesson, ask:

- Did students listen to one another as they read or performed sound effects?
- Was the choral reading spirited but not confused?
- Did students pick up on Macbeth's darkening resolve and desperation in 4.1.39–177?

To evaluate plot and character comprehension at the end of Act 3, give the optional Act 3 exam, Handout 6.

૨௫

HANDOUT 5

A CHORAL READING FOR WITCHES AND SOUND EFFECTS

Group 1—Sounds of wind
Group 2—Owls hooting
Group 3—Dogs howling

FIRST WITCH Thrice the brinded cat hath mewed.	1
SECOND WITCH Thrice, and once the hedge-pig whined.	1
THIRD WITCH Harpier cries "'Tis time, 'tis time!"	1
FIRST WITCH Round about the cauldron go;	2
In the poisoned entrails throw.	2
Toad, that under cold stone	2
Days and nights has thirty-one	2
Sweltered venom sleeping got,	3
Boil thou first i' th' charmèd pot!	3
ALL Double, double toil and trouble;	3
Fire burn, and cauldron bubble.	1 & 3
SECOND WITCH Fillet of a fenny snake	1 & 3
In the cauldron boil and bake.	1 & 3
Eye of newt and toe of frog,	2
Wool of bat and tongue of dog,	2
Adder's fork and blindworm's sting,	2
Lizard's leg and howlet's wing,	1
For a charm of powerful trouble,	1
Like a hell-broth boil and bubble.	1
ALL Double, double toil and trouble;	1, 2, & 3
Fire burn, and cauldron bubble.	1, 2, & 3
THIRD WITCH Scale of dragon, tooth of wolf,	3
Witch's mummy, maw and gulf	3
Of the ravined salt-sea shark,	3
Root of hemlock digged i' th' dark.	1 & 2
ALL Double, double toil and trouble;	1, 2, & 3
Fire burn, and cauldron bubble.	1, 2, & 3

૨௫

HANDOUT 6

MACBETH EXAM—ACT 3

Choose eight of the ten following quotations from *Macbeth* and (a) identify the speaker, (b) identify to whom he or she is speaking, and (c) explain what is happening in the play at the time the words are spoken.

1.   O, proper stuff!
This is the very painting of your fear.
This is the air-drawn dagger which you said
Led you to Duncan.

2.   The time has been
That, when the brains were out, the man would die,
And there an end. But now they rise again
With twenty mortal murders on their crowns
And push us from our stools.

3. Thou hast it now—King, Cawdor, Glamis, all
As the Weïrd Women promised, and I fear
Thou played'st most foully for 't.

4.   I am in blood
Stepped in so far that, should I wade no more,
Returning were as tedious as go o'er.

5. (To leave no rubs or botches in the work)
Fleance, his son, that keeps him company,
Whose absence is no less material to me
Than is his father's, must embrace the fate
Of that dark hour.

6.   To be thus is nothing,
    But to be safely thus. Our fears in Banquo
    Stick deep, and in his royalty of nature
    Reigns that which would be feared.

7. Thou art the best o' th' cutthroats,
    Yet he's good that did the like for Fleance.
    If thou didst it, thou art the nonpareil.

8. We hear our bloody cousins are bestowed
    In England and in Ireland, not confessing
    Their cruel parricide, filling their hearers
    With strange invention.

9.   Better be with the dead,
    Whom we, to gain our peace, have sent to peace,
    Than on the torture of the mind to lie
    In restless ecstasy.

10. Then comes my fit again. I had else been perfect,
    Whole as the marble, founded as the rock,
    As broad and general as the casing air.
    But now I am cabined, cribbed, confined, bound in
    To saucy doubts and fears.—But Banquo's safe?

LESSON 16 "Nightmare, Death, Heaven"

Reports from Act 3 Word Journals

WHAT'S ON FOR TODAY AND WHY

Students will discuss their word journal work, first with members of their word groups, then with the class. Enlightened by the work they did in Lesson 11, and tempered by the length of time they have spent thinking about the repeated use of a single key word in the play, students will have the opportunity to see how their word affects the characters who use it, the audience that hears it, and *Macbeth* as a whole.

WHAT TO DO

1. Word Journal Groups

Divide students into groups according to which word they researched: *blood, hand, night,* or *sleep.* In each group there will be some students who researched their word for Act 2 and some who kept word journals for Act 3. Ask the latter to lead their group in a discussion of their findings, giving special emphasis to the "conclusions" section (part c) of the assignment, which focuses on how the word's meaning is affected by the character who uses it and by the events occurring in the play at the time of its use.

All group members should have something to say about the evolution of "their" word, since all will have kept a word journal by this time. This should take about 15 minutes.

2. Making a Web from the Word Journal Findings

Tell each student to select a passage from his word journal that he especially likes and, using the word association lists he created in Lesson 8, choose three words that he strongly associates with that passage. For example, those tracing the word *night* might have the following results:

BANQUO "How goes the night, boy?" Silence, mystery, black.

MACBETH "Tonight we hold a solemn supper, sir, / And I'll request your presence." Darkness, fear, evil.

BANQUO "Go not my horse the better, / I must become a borrower of the night / For a dark hour or twain." Nightmare, death, heaven.

As in Lesson 11, divide the board into fourths. Write one of the key words in each quadrant.

Reconvene the entire class and call one group at a time to the front of the room to make a word web. See Lesson 11 for instructions.

Collect word journals.

TOMORROW AND TOMORROW AND TOMORROW

Assign 4.2 for reading.

HOW DID IT GO?

Listening in on the group discussions and monitoring the group reports to the class should help you to see if students were able to infer from key words messages about the people and ideas in *Macbeth.* To evaluate Act 3 word journals, see Lesson 11.

LESSON 17 "All My Pretty Ones?"

Looking at Macduff

ও❧

PLAY SECTIONS COVERED IN THIS LESSON

4.2 Macbeth's murderers kill Macduff's family.

LINES: Lady Macduff, 42; Ross, 20; Macduff's son, 22; Messenger, 10; Murderer, 4

4.3 Although skeptical at first, Malcolm tells Macduff he will fight for the Scottish throne. Macduff hears about his family's murder and vows to avenge their deaths.

LINES: Malcolm, 146; Macduff, 91; Doctor, 5; Ross, 40

ও❧

WHAT'S ON FOR TODAY AND WHY

Today's lesson uses the events of 4.2 and 4.3 to reveal Macduff's character. Because 4.3 is a long scene, we will summarize parts of it, as well as the first section of 4.2, so we can work in a staged reading and discussion.

Again, we will present film excerpts. Cue the video to 4.2. Also, we will need to prepare handouts for the passages in section 3 of "What to Do" or write the passages on the board or transparency.

WHAT TO DO

1. Staging 4.2.71–98

Assign parts (Messenger, Lady Macduff, Murderer, and Son) and read from line 71 to the end of the scene. Ask leading questions: What words describe how the messenger feels in this scene? How do these feelings translate into behavior? What does Lady Macduff's response tell you about her frame of mind? What do the son's words show about his character?

Canvass the class for suggestions about how this scene should be played. Ask four new volunteer actors to perform it. Discuss how it went, what further modifications should be made in the performance.

2. Film Excerpt: The Murder of Macduff's Family

Explain that the portion of 4.2 which the class just performed is preceded by an exchange between Lady Macduff and her son. Summarize the exchange. Then show a film performance of the entire scene.

Discuss students' reactions to characterization and staging.

3. Macduff's Reaction as Seen in Key Passages of 4.3

Explain that the play's setting shifts after 4.2. Then summarize 4.3.1–181.

Next, explain that Ross arrives in England and delivers to Macduff the news of the murder of Macduff's wife and children.

Write the following passages on the board or distribute them to students on a handout and explain that they are spoken by Macduff after he receives this news.

> My children too?
> And I must be from thence? My wife killed too?
>   (4.3.248, 250)

> He has no children. All my pretty ones?
> Did you say "all"? O hell-kite! All?
> What, all my pretty chickens and their dam
> At one fell swoop?   (4.3.255–258)

>   Did heaven look on
> And would not take their part? Sinful Macduff,
> They were all struck for thee! Naught that I am,
> Not for their own demerits, but for mine,
> Fell slaughter on their souls. Heaven rest them now.
>   (4.3.263–267)

> O, I could play the woman with mine eyes
> And braggart with my tongue! But, gentle heavens,
> Cut short all intermission! Front to front
> Bring thou this fiend of Scotland and myself.
> Within my sword's length set him. If he 'scape,
> Heaven forgive him too.   (4.3.270–275)

Explain that these passages reveal, in sequence, Macduff's reactions to the murder of his family. Call four new volunteers to the front of the room and ask them to read the passages in a straightforward way. Paraphrase the lines and ask the class for suggestions about what emotion or emotions underlie each passage (i.e., shock, horror, anger). Now ask the volunteers to deliver their lines in sequence, attempting to capture the appropriate emotion.

4. Film Excerpt: Macduff's Reactions

View 4.3.182–282 on film. Compare the Macduff on film to the Macduff as acted in class—how did each react to the catastrophic news? Answer questions about what happened and how the scene ends.

TOMORROW AND TOMORROW AND TOMORROW

Journal entry: Summarize an incident that caused you to feel several different emotions in rapid succession. Then write a dialogue that reveals those changing emotions in stages.

Assign 5.1 for reading.

HOW DID IT GO?　　　　Student questions, discussion, and dramatic reading should show an understanding of the plot and characterization:

- Did students follow the shift of setting?
- Did students assign appropriate emotions to each of the Macduff passages in 4.3.182–275?
- Were students able to connect plot and character development in Act 4 with those in previous acts?

　　If students are confused about plot and character, stop and get the story straight. Call on students to piece out the narrative and talk about each major character.

LESSON 18 "Hell Is Murky"

Lady Macbeth's Decline

ॐ

PLAY SECTION COVERED IN THIS LESSON

5.1 Lady Macbeth sleepwalks.

LINES: Doctor, 37; Gentlewoman, 26; Lady Macbeth, 21

ॐ

WHAT'S ON FOR TODAY AND WHY

Students will start this lesson with a quick exercise to familiarize them with lines from Act 5. After reading 5.1 aloud, students will contrast some of the lines from Lady Macbeth's sleepwalking speech with selected lines from previous scenes to highlight the changes that have occurred in Lady Macbeth's character.

WHAT TO DO

1. Tossing Lines from Act 5

Push back the desks, place six chairs in a small circle at the front of the room, and ask for six volunteers to take those seats. Give each one a card containing one of the following lines from Act 5 of *Macbeth:*

Out, damned spot, out, I say! (5.1.37)

I have lived long enough. My way of life
Is fall'n into the sere, the yellow leaf . . . (5.3.26–27)

Tomorrow and tomorrow and tomorrow
Creeps in this petty pace from day to day . . . (5.5.22–23)

Ring the alarum bell!—Blow wind, come wrack,
At least we'll die with harness on our back. (5.5.58–59)

They have tied me to a stake. I cannot fly,
But, bear-like, I must fight the course. (5.7.1–2)

Macduff was from his mother's womb
Untimely ripped.   (5.8.19–20)

I will not yield
To kiss the ground before young Malcolm's feet. . . .
                    (5.8.32–33)

Lay on, Macduff,
And damned be him that first cries "Hold! Enough!"
                    (5.8.38–39)

Allow each student volunteer a moment to become familiar with his quotation. Then ask him to shout it out as the rest of the class listens. After each volunteer has been heard, give one of them a tennis ball: he is to shout out his line, then toss the ball to another person in the circle. The recipient calls out her line and passes the ball to another reader in the circle, and so on. After several rounds, put the ball away and ask the class to join in and recite each line in chorus.

2. Reading 5.1

Assign parts and read the scene aloud. Follow up with questions: What's going on here? What is the mood? What kind of lighting would you use to communicate that mood? Where would you position these characters onstage?

3. Lady Macbeth Now and Then

Break the class into nine groups and distribute Handout 7: Lady Macbeth Now and Then.

Assign one pair of lines (A through I) to each group. Review the instructions on the handout. Give students 10 minutes to do the work.

4. Face to Face

Tell each group to place two chairs facing one another and ask two group members to sit in them. One says the line from Act 5 aloud to the other. The second student reads aloud the line from the earlier act. Here's an example for the group doing pair "A":

SAMEER   Hell is murky.

ALICIA   Come, thick night, / And pall thee in the dunnest smoke of hell.

Ask for student comments. (For example, students might say that although both lines reflect Lady Macbeth's preoccupation with hell and darkness, she has undergone significant change between the times that she speaks them.)

Talk about ways to convey the difference in attitude between the two lines—for example, tone of voice, gestures, posture, inflection, stress, volume, speed, pacing, and pauses. Do this enough times for everyone in the group to have a chance to sit and deliver. Group members who are not speaking might serve as directors, offering advice to those who are speaking.

Now call people from each group to the front of the room. Tell them to deliver their lines, complete with embellishing tone of voice, body language, etc., then briefly explain the incident or situation the lines refer to and summarize the change Lady Macbeth has undergone.

Collect summary paragraphs done for Handout 7.

TOMORROW AND TOMORROW AND TOMORROW

Tell the students to finish reading Act 5.

HOW DID IT GO?

Student understanding should be evident from their performances and their preparatory summary paragraphs.

To evaluate this lesson, look over the summary paragraphs students did for Handout 7 and think back to their face-to-face performances. Ask:

- Did students grasp the two situations?
- Could students convey in writing the two situations?
- Did students use acting tools (tone of voice, pause, stress, inflection) to convey the difference between the two situations?

ಎ

HANDOUT 7

LADY MACBETH NOW AND THEN

Lady Macbeth said each of the paired lines below. Each pair contains a line from her sleepwalking scene and a line she said in an earlier scene. They have been paired because they refer to a common incident or situation, primarily the murders the Macbeths have committed. Some of them use an important common word.

1. Open your book to the line from the earlier scene, reacquaint yourself with the situation in the play at that time, and write a summary paragraph of that situation and a summary paragraph of how the character feels as she delivers the line.

2. Look back to the line from Act 5 and write summary paragraphs of the situation and the character's feelings as she delivers the line.

3. Make any conclusions you see fit.

A. "Hell is murky." (5.1.38)

> "Come, thick night,
> And pall thee in the dunnest smoke of hell . . ." (1.5.57–58)

B. "Fie, my lord, fie, a soldier and afeard?" (5.1.38–39)

> "What, quite unmanned in folly? . . . Fie, for shame!" (3.4.88, 90)

C. "Yet who would have thought the old man to have had so much blood in him?" (5.1.41–42)

> "Give me the daggers. The sleeping and the dead
> Are but as pictures. . . .
>   If he do bleed,
> I'll gild the faces of the grooms withal . . ." (2.2.69–70, 71–72)

D. "The Thane of Fife had a wife. Where is she now?" (5.1.44–45)

> "My hands are of your color, but I shame
> To wear a heart so white." (2.2.82–83)

E. "What, will these hands ne'er be clean?" (5.1.45)

> "A little water clears us of this deed.
> How easy is it, then!" (2.2.86–87)

F. "Wash your hands. Put on your nightgown. Look not so pale." (5.1.65–66)

> "Get on your nightgown, lest occasion call us
> And show us to be watchers." (2.2.90–91)

G. "I tell you yet again, Banquo's buried; he cannot come out on 's grave." (5.1.66–67)

"Why do you make such faces? When all's done,
You look but on a stool." (3.4.80–81)

H. "To bed, to bed. There's knocking at the gate." (5.1.69–70)

"I hear a knocking
At the south entry. Retire we to our chamber." (2.2.84–85)

I. "What's done cannot be undone." (5.1.71)

"What's done is done." (3.2.14)

<hr>

LESSON 19 "Hold, Enough!"

Concluding the Reading of the Play

ෑ _____

PLAY SECTIONS COVERED IN THIS LESSON

5.2 The Scottish and English forces meet in Birnam Wood.

LINES: Menteith, 10; Angus, 9; Caithness, 11; Lennox, 7

5.3 Confident that Malcolm cannot win because he was of woman born, and certain that Birnam Wood cannot come to Dunsinane, Macbeth gears up for battle.

LINES: Macbeth, 61; Servant, 3; Seyton, 3; Doctor, 9

5.4 Malcolm's army joins up with the Scottish forces. Malcolm orders the soldiers to camouflage themselves with boughs from Birnam Wood.

LINES: Malcolm, 11; Menteith, 2; Siward, 10; Soldier, 1; Macduff, 3

5.5 Macbeth learns of Lady Macbeth's death. He hears reports that Birnam Wood appears to be advancing on the castle.

LINES: Macbeth, 48; Seyton, 2; Messenger, 9

5.6 Malcolm's forces reach the castle.

LINES: Malcolm, 6; Siward, 3; Macduff, 2

5.7 In battle, Macbeth kills young Siward. Macbeth's army breaks down as many soldiers join Malcolm. Malcolm enters the castle.

LINES: Macbeth, 11; Young Siward, 7; Siward, 6; Macduff, 10; Malcolm, 2

5.8 Macbeth meets Macduff. Certain he will win and wanting no more of Macduff's blood on him, Macbeth is reluctant to fight Macduff. But when Macduff tells Macbeth that he was early ripped from his mother's womb, Macbeth knows he is done for. Macduff brings Malcolm Macbeth's head, and all hail the new king of Scotland.

LINES: Macbeth, 26; Macduff, 20; Malcolm, 21; Siward, 13; Ross, 10

ෑ

WHAT'S ON FOR TODAY AND WHY

Despite its many scenes—or perhaps because of them—Act 5 rushes to closure, and so should this unit. Use this play's accelerating pace to wrap up the reading quickly. Take one of two approaches to concluding the play: either play an except of these scenes, or conduct a final reading aloud.

This lesson will take two or three days.

WHAT TO DO

1. Guides for Reading 5.2 Through 5.8

List on the blackboard the scene changes for scenes 2–8, and briefly identify the play's new major characters:

- Menteith, Caithness, and Angus: noblemen loyal to Malcolm
- Seyton: officer attending Macbeth
- Siward: general of the English forces
- Young Siward: Siward's son

2. Moving Through the Scenes

Show a videotape of 5.2 through 5.8 or cast the various scenes and read them. Stop at the end of each scene to answer questions about what was just covered and to introduce the upcoming setting and characters.

If reading aloud, divide students into the three groups listed below. (Each group will be responsible for about the same number of lines.) Assign each group member a speaking part or the role of director. Ask each group to prepare a staged reading of their assigned lines. (For large classes, make more parts by assigning more than one director per group and/or spotlighting one of the lengthier speeches and assigning it to another actor—i.e., even though David does Macbeth in 5.2–3, Belinda steps in and does Macbeth's long speech in 5.3.23–34 during the performance.)

- Group 1: 5.2–3
  Cast: Menteith, Angus, Caithness, Lennox, Macbeth, Servant, Seyton, Doctor, director.
  Lengthy speech: Macbeth, 5.3.1–11 or 23–34

- Group 2: Scenes 5.4–6
  Cast: Malcolm, Menteith, Siward, Soldiers, Macduff, Macbeth, Seyton, Messenger, director.
  Lengthy speech: Macbeth, 5.5.20–31 or 44–59

- Group 3: 5.7–8
  Cast: Macbeth, Siward, Macduff, Young Siward, Malcolm, Ross, director
  Lengthy speech: Macduff, 5.7.19–28; Macbeth, 5.8.21–26 and 32–39; or Malcolm, 5.8.72–88.

The job of the directors is to read their scenes or sections carefully and prepare a staging for it. They will direct their group's readers when their pair of scenes are read aloud in class. The job of the readers is to study their lines carefully and be prepared to read them as smoothly and with as much vocal interpretation as possible.

3. Speaking a Speech from Act 5

Once the class has finished hearing the play, tell each student to choose one of the following longer speeches from 5.2–8 and prepare a somewhat polished dramatic reading for the next class:

Macbeth:	5.3.1–11
	5.3.23–34
	5.5.20–31
	5.5.44–59
	5.8.21–26 and 32–39
Macduff:	5.7.19–28
Malcolm:	5.5.72–88

Set aside a day for presentations.

TOMORROW AND TOMORROW AND TOMORROW

Tell students to bring their word journals ("Tracing a Word") and journals for use in a final discussion of the play.

HOW DID IT GO?

The actors' readings, the directors' stagings, and the related discussions will help you to gauge students' understanding of Act 5:

· Did students respond to the rapid pace of the short scenes?
· Did students follow the actions and inner actions of the major characters? Even the new ones?
· Did students respond to and convey the thoughts of Macbeth, Malcolm, and Macduff as they performed the longer speeches?
· Did students connect the concluding action with the rest of the play?

LESSON 20 "Out, Out Brief Candle"

The Concluding Word Web

WHAT'S ON FOR
TODAY AND WHY

Word journal groups—"Bloods," "Hands," "Nights," and "Sleeps"—will use findings from their word journal work to discuss and diagram the connections between their word and those of the other groups and to discuss the play's themes.

Any student who has been through this unit will have in her mind a wealth of words, images, characters, ideas. And she can connect them in hundreds of ways. By herself. With no teacher intervention. But in this lesson we want to give her an opportunity to verbalize her connections, so we will lead an open-ended wrap-up discussion in which we will invite students to talk about memorable ideas, actions, writing strategies, and effects.

Also, we will introduce the acting companies and culminating performance assignment. Lessons 4 and 18 of *A Midsummer Night's Dream* and Lesson 23 of *Romeo and Juliet* give additional ideas about how to organize students for this project. Before class today, we need to think carefully about the combination of actors in companies, balancing students as described in the lessons above, and bring to class rosters of group members.

WHAT TO DO

1. The Macbeth Web

To begin the discussion, print, in the center of the blackboard, *Macbeth* and circle it. Beneath it, add the word *murder*, also circled.

Invite a student to come to the board, place a word of his choice anywhere in relation to *Macbeth* or *murder*, and explain to the class the connection he sees between his word and *Macbeth* or *murder*. Then discuss the significance of the word to the play as a whole.

One by one, ask students to add their words to the board. Tell them they might also consider placing a word in a specific location. If they do, ask them to explain their choice of location. Soon, a web of words will exist. As each student adds a word, the student should try to connect it to at least two others that are already on the board and explain the connection. It will soon become obvious that a three-dimensional model is needed to connect all the related words. To ease this problem, and to clarify connections, students may also add the names of key characters to the web and repeat words.

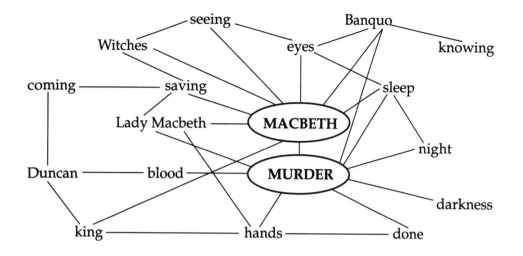

2. Wrap-up Discussion

Lead students to connect ideas. Ask: What is the main idea of this story? What can we learn from these characters? Do you see recurring images, words, deeds, situations, consequences, mistakes?

Direct their attention to Shakespeare the playwright. Ask: What can you say about how Shakespeare put this play together? How did he manipulate action, information, characters, moods, emotions?

Ask them to reveal the overall effect of *Macbeth* on them: What memories of *Macbeth* will you take with you? On a scale of 1–10, how well do you understand *Macbeth*?

3. Introduction to the Culminating Performances

Tell students that for their final project they will form acting companies and prepare a scene from *Macbeth* for presentation to the class. Announce the group rosters and send students to their acting companies with Handout 8: *Macbeth* Scenes for Final Performance. Tell each group to look over the scenes and give you a list of their first, second, and third choices.

TOMORROW AND TOMORROW AND TOMORROW

Ask students to reread Handout 8.

HOW DID IT GO?

Think back to students' comments during this lesson. Did someone insist that *Macbeth* is really a play about "hands"? (Or "blood" or "sleep" or "night"?) Did someone put forth the theory that the short, violent scenes of Act 5 hit Macbeth like death blows? Did someone connect the "tale told by an idiot" line with the witches' gibberish? If so, students have made sense out of the play. More particularly, they have made a play—they have taken typeset words, examined them, spoken the lines, seen mental pictures of the characters, heard the characters speak, followed the characters through many tricky turns in Scotland, and now they are certain enough of this play's existence that they argue about various aspects of it.

It would be a fine measure of success if at the end of this lesson we could look into students' brains and see that they are disturbed. After all, they have put up with frustrating characters and wrestled with powerful issues. It is entirely appropriate for their brains to be weary but full of sparks.

HANDOUT 8

SCENES FOR FINAL PERFORMANCE

The following *Macbeth* scenes are recommended for a final acting performance by student acting companies. Look at them carefully and choose the best scene for your group. If you have more actors than parts, divide one or more of the parts. If you have fewer actors than parts, combine two or more parts. If your group wishes to perform a scene not listed here, clear this with your teacher.

Here are some issues to consider when choosing a scene:

- It's okay for more than one group to do the same scene.

- Memorizing lines is encouraged but not required.

- The group will make a shoe-box stage showing the set as students would like it to be.

- Actors will design costumes, make a script, and analyze the characters they are playing.

- Your performance will be graded on careful reading and rehearsal, understanding of characters, understanding of plot, understanding of language, ability to use language to portray character, well-planned movements, well-planned use of props and costumes, and anything extra you add to the production.

1.3   Soon after the three witches prophesy that Macbeth will be the thane of Cawdor, Ross and Angus arrive with the news of Macbeth's new title. Macbeth then contemplates the witches' other prophesies: that Banquo will be the father of kings, and that Macbeth will be king.
Lines: First Witch, 35; Second Witch, 12; Third Witch, 14; Macbeth, 50; Banquo, 42; Ross, 16; Angus, 12

1.5   Lady Macbeth reads the letter from Macbeth and plots murder.
Lines: Lady Macbeth, 77; Messenger, 5; Macbeth, 4

1.6–7 Duncan's visit to Macbeth's castle is followed by Macbeth's second thoughts about doing the deed.
Lines: Duncan, 19; Banquo, 9; Lady Macbeth, 54; Macbeth, 50

2.2   Macbeth murders Duncan.
Lines: Lady Macbeth, 52; Macbeth, 43

2.3   Macduff discovers Duncan's murder.
Lines: Porter, 38; Macduff, 41; Lennox, 20; Macbeth, 33; Lady Macbeth, 6; Banquo, 11; Donalbain, 8; Malcolm, 14

3.4   The banquet scene. Macbeth sees Banquo's bloody ghost while entertaining the court.
       Lines: Macbeth, 111; Lords, 3; Lady Macbeth, 43; Murderer, 6; Lennox, 6; Ross, 7

4.1   The witches cook up a charmed pot of hell-broth. Macbeth consults with the three witches.
       Lines: First Witch, 41; Second Witch, 28; Third Witch, 29; Hecate, 5; Macbeth, 81; First Apparition, 2; Second Apparition, 4; Third Apparition, 5; Lennox, 6

4.2   Macbeth's murderers kill Macduff's family.
       Lines: Lady Macduff, 42; Ross, 20; Macduff's son, 22; Messenger, 10; Murderer, 4

5.1   Lady Macbeth sleepwalks.
       Lines: Doctor, 37; Gentlewoman, 26; Lady Macbeth, 21

5.8   Macbeth meets Macduff. Certain he will win and wanting no more of Macduff's blood on him, Macbeth is reluctant to fight Macduff. But when Macduff tells Macbeth that he was early ripped from his mother's womb, Macbeth knows he is done for. Macduff brings Malcolm Macbeth's head, and all hail the new king of Scotland.
       Lines: Macbeth, 26; Macduff, 20; Malcolm, 21; Siward, 13; Ross, 10

LESSON **21**   **"Hang Out Our Banners"**

Culminating Performances

WHAT'S ON FOR TODAY AND WHY

As in the study of *A Midsummer Night's Dream* and *Romeo and Juliet*, students will have a chance to put together all they have learned about *Macbeth* characters and how to portray them as they stage a scene from the play. Though far from perfect, these scenes will be more polished since we give students five days to plan and rehearse this project.

To prepare for this lesson, teachers should review the list of scene choices in Handout 8 and assign each group a scene. If possible, we want a variety of scenes from throughout the play; however, we saw in film clips how the same scene can be done more than one way, so assigning two groups the same scene is not an inferior plan.

To help students use their rehearsal time wisely, teachers need to broadcast clear goals for each of the five preparation days and give each student a copy of the Performance Evaluation Form. These five days will be hectic for teachers, for as the artistic consultants to the acting groups they will be called on to solve all kinds of problems. It might help to keep this thought in mind: As years pass, students will forget much of *Macbeth,* many of the activities, most of your wise advice, but they will remember that they *acted* Shakespeare, that they *were* Macbeth (or Macduff or the porter).

WHAT TO DO

1. Day 1: Establishing the Criteria

Announce and post the scene assignments.

Tell students that they will have five days to prepare a group performance of their scene. Their performance can be given live or recorded ahead of time.

Distribute Handout 9: The Director's Notebook and review it with students.

Answer questions. Here are some that students frequently ask before they begin. Let your knowledge of your students guide your responses.

- *"Do we have to memorize lines?"* When students have memorized lines, they can usually give more attention to performance. However, requiring memorization can keep some students from even starting. Therefore, we encourage but do not require actors to memorize lines.
- *"Do we have to do this for homework?"* If the students are using experimental techniques, or if the product is to be a filmed performance, it will probably be necessary for them to rehearse outside of class. However, it is possible, even expected, for students to create a superior performance in the time given in class.
- *"Do we have to perform the whole scene?"* No, and you probably shouldn't.

However, in deciding what portions or lines of a scene to cut, keep in mind the number of actors in your group and the flow of the plot in the scene.

- *"How will we be graded for this?"* Each group will receive two grades: one on the director's notebook and one on the performance. It's likely that most group members will have had little if any acting experience. Therefore, thoroughness of preparation should count for a lot. If there's a Tony out there, fine, but don't make this the bottom line. Your performance will be graded on the criteria listed in Handout 8. Your director's notebook will be graded on the thoroughness with which you completed each task: script, costume design, character analysis, set and props, and music.

- *"Who has to do the director's notebook?"* Everybody. For instance, each actor does a script. Each actor does costume design. Each actor does a character analysis. Everybody does the shoe-box set. Then you put it all together in some neat and organized way and turn it in after your performance. The person in charge of organizing it and turning it in is the director.

After all this information, let the acting companies meet to begin preparations. By the end of the period, tell companies to (1) furnish the teacher with the name of the director, (2) decide on a set and/or concept for their scene, and (3) work through section 1 (Script) and section 2 (Costumes) of Handout 9: Director's Notebook.

Homework for day 1: Tell students to make promptbook pages for their scene. (See the script section of Handout 9: Director's Notebook.) Remind them that they need to get to a copy machine to do this, so they must plan well.

Tell students to sketch their costume concepts.

2. Day 2: Planning the Staging

Send students to their acting companies with the promptbook pages they prepared the night before. Tell each group to read their scene, make cuts, and plan movements, vocal inflections, etc. Tell each actor to mark his promptbook script the way the acting company decided the scene would be done.

Also, before the day is out, make sure that each group gets its scene on its feet. Students should be moving around saying lines, not sitting down and talking about them.

Homework for day 2: Tell each group to bring a shoe box, markers, small objects, and other material so that tomorrow they can make their shoe-box stage and do section 4 of Handout 9: Director's Notebook.

Tell actors to practice memorizing lines.

3. Day 3: Practicing the Movements

Tell each group to work through staging, section 4 of the director's notebook, constructing a shoe-box set and using objects such as coins or Legos to test the movement. After they have made adjustments and marked their scripts accordingly, tell the companies to get the actors on their feet going through the movements they decided on.

Take the last 15 minutes of class and ask each student to prepare a character analysis, section 3 of the director's notebook.

Homework for day 3: Tell students to practice memorizing their lines and to put together their actual costumes.

4. Day 4: The Scene in More Detail

Tell groups to make a more detailed sketch of their proposed set, as in section 5 of the director's notebook. Tell them to make a list of props and decide who will bring what. Also, tell them to discuss music (as in section 6, director's notebook) and plan what they will use and how they will handle it.

On this day, groups should run through their scenes at least twice.

Homework for day 4: Tell students to practice memorizing their lines and to do any assignment their group made for them.

5. Day 5: Final Rehearsals and Finishing Touches

Tell students to complete their director's notebook and have it ready to turn in tomorrow.

Let them rehearse their scene.

Ask them to spend the last few minutes reviewing the Performance Evaluation Form and reminding company members who will bring what for tomorrow's performance.

Homework for day 5: Memorize your lines. Get to class with the props, costumes, scripts, and any other equipment necessary for your performance.

6. Day 6: Performance

૨૭

HANDOUT 9

DIRECTOR'S NOTEBOOK

In preparation for its performance, each group will keep a director's notebook in which it will record its insights about the delivery of lines, costuming, characterization, staging, music, and set and prop choices.

Required Contents of the Notebook

1. *Script:* Copy your scene and cut, trim, and paste each page onto a larger piece of plain paper. Cross out any lines you intend to cut. Make sure you have room in the margins to enter the following pieces of information to indicate how the scene will be played:

• Vocal pauses, stresses, and inflections
• Tone of voice
• Gestures and facial expressions (those that are explicit in the script as well as those that are not)
• Notes or diagrams of actions and movements
• Definitions of words or phrases you do not understand

2. *Costumes:* Design two costumes: (1) the conceptual costume (the one you would wear if money were no object), and (2) the actual costume (the one you will improvise for this performance). You may draw these, construct them from magazine cuttings, or simply write out a detailed description explaining your choices (styles, materials, colors, etc.), but tell about both your conceptual and actual costumes. (In the director's notebook, there should be costume descriptions from each actor.)

3. *Character Analyses:* Write an analysis for each character who appears in the scene. As you prepare these analyses, question yourself about the characters' motivations in this passage or scene. Also consider what you know about the character up to this point in the play. The following questions should help to guide you:

• What does each character want?
• Do the characters' objectives change in this scene? If so, when and why? Do tactics change? If so, how and why? What obstacles stand in each character's way? What happens when objectives meet obstacles?
• What is distinctive about the way the characters speak? (For example, who uses plain language? Elaborate language? Puns? Riddles? Sarcasm? Why does the character speak this way?)

4. *Staging:* Plan the staging. Draw the set. Then make a model of it using the shoe box or posterboard. With script in hand, read the scene and move objects such as Legos, buttons, coins, or dolls to represent the characters. These actions will anticipate the movements the performers will make during your performance. Mark your scripts as you plan the movements.

5. *Set and Props:* Plan a simple set using classroom furniture for the most part. If you want to add special pieces, draw them or use magazine clippings to represent them. Keep props simple. Improvise them from objects at hand. In the director's notebook, include a drawing of the set (the director's responsibility) and a list of props. Briefly explain your choices.

6. *Music:* Select appropriate music to play as an introduction to your performance. If you like, let the music be heard during the performance as well. The characters, action, and mood of your scene should guide your choices.

ॐ

PERFORMANCE EVALUATION

ACTING COMPANY NAME:

SCENE PERFORMED:

CHARACTER	PLAYED BY	COMMENTS

POINTS POSSIBLE	POINTS AWARDED	TO WHAT EXTENT DOES THE PERFORMANCE SHOW:
15		Careful Reading and Rehearsal
15		Understanding of Characters
15		Understanding of Plot
20		Understanding of Language
15		Ability to Use Language to Portray Character
10		Well Planned Movements
10		Well Planned Use of Props and Costumes
(BONUS)		Something Extra
100 TOTAL (+ BONUS)		

COMMENTS:

ॐ